THE KING OF NAZI PARIS

THE KING OF NAZI PARIS

HENRI LAFONT AND THE GANGSTERS OF THE FRENCH GESTAPO

CHRISTOPHER OTHEN

This paperback edition published in Great Britain in 2021 by
Biteback Publishing Ltd, London

ISBN 978-1-78590-659-6

10 9 8 7 6 5 4 3 2 1

A CIP catalogue record for this book is available from the British Library.

Set in Minion Pro and Trade Gothic

Printed and bound in Great Britain by
CPI Group (UK) Ltd, Croydon CR0 4YY

CONTENTS

PREFACE TO THE PAPERBACK EDITION

THE KING OF NAZI PARIS began when I was living in a *fin de siècle* apartment in Brussels with high ceilings and a view of the Parc du Cinquantenaire. The place belonged to the Polish government and housed a diplomat who went to mass twice a week and thought a relationship with an English writer might work. She soon discovered otherwise and began emailing me regular bullet-point lists of things that needed to change. The lists evolved over time, but point three usually involved my immediate conversion to Catholicism and point eleven demanded a spontaneous romantic gesture once a week, preferably on Friday evenings.

That summer we took a week's holiday in Paris to try to save the relationship, even though it felt a lot like grappling with the controls of a crashing aircraft. We went on a Friday evening so I could cross a bullet point off the list and stayed with a friend at the Polish Academy of Sciences somewhere deep in the sixteenth arrondissement. An iron and glass gate creaked open to reveal a four-storey maze of conference rooms and bedrooms and an extensive basement, all curled around a rectangular concrete courtyard. The building had been a hotel before the war and a private residence before that. A plaque on the wall by the worn marble stairs noted that Marcel Proust used to visit the family who once lived here. Our room looked out at slick grey Paris rooftops and we were woken every morning at seven by rubber thwacks from the squash club next door. Then we explored the city.

I loved Paris instantly. It's a cliché but that doesn't stop it being true. That place tore the heart right out my chest and served it up with garlic and shallots and a glass of red wine. I would have happily paid double and tipped the waiter. History, architecture, restaurants, cafés, the flowing Seine, the chic passers-by and the prime real estate given over to bookshops and art galleries. It was paradise on earth. My diplomat girlfriend had studied here a decade back and wanted to show me the tourist spots: the Eiffel Tower, the Musée d'Orsay, Notre-Dame, Montmartre. Before we left Brussels she had asked if there was anything I wanted to see in the French capital. I had a list including Ernest Hemingway's apartment, the grave of Charles Baudelaire and a few other things.

I also vaguely remembered having read about wartime gangsters in Paris years earlier during one of those internet sessions when you intend to spend five minutes checking emails and find yourself still there six hours later watching videos of real-life helicopter crashes in Russia. Somewhere between the spam and flying rotor blades was the story of the Bonny-Lafont gang.

This group of crooks, corrupt cops and fallen celebrities had been led by the orchid-loving thief Henri Lafont and his disgraced policeman sidekick Pierre Bonny. They worked for the Nazis and lived like royalty until the Allies arrived. But while the going was good, Lafont reigned as the king of Nazi Paris out of his headquarters at 93 rue Lauriston. Even members of the collaborating French government at Vichy, who supposedly enjoyed the support of Berlin, came to No. 93 and begged for favours. One of Lafont's gang had been the former captain of France's 1930 football World Cup team. Another ran the famous French Connection heroin smuggling ring. A third was France's first Public Enemy Number One.

The building was still standing. A memorial plaque to their victims hung on the wall outside. I wanted to see it and pay my respects.

'Do you think we can find 93 rue Lauriston?' I asked.

'It's not difficult,' my diplomat replied. 'We're staying at No. 74.'

It was the first of a blizzard of coincidences that pushed me into writing the book. A biography of French gangster Jo Attia I'd picked up second-hand in Brussels a week before the holiday turned out to involve the gang. Attia had been a prominent member, at least until he had second thoughts. I opened a glossy photobook in a Paris museum gift shop and discovered that a familiar picture of two lesbian drinkers at the Chameleon Club, seen in various contexts many times before, apparently featured Violette Morris, a collaborator and friend of the gang. Infamous wartime serial killer Marcel Petiot had counted a member of the gang among his victims. I'd read – for some reason – two separate biographies of the good doctor but only discovered the Bonny-Lafont connection during this holiday.

The biggest coincidence of all was in a book about wartime Paris, picked up from a four-storey Gilbert Joseph shop in the centre of the city, which noted in passing that during the war 74 rue Lauriston had housed members of the gang's paramilitary unit, the Brigade Nord-Africaine. We were staying in a building, possibly even in one of the rooms, where Lafont's Moroccan mercenaries had slept during the spring of 1944 while the resistance movement strengthened and the Allies waited in the wings of Europe.

The King of Nazi Paris wanted to be written. I'd had other ideas for my fifth book but clearly something was pushing me in Lafont's direction and I had no choice in the matter. I told my girlfriend about it as we sat outside a café near the Champs-Élysées. She nodded and leaned across the bronze tabletop.

'I think God wants you to write this book,' she said earnestly.

'I don't think God wants me to write a book about gangsters who collaborated with the Nazis,' I replied. 'But I'm going to anyway.'

She laughed at that, something so unprecedented that her lipstick cracked in three places, but our Parisian holiday couldn't save the relationship and I moved to Warsaw a few months later. At first there was lot of staring at the falling snow outside my windows with a glass of whisky in hand, but then I met someone who turned on the lights and my life was better than it had ever been before. Through it all *The King of Nazi Paris* called out to be written.

• • •

There was research, an agent, a contract, more research and then the writing. Sitting in my apartment hacking at the laptop keyboard, the coincidences that had inspired the project remained lodged in my mind even as other kinds of parallels began to emerge.

Polish friends were permanently astonished that I wasn't writing a book about their country, but still managed to remain polite about it. When I explained the subject of my book they would nod and say, '*Dobrze*. So just like Abraham Gancwajch?'

I knew the name. Since returning to Poland I had been living in a post-war block of flats on the site of what once had been the outer boundary of the Warsaw Ghetto. In 1940 the invading Nazis walled up 400,000 Jews in 1.3 square miles of city centre as part of their Manichean racial war. SS soldiers starved the Ghetto inhabitants, beat them, and were still surprised when the Jews rose up in early

1943 and took on the Germans in an act of suicidal resistance. The battle was only ever going to end one way.

Today there isn't much left of the Ghetto except a few crumbling red brick walls and some tramlines that abruptly terminate in the middle of the street. The Israeli school parties that come here every summer look both moved by the memories and disappointed to find themselves walking around a zone filled with modern hairdressers and supermarkets.

While the Ghetto still stood here, Abraham Gancwajch was its Jewish king. His gang was known as the 'Trzynastka' ('Thirteen') after the address of Gancwajch's headquarters in ulica Leszno. Amazingly the building still stands, five minutes from my apartment, although post-war rebuilding has concealed it behind a new number and road name. Unlike Lafont, the Jewish Pole hadn't started out as a gangster but worked instead as a journalist with a strong line in Zionism. All that crumbled when the Nazis invaded Poland and Gancwajch agreed to spy on his own people for the German intelligence services. By December 1940 he had been inserted into the Warsaw Ghetto to undermine the existing Jewish authorities, which were proving too independent-minded for the Germans.

With the establishment of the Trzynastka, Gancwajch became a gangster. His group was officially supposed to combat extortion and price gouging. In reality it did the opposite, blackmailing Ghetto inhabitants, threatening others and running the black market that Gancwajch publicly claimed to be stamping out. He became rich and powerful, eating well as other Jews starved and smuggling goods into the Ghetto with the help of corrupt German officers. Gancwajch sent regular intelligence reports back to the Gestapo and set up his own brothel where the Trzynastka inner circle drank and whored their days away.

After the Ghetto uprising he took his family into the Aryan side of Warsaw, still working for the Nazis, and helped hunt down Polish resistance fighters. Jewish gangsters were a lot more disposable than French ones and Abraham Gancwajch disappeared in 1943, probably executed by the Germans once his usefulness ran out.

The parallels between Lafont's and Gancwajch's activities were clear, but there was an ocean of difference between the circumstances of a Catholic Frenchman and a Jewish Pole living under Nazi rule. A Dutch expatriate I knew in Warsaw, who claimed to have deserted from the French Foreign Legion and now corrected the subtitles for video games, told me that a Dutchman named Dries Riphagen provided a closer match to Lafont.

A merchant seaman who spent some time in America learning from the local crime gangs, Riphagen became a big name in the Amsterdam underworld for his involvement in pimping, gambling and stolen cars. Unlike Lafont he was political and carried a membership card for the Nationaal-Socialistische Nederlandsche Arbeiderspartij (National Socialist Dutch Workers Party), a far-right group who prayed for the day Germany would absorb their country. Their prayers were answered in 1940 and Riphagen immediately began working for the German security services. In other corners of the Nazi empire, Lafont and Gancwajch were doing the same.

The Dutch gangster combined his existing criminal schemes with tracking down Jews and resistance fighters for the Nazis. He roped other crooks into his network and eventually graduated to membership of the Henneicke Column, a group of crooks and fascists that collected a bounty for each Dutch Jew they arrested. When the war was over Riphagen escaped to Argentina and managed to avoid extradition by cosying up to the Perón regime. He spent his last years in Madrid as an ageing gigolo kept by wealthy women.

Every occupied country seemed to have produced someone like Lafont or Gancwajch or Riphagen during the war. Nazi intelligence services obviously had no objection to employing foreign gangsters. Neither did the Allies. America used mobster Charles 'Lucky' Luciano to smooth the 1943 invasion of Sicily, while the British sent safecracker and career criminal Eddie Chapman undercover into occupied Europe as Agent Zigzag. As I worked on *The King of Nazi Paris* it became clear that what made Henri Lafont so unique was not his background but the sheer influence he exercised. The other gangsters operated within strictly monitored boundaries, but Lafont was everywhere, his tentacles creeping into every crevice of the occupation. By 1944 he was the most powerful Frenchman in Paris, with the ability to pressure senior SS officers into releasing prisoners, bully important collaborators, and remain unafraid of even the most feared Nazi officers in the capital.

It was a Faustian pact with the occupier and even Lafont found it hard to be surprised when it all came tumbling down. He had brought enough pain and suffering to others on the way to deserve his fate. The stone plaque outside rue Lauriston that I saw on that trip to Paris commemorates his victims. There is always a fresh bunch of flowers in a blue, white and red wrapper hanging beneath it.

Eventually I finished writing the book. A journey which began in Brussels had ended in Warsaw, but its dark heart always remained that gang of men who could not recognise true north on the spinning moral compass of wartime Paris. They all paid the price, one way or another.

INTRODUCTION

IN A STATION OF THE MÉTRO

DRINKERS IN CHEZ LA Mère Laval scrambled for cover as Henri Lafont chased the pimp out of the bar and into the street, pulling a gun from his jacket pocket. The shooting started in the blackout of rue d'Aboukir.

A few minutes earlier, a pimp named Tanguy had been taking a drink after a day spent slapping around girls who kept money back at the brothel. Now he was running for his life towards the mouth of the Métro Strasbourg – Saint-Denis as Lafont's shots lit up the street around him.

He almost made it. Tanguy was at the Métro entrance when a bullet hit him somewhere vital and he tumbled, tried to get up, went down again and lay there like a petal stuck to a wet branch. He was bleeding all over the stone steps when a German patrol in feldgrau arrived. Lafont showed them an identity card with French text: '*Le porteur du présent papier ... est Officier ... Il est authorise de...*' ('The bearer of this document ... is an officer ... he is authorised to...') and a black and white photograph of his flat face, with its lacquer-dark hair and hint of a double chin.

'He's a terrorist,' said Lafont.

Somewhere in the darkness Tanguy coughed up blood on the

Métro stairs. It was a late November evening in a surrendered city, close to curfew. Lafont had erased another threat to his criminal empire. The man had been his friend for years.

In wartime Paris, a gang of crooks, corrupt police and fallen celebrities led by the orchid-loving thief Henri Lafont worked for the Nazis and lived like kings until it all came down and a price had to be paid. The Allies called them 'the Bonny-Lafont gang', after the group's leaders; the Germans knew them as '*Active Gruppe Hess*', after a Nazi contact man in rue des Saussaies; its members called themselves 'the Carlingue', underworld slang for the firm or the outfit. Locals called them 'the French Gestapo'.

They were a tribe of murderers, thieves, gold traffickers, pimps, stick-up men, fake French barons, Russian princesses, self-taught art experts, disgraced former policemen and the one-time captain of the French national football team. They even had their own Rasputin, a bearded Bulgarian mystic, who was obsessed with magical pentacles and underage girls.

The twin suns of this French wild bunch were a petty criminal who went by the name of Henri Lafont and his former policeman sidekick, Inspector Pierre Bonny. The pair wore the best clothes, ate at the best restaurants and did whatever they wanted in occupied Paris. They lived on a poisoned honeycomb.

Lafont's real name was Henri Chamberlin. Tall and flabby-faced under brilliantined dark hair, he could look almost respectable in the right light, like a bank clerk caught with his hand in the till. In the wrong light he was a barely literate racketeer. Before the war he'd been an unsuccessful small-time crook constantly in and out of prison. Money was never happy to see him.

'I had a bare arse and empty pockets,' he said.[1]

His friend Bonny was lean as whalebone. As a police inspector,

Bonny had been involved in some of the biggest cases in 1930s Paris. His role in the Alexandre Stavisky affair got front-page attention when the investigation sparked nationalist riots in the Place de la Concorde. Later, it emerged that Bonny was as corrupt as the crooks he had chased. The police force kicked him out into disgrace and poverty.

The Second World War changed everything. German tanks rolled through France in the summer of 1940 and ended the Third Republic's seventy years of political compromise and empire building. Some Frenchmen crossed the Channel with General Charles de Gaulle to continue the fight from London, but the rest accepted defeat.

The 84-year-old Marshal Philippe Pétain had been trudging towards retirement as the French ambassador to Spain when the war began. He returned during the days of retreat to join Paul Reynaud's tottering government and negotiate a ceasefire with Germany; a position taken as pragmatism by some and treason by others. Fellow ministers fled to London, but the marshal stayed behind to head up a puppet government in the peaceful spa town of Vichy. His ministers launched a Révolution Nationale that salvaged as much French pride as the Nazi gauleiters would allow.

The Germans took Paris for themselves, flew a swastika from the Eiffel Tower and recruited local help. Chamberlin was a perfect candidate. A chance encounter in a prison camp led him to a life of luxury running a ruthless mob of gangsters who looted the city on behalf of the German occupiers. All it took was a taste for treason, treachery and deceit.

The same wheel of fortune brought Pierre Bonny out of humiliation and back into the high life. The former inspector tried to pretend that he was still a policeman as the gang rode a crime wave through the capital.

Chamberlin and Bonny looted Jewish properties; bought low and sold high on the black market; scammed illegal gold deals; stole priceless art; ran protection rackets; intercepted parachute drops; infiltrated resistance groups; gunned down rivals; and sprung anyone from prison for the right price. They drafted in Chamberlin's old gangster friends from prison and the underworld. Soon they had an all-star team made up of France's most-wanted crooks. The gang's Nazi handlers gave them all immunity in exchange for a cut of the profits and any useful information that came their way.

Chamberlin and Bonny moved into a blank-faced town house at 93 rue Lauriston, which was a narrow urban canyon of a road between the Place de L'Étoile and the Trocadéro. The first floor of their new home hosted parties where collaborationists mixed with young socialites and well-mannered German officers. Henri Chamberlin showed off the orchids that he loved so much and everyone drank champagne while the gramophone scratched up a shellac 78. Then the party would head off to a nightclub in one of Chamberlin's white Bentleys with headlights cutting through blackout Paris, German soldiers saluting as they passed. The rest of the gang stayed behind to torture prisoners down in the rue Lauriston cellars.

Some of Chamberlin's men, like Abel 'Le Mammouth' Danos, tortured people to get information and money. Others, like Paul Clavié, with his dark eyes and pimp's moustache, just liked to watch people suffer.

The Bonny-Lafont gang climbed its way up the collaborationist hierarchy. The gang became untouchable when Chamberlin manoeuvred himself into a role hunting down members of the resistance and the Nazi authorities handed over German police identity cards and the licence to carry guns. By 1943, Monsieur Henri was the most powerful Frenchman in Nazi Paris.

• • •

Tanguy the pimp signed his own death warrant when he carved up two of Chamberlin's gangsters in a Montmartre bar fight. The underworld knew Jean Sartore as 'Le Chauve' (The Bald) for his sparsely covered scalp. His friend Auguste Jeunet was a pimp called 'Cajac', who had a soft black moustache and a right eye that stared off at an oblique angle from a nest of scar tissue.

The two men never told anyone how the fight with Tanguy started. Protection money, gambling debts, stolen silverware, swaggering machismo, perhaps something to do with an Arab prostitute called Matilda who ended up dead in a ditch after trying to shoot her gangster boyfriend. Whatever the cause of the disagreement, it finished with Sartore's intestines hanging out through his silk shirt and Jeunet bleeding deep from slashes on his skull.

Chamberlin visited the pair in hospital to hear that a pimp they knew only as 'Phono' had done the damage. Sartore and Jeunet asked their boss not to retaliate; they'd take care of business when they had recovered. Chamberlin gave them an oily smile and promised nothing.

A few weeks later, Tanguy was sitting at a bar in the rue d'Aboukir when someone connected him to the nickname Phono and made a quick telephone call. Chamberlin and his men arrived in their white Bentley. Tanguy and Chamberlin realised that they knew each other, and had even been good friends once, but this did not stop the confrontation. There were words from Monsieur Henri that might have been an attempt to make an arrest, which was followed by raised voices and then fists. Finally Tanguy broke free and ran. Chamberlin shot him in the back at the entrance to the Métro Strasbourg – Saint-Denis. Tanguy died in hospital.

Bonny typed up a report for his Gestapo contacts that remodelled the dead pimp as a dangerous resistance fighter and turned the gangland vendetta into a righteous political act. The men in black leather coats didn't believe any of it, but Chamberlin was too valuable, too rich and too powerful for them to openly doubt his version of events.

The Bonny-Lafont gang continued to rule Paris from its sixteenth-arrondissement headquarters and began looking to grab some political power. Chamberlin told other gangsters that he saw himself as a future police prefect of the city, perhaps even mayor. He had plans to help the poor. Fellow collaborator Robert Brasillach described him as an 'intermediary between the Renaissance and Scarface'.[2]

Famous and infamous faces came to pay homage to Lafont at rue Lauriston. Singer and actor Maurice Chevalier came to ask for a favour; Jewish scrap metal millionaire Joseph Joinovici had deals to finance; bisexual race-car driver and champion weight-lifter Violette Morris came to socialise. Somewhere out there on the streets of Paris was a notorious doctor with a secret life as a serial killer on a collision course with the gang.

By early 1944, the Carlingue was so enmeshed in the German wartime framework that its gangsters officered and ran the Brigade Nord-Africaine, a paramilitary outfit of Moroccan and Algerian émigrés operating out of Tulle. It robbed, raped and murdered the locals under cover of fighting the resistance. Chamberlin hoped to build a political empire out of France's North African population, with the brigade as its foundation stone. Then the Allies came.

De Gaulle's soldiers kicked open the doors of 93 rue Lauriston to find the smouldering remains of Bonny's files in the garden and graffiti on the cellar walls. The building was empty. It was the end of easy money, expensive clothes, champagne every night, pressed duck at the Tour d'Argent and the parades of girls in fur wraps, who all claimed to be countesses and loved opium and threesomes but looked familiar to anyone who knew the chorus lines in the sleazier revues of Paris.

'For four years, I had all the most beautiful women, orchids, champagne and caviar by the bucketful,' said Chamberlin. 'I lived the equivalent of ten lives.'[3]

The war had transformed Chamberlin from wanted man into the godfather of Nazi Paris. The German defeat sent him back to where it all began like a Möbius strip; and he was once again on the run with death one step behind him.

PART I

FROM THE UNDERWORLD TO THE ABWEHR

1

THE MAN WHO LOVED ORCHIDS

ON A SUMMER'S DAY in the middle of June 1940, a fleet of Stuka dive-bombers came screaming out of the sun in northern France. Whatever sadist designed the aircraft had built sirens into its landing gear, with no other purpose than to traumatise civilians on the ground already terrorised by Panzer tanks and jackboots. The Stuka siren provided the soundtrack for German victories in the first year of the Second World War through Poland, Norway and Belgium.

The sirens sent a prisoner column scrambling into ditches along a country road, located a few days' march from Paris. When the first bombs hit, three prisoners jumped up and took off across a road through all of the noise and smoke. They made it into a field and kept going through the high grass. The tall man, who was trying to hunch over as he ran, was Henri Louis Chamberlin, a petty criminal who loved flowers and fraud and had spent his adult life trying to stay out of prison.

Chamberlin grew up in a poverty-stricken household in the thirteenth arrondissement of Paris to a working-class printer and his wife. He was an orphan by the age of thirteen with a handful of relatives scattered around the country who had no time for him. He told friends about spending one birthday curled up asleep on his father's grave. His childhood was spent living on the streets and eating out of dustbins. Chamberlin got his education from beggars and crooks and street gangs. As a teenager he landed a job as a butcher's delivery boy, but petty crime was already deeply embedded in his bones.

In 1919, the police picked up seventeen-year-old Chamberlin riding a stolen work bicycle down to Toulouse in the south-west of France, where he hoped to visit his sister. He was arrested and served three months in prison. Chamberlin was barely back on the streets when the police arrested him again, this time for stealing rabbits. He was put in a correctional centre for criminal teens; institutions designed to rehabilitate, but full of bullying and exploitation and the ammonia stink of piss.

After Chamberlin's release, the army grabbed him for national service on his eighteenth birthday. He did two years in the Tirailleurs Algériens and was one of the few white faces among the Algerian colonial troops. Chamberlin came out of the armed forces with a good conduct record; if he stole anything while he was overseas no one found out. By this time, he was a big, hard man with a surprisingly high voice and a love of orchids. Something about the lush soft blooms meant a lot to him, but no one mocked him about it more than once.

The adult Chamberlin had a talent for deception and small horizons. He had become the kind of man who could make friends with anyone in a café and would count it a good day if he stole their wallet when they visited the toilets. He was tough enough when it came to a fight, but preferred to leave violence to the professional thugs, unless there was a point to be made. He lied all the time, for good reason or just out of habit.

Chamberlin's return to civilian life led to more stealing and more arrests. He briefly joined a circus then did a six-month stint in prison for theft. He moved to Marseille, bought a van and started his own moving business. One day the gendarmes arrived to find him working on a stolen car. Chamberlin claimed the vehicle belonged to one of his friends, but the judge gave him a two-year sentence. While still behind bars he married his girlfriend Rebecchi Arzia, and the couple later had a son and daughter.

Chamberlin would serve another five prison sentences, which ranged from six months to a year. Almost all were for theft. He became used to the clanging cell doors, bad food and shuffling around an exercise yard with men who had tattoos of dotted lines and 'cut here' circled around their necks because France still executed criminals by the guillotine.

Chamberlin's cellmates included an outwardly respectable war hero-type called Lionel de Wiet, who dropped heavy hints about a blue-blooded background. Behind the good manners and nice accent, de Wiet was neither an aristocrat nor a soldier, just a cocaine addict from a good family who had made a career out of fraud.

Another prison friend was Adrien Estébétéguy, who was known to the underworld as 'The Basque' or 'Adrien la Main Froide' (Cold Hand Adrien). Estébétéguy had a stern face, thinning hair and eyebrows like black caterpillars. He could be thuggish, and had a taste for beating up policemen, but his relish for verbal violence was enough to make other gangsters avoid him. Estébétéguy spent most of his criminal career around Toulouse and had done eight stretches in prison for robbery. 'An individual of more than doubtful morality,' said his police report.[1]

Chamberlin was not in the same league as his new prison companions. He was just a habitual petty criminal, never good enough to make a living out of crime and never honest enough to stick to a straight job. He moved his family to Saint-Jean-de-Maurienne in south-eastern France and worked in a store. In 1937 his wife took the children and 2,000 francs from the store cash drawer and ran off with another man. Chamberlin was blamed for the theft. At the prospect of serving more prison time, he left town and spent the next few years bouncing between Paris and the south of France under a fistful of fake identities.

As the 1930s came to an end, Chamberlin was as crooked as ever and just as unlikely to tell the truth. Even his friends didn't trust his stories.

'Monsieur Henri had a little problem with exaggeration,' said the owner of a café where Chamberlin went a few days a week to drink and chat. 'It amused him to put us on. He pretended to have been in a German prison with Monsieurs Hitler and Hess.'[2]

No one in the café believed a word he said. The owner advised him to write a novel.

It was a strange time to be boasting about knowing Adolf Hitler. Years of bitterness about the First World War and the Versailles Treaty had pushed the Nazis into power in Germany. Imperialism came back on the menu and as the end of the decade approached, war became inevitable.

On 1 September 1939 Germany invaded Poland; Britain and France declared war on Germany; and a conflict began that would go on to affect every corner of the world. Hitler's allies in the Soviet Union swallowed up the eastern half of Poland in mid-September, before taking the Baltic States and then invading Finland in November. German tanks sat on the French border, while Hitler hoped for peace in the west but spent his time planning for war.

Among all the panic and military preparations, Chamberlin was leading an outwardly respectable life and working as a sub-agent for

Simca, a recently established car manufacturer that was backed by Fiat. He ran a showroom for the company near the Porte des Lilas in Paris under the name Henri Normand. In April 1940 he branched out to help administer the canteen at his local police station. He had managed to manoeuvre himself into the precinct on the back of the goodwill received after donating a car, that probably didn't belong to him, as a prize in a police charity raffle.

Chamberlin had barely started work with the police canteen when German tanks made an unexpected thrust through the Ardennes. The French army called up anyone with a pulse and a working trigger finger to fight for their country, but Monsieur Henri had no interest in saving a society whose morality meant nothing to him. He stole as much money as he could get his hands on in the canteen and vanished.

The fraud was discovered by Inspector Albert Priolet, who was famous for having arrested the Dutch spy Mata Hari back in the First World War. Chamberlin was picked up in his new role helping set up concert tours for the army. He spent a few weeks in Cherche-Midi prison before being transferred to a new camp at Cépoy, a disused riverside factory seventy miles south of Paris. From there, the authorities planned to ship him out to a penal colony in French Guiana.

While in Cépoy, Chamberlin became friendly with a Swiss cell-mate interned on espionage charges. Max Stöcklin was a big-jawed 39-year-old from Basel who got into the spy game following years of roaming Germany and France as an unsuccessful salesman for gasogene boilers. He bottomed out in Brussels with two divorces to his name and bankruptcy looming over him.

In 1934 Stöcklin met a high-living German called Hermann Brandl, who claimed to represent Belgian boiler makers but got his real pay cheque from the Abwehr, the German military intelligence service. Brandl was a cheerful blond spy with good manners and a square head. He put Stöcklin through a few years of loaded questions before recruiting him as an agent. Money was not a problem for Stöcklin anymore.

Nine months into the Second World War, French agents discovered that Stöcklin had been transmitting information about military manoeuvres from a house in Paris and locked him up. In Cépoy he became friendly with Chamberlin and another German spy called Karl Hennecke. The trio began plotting their escape and finally got their chance when the authorities evacuated the camp in the middle of June ahead of the arrival of the approaching German army.

Stuka bombers came down on the procession of prisoners as they tramped along a country road carrying suitcases and overcoats. Chamberlin, Stöcklin and Hennecke managed to make their escape in the chaos.

The spies needed to get back to Paris and Chamberlin knew the best way to reach the city. They arrived in the capital to see German troops parading down the Champs-Élysées; the swastika flying from the top of the Eiffel Tower; signposts in Gothic German script near the city's landmarks; sandbags everywhere; and a newly imposed curfew. Most Parisians had already fled the metropolis in cars and carts loaded high with furniture. Over at the Hôtel Ritz, waiters were serving poached sole and scalloped eggs to German officers and American war correspondents. Table talk was about the odds of a quick surrender from the British, who were still fighting from across the Channel.

Hennecke disappeared into the city on a personal mission and the other two escapees never saw him again. Stöcklin discovered that his old Abwehr spymasters had set up their headquarters at the Hôtel

Lutetia on boulevard Raspail and were filling up the place with a mess of boxes and papers and men in uniform. Straight-backed officer types appeared happy to see Stöcklin and politely shook hands with Chamberlin before escorting him out of the building. He tried to get his job back at the police canteen, but Inspector Albert Priolet chased him away. 'He threw me out like something dirty,' said Chamberlin, outraged by the violation of some obscure moral code.[3]

The ex-prisoner then drifted through Paris and attempted to reconnect with his old friends and acquaintances. He discovered that his former cellmate Estébéteguy was in Fresnes prison for circulating counterfeit money before the war, and everyone else he knew had fled the city. The capital was in chaos: the Germans had requisitioned many apartments and hotels, most shops had closed down and food had become scarce.

Chamberlin had no friends to call on and nowhere to go. He returned to the Hôtel Lutetia and asked the Abwehr for work.

• • •

The Abwehr was born out of the defeat of the First World War. After the war, Allied troops were stationed across Germany and the Versailles Treaty had all but destroyed what was left of the Kaiser's army. Prussian officers saw the benefits of establishing an intelligence outfit that was able to creep around in the shadows of their country without alerting the Allies. The Abwehr set up spy networks and filed intelligence reports and waited for the day that Germany would rise from the ashes of defeat.

A merger with Reichsmarine intelligence gave the military outfit a naval flavour. The white-haired sea-dog Admiral Wilhelm Canaris was in charge of the Abwehr by the time that the Nazi government started planning for war. In August 1939, Canaris's men supplied the Polish uniforms used in a false flag attack on a German radio station in Gleiwitz that gave the Panzer tanks an excuse to start rolling into Poland. In the coming months Abwehr agents armed Ukrainian nationalists, funded a Hindu underground cell seeking to end British imperialism and followed the victorious German army through country after country.

A year later, Abwehr men were in the Hôtel Lutetia looking on as a defeated France was dismembered. The Germans lacked the manpower to effectively police the whole territory and settled for occupying the industrial north of France and a thick western coastal strip that ran all the way down to the Spanish border. The Italians were granted a chunk of land near the Alps in the south-east of the country. What remained became the Zone Libre (Free Zone) under the rule of a nominally independent French government led by Marshal Philippe Pétain from the spa town of Vichy. Officially Pétain's authority extended across all France; in reality, the Germans had no intention of allowing him any genuine power outside the Zone Libre beyond some low-level bureaucracy.

Pétain's administration danced on strings that were being pulled in Berlin, but following the shock of defeat many French people found comfort in its pragmatic acceptance of the new order. The Troisième République that had ruled France since the Franco-Prussian war was dead and members of the right wing cheerfully tap-danced on its grave.

'An old syphilitic whore ... stinking of patchouli and yeast infection, still exhaling her bad odours, still standing on her sidewalk,'[4] said Robert Brasillach, writing about the republic from a prisoner-of-war camp where he and 1.5 million other French soldiers were languishing.

The German occupying authorities fully established themselves in Paris. Flags flew, soldiers marched and intelligence agencies sent their tentacles slithering through the city streets and avenues. Abwehr chiefs began a recruitment campaign among the local inhabitants. Stöcklin was happy to see Henri Chamberlin when he reappeared in the lobby of the Hôtel Lutetia on boulevard Raspail. The feeling was mutual.

'There was the Hôtel Lutetia, where I had made friends, thanks to my Swiss chum, Max Stöcklin,' said Chamberlin about that period. 'I paid him a visit and he said: "Let's see, we'll find something for you."'[5]

Stöcklin introduced his former cellmate to Captain Wilhelm Radecke, a Wehrmacht officer who had been seconded to the Abwehr. The former banker from Berlin liked to act the playboy and loved good food, making money as easily as possible and pretty girls who weren't his wife. Chamberlin turned on the charm with his high voice and offered to take the captain on a tour of the city and show him what the city's nightlife had to offer.

The hedonistic fairground that was Paris was whirling back to life, fuelled by all the money that was being thrown around by the occupiers. German soldiers packed out every café, cabaret and strip show. They drowned in beer and wine and a sea of female flesh. The pimps of Paris got rich quick, and for some French women, the tall, jackbooted men of the Wehrmacht were hard to resist, especially for those whose husbands were far away in prison camps.

As a former street rat, Chamberlin knew every sleazy nightclub and gangster bar in the city. He got the seats near the band, knew the good madams and the best girls and could push his way into the few restaurants that were still open. Radecke enjoyed himself enough to propose his new French protégé a post as an Abwehr agent. Chamberlin didn't hesitate.

'Fucking hell, at thirty-eight years old I was in total shit and here comes Fritz to offer me money, honours, respectability, the good life,' he said. 'They shake my hand, feed me, treat me with respect, not like the French who want to send me off to Guiana. I'd have to be the king of idiots to refuse and I'm not the king of idiots.'[6]

Chamberlin received an Abwehr identity card and became agent number 10.474.R. He had joined the organisation at just the right time. Everybody working for the Nazis in Paris was about to have the opportunity to get rich.

Reichsmarschall Hermann Göring was visiting the defeated capital to spread the word about the official Nazi occupation policy. The overinflated Luftwaffe chief settled in at the Hôtel Ritz and spent his days buying up perfume, jewellery, paintings, statues and a diamond-studded marshal's baton handcrafted out of gold at Cartier. He settled his hotel bill with a 90 per cent discount, paid even less to Cartier, and looted everything else he could get his hands on. When the shopping expedition was over, Göring assembled his underlings at Maxim's restaurant to relay the orders that he had been given in Berlin. 'You must turn yourself into hunting dogs,' he announced. 'Be on the trail of anything which might be useful to the German people.'[7]

Marshal Pétain's defeated nation would be forced to sell off everything Germany needed for its war effort, from copper to art, leather to foie gras, petrol to champagne. Money would not be a problem. The new Vichy government had been ordered to pay 20 million Reichsmark a day towards German occupation costs, at the artificially high rate of twenty francs to the Reichsmark when the real value was closer to twelve. This money would be used for the Nazi spending spree. France was funding its own exploitation.

Kriegsmarine officers of the German naval force were the first to set up a buying office in Paris, on the rue Saint-Florentin.

Other military organisations quickly followed. Stöcklin's former spy boss Hermann Brandl arrived from Brussels to set up the Abwehr contribution, which became known as the Amt Otto chain. Chamberlin took an interest in the operation and suggested to Radecke that some of his old criminal associates would make good buyers, if only they weren't in prison.

Radecke agreed, still impressed by his guide to the Paris nightlife. He assigned two German soldiers to accompany Chamberlin as muscle but stressed that the local Abwehr boss, Colonel Friedrich Rudolf, could never discover what was going on. Rudolf was a strait-laced gentleman warrior of the old school, who lived for espionage, but hated the vulgarity of petty crime.

Chamberlin headed down to the Paris courts and demanded access to the files on all recent fraud and theft cases, while calling himself a German police agent. The intimidated clerks handed over everything that was available and watched him walk out the door with his arms full of paperwork.

The next day agent 10.474.R and his German sidemen appeared at Fresnes prison in the southern suburbs of Paris. Chamberlin spoke to the prison authorities and demanded the release of five prisoners. The two soldiers who stood glowering over his shoulder quashed any doubts the prison staff had and Chamberlin got his men. The prisoners he had freed were smugglers and traffickers and were all tied to a case that involved the bribery of police officers. Four of the men were career crooks, but the round-faced fifty-something Paul Maillebuau, nicknamed 'Gros Paul' (Big Paul), was a corrupt police inspector who had been kicked out of the force for extorting his own men.

Chamberlin returned two days later for another twenty-one prisoners, and then came back the next day for two more. Most of the men he selected came from his criminal past in Paris or in the south of the country, and all were professional crooks with long records. Famous faces included his old prison friend Adrien Estébétéguy; André Girbes, known as 'La Rigole' (The Laugh), who was a hardened thief with a reputation in the French underworld; his friend Robert Moura, nicknamed 'Le Fantassin' (The Footsoldier), who was a pimp with a recent conviction for 'hiring women for the purpose of debauchery'. There was also Lucien Prévost, who had four convictions for dealing in stolen goods, had strong connections to a notorious arms dealer, and had partnered Estébétéguy in the gold scam that put them both in prison in the first place. Other crooks included Tissier, Carrier, Pinardel and others. And now they all worked for Chamberlin.

The news about Chamberlin's fledgling criminal enterprise spread throughout gangland Paris, from the whorehouses of Pigalle to the dimly lit bars of Montmartre. Monsieur Henri had the power to spring anyone he wanted. A 38-year-old petty criminal who'd spent most of his career getting caught was now a serious '*caïd*', a gang boss.

Chamberlin had barely assembled his team when a panicking Radecke approached him and pushed a train ticket to the French coast into his hand. Chamberlin needed to take an urgent holiday. Colonel Rudolf had found out about Chamberlin's recruitment drive among the cells of Fresnes, and he wasn't happy.

The colonel was especially upset about specific rumours that some prisoners had only been freed after their families had paid off Chamberlin with bribes. Apparently, a lot of money had changed hands. Rudolf was talking about putting Chamberlin on trial. Radecke told his new hire to stay out of sight until the situation calmed down.

Monsieur Henri headed for Bordeaux, while looking for a way to persuade the Abwehr to take him back. He would eventually find it through a Belgian spy who was hiding from the Germans in Toulouse. Chamberlin was moving on from petty crime to treason.

2

ONE HOUR BEHIND GERMANY

THE OLD MARSHAL HAD lines around his eyes like fishing nets and a dusty white, neatly trimmed moustache. By the time of the occupation, Pétain was eighty-four years old. On 30 October 1940, he made a formal address to the French people. His voice was firm and soothing as it came through radio grilles across the country.

'This first meeting, between the victor and the vanquished, marks the first step toward the recovery of our country. I freely accepted the Fuhrer's invitation. I acted under no compulsion, nor did I follow any diktat. Collaboration was proposed between our two countries, and I accepted the principle.'[1]

Marshal Henri Philippe Benoni Omer Joseph Pétain had lived long enough to remember Napoléon III ruling over the Second Empire, horses clip-clopping on cobblestones through flickering shadows cast by the Paris gas lights and Georges-Eugène Haussmann gutting the heart of the city to build his model metropolis. Now the marshal was an old man hoping to rescue something from the wreckage of defeat.

A lot of things had changed in the country since the summer of 1876, when a young Pétain left his family farm to enlist as a soldier in the service of France. Years of staff and regimental postings had kept the career military man off the colonial battlefields but allowed him to build a reputation as a dependable homeland officer, although not one who could always be trusted with other men's wives. During his time in the forces, he saw the sword replaced by the pistol, and the rifle upgraded to the machine gun, and understood that future wars would be mechanised slaughterhouses; '*Le feu tue*,' Pétain said. Firepower kills.[2]

His understanding of modern warfare meant that he was one of the few French generals to come out of the First World War with his reputation intact. Politicians appreciated his cautious yet solid defence tactics. Soldiers welcomed his leniency with those men who cracked under the pressures of trench warfare. The interwar years saw Pétain take up more military staff positions, embark on a campaign against Rif rebels in Morocco, dabble in conservative politics, serve a stint as the French Minister of War and finally take up the position of ambassador to Spain.

Paul Reynaud's government recalled Pétain in May 1940 in an attempt to stop the German tanks powering through the Ardennes. Pétain checked the maps, did some calculations, then argued for an armistice. On 16 June he replaced Reynaud as Prime Minister of France. Soon after, the German troops took control of Paris and the fighting ceased.

Pétain hoped for an honourable peace for his country, but instead he got an occupation that bled France dry and butchered its corpse. Nazi organisations began looting everything of value, while Wehrmacht mapmakers divided the country into 'Occupied' and 'Unoccupied' zones, before hacking away some more to make additional 'Reserved', 'Forbidden' and 'Attached' zones. Alsace-Lorraine became part of Germany. Another piece of France down in the south-east along the Alps went to Italy. All of the zones had different administrations and were divided by hard demarcation lines dotted with soldiers, sandbags and identity checks. The Occupied Zone ran on Berlin time, which was an hour ahead of the other sectors. It was a humiliating system, even to those French fascists who had initially welcomed their new German overlords, like far-right novelist Pierre Drieu la Rochelle. 'A hierarchy of nations is not internationalism,' he wrote in his diary.[3]

The bitterness of occupation was sweetened slightly when Berlin authorised nominal French self-rule. This saw Pétain pupate into a dictatorial Chief of the French State and sign the armistice on 22 June 1940. Later he posed with Adolf Hitler in front of clicking cameras. Germany's apparent concession was Machiavellianism disguised as charity. The true purpose of granting of self-rule was to soothe Britain into a peace deal and to stop rogue French military leaders fighting on against Germany from the colonies.

Vichy obediently took its place in the Nazi new order and was immediately caught in the crossfire. In July 1940, over 1,000 sailors died at the Algerian port of Mers-el-Kébir when the British Royal Navy bombarded the French ships to prevent them being used in the German war effort. The next month, Pétain's former subordinate General Charles de Gaulle – who had fled France in disgust at the armistice – left his London exile to occupy French Equatorial Africa and launch a failed invasion of the West African port of Dakar at the head of his rebel Free French forces.

This civil war in miniature led to the deaths of French soldiers on both sides and left the public at home in desperate need of reassurance. Marshal Pétain gave it to them. On 30 October, millions tuned into Radio Nationale to be told that surrender was not shameful and that humiliation was not fatal.

> To all those who await the salvation of France, I wish to say that salvation is already in our hands. To all those who would doubt the noble sentiment of our thoughts, I wish to say that a Frenchman's first duty is to have faith. To the doubters and the defiant, I would remind [them] that the virtues of reserve and pride, when taken to an extreme, become mere stubbornness.[4]

Pétain's broadcast formally accepted that the German occupation was permanent. The old marshal couldn't understand why Britain continued to fight the Nazis, and many French citizens felt the same way. In London, the Jewish author André Maurois, who had been caught overseas as a result of the occupation, had a row with National Gallery director Kenneth Clark about the British refusal to make peace. 'He said that our obstinacy was an insult to France, a menace to Europe and a crime against history,' stated Clark. 'I realised that at this moment the French, having failed to fight the Germans, felt they must fight someone.'[5]

The moral complexities of collaboration or resistance meant nothing to Henri Chamberlin. His only concern was to avoid a return to the pre-war days when he had empty pockets and a grumbling stomach. In the autumn of 1940 this meant that he had to prove his value to the Abwehr and find a way back to Paris.

At first, Chamberlin spent the days of his imposed exile drinking in Bordeaux cafés and getting used to his newly adopted pseudonym of Henri Lafont. There was not much else to do in the flat port city on the river Garonne. His fortunes changed when the local German commander, Colonel Lorscheder, invited him to dinner. Agent 10.474.R turned up the charm and made it a memorable evening for all concerned, full of wine and jokes. By the time that dessert was served, Chamberlin was listening intently as Lorscheder complained about the problems that he was having in tracking down an enemy agent.

Before the Second World War, a Belgian spymaster named Otto Lambrecht had managed a network of contacts across Europe. He disappeared from his homeland when Brussels fell to the Germans in May 1940, and re-emerged in Toulouse, a coral-coloured town full of restless Mediterraneans deep in France's Zone Libre. In this part of the country, the German occupiers had no official presence and the local police remained eagle-eyed and patriotic.

Lorscheder wanted Lambrecht and his spy network closed down but did not seem to be too concerned about the situation. The resistance in France remained embryonic. De Gaulle's call to arms on BBC radio on behalf of the Free French had been heard by few and obeyed by less. There were episodes of defiance: a handful of German soldiers in Paris were attacked on the street and an ambush near the Bois de Boulogne put three soldiers in hospital. The occupying authorities talked about taking hostages, but the attacks stopped and nothing came of it.

Most French people were too stunned to think about resisting the occupation. Chamberlin barely even understood that some of his compatriots were fighting back. 'If the guys on the other side, the resistance, had suggested something to me, I would have done it, no question,' he later remarked. 'But in July and August 1940, I didn't know about the resistance and hadn't seen anything. I didn't even know what it was.'[6]

Lorscheder's table talk about the rogue Belgian spy gave Chamberlin an idea. He had been arrested in Toulouse back in the late 1920s and knew the area well. He offered to make a trip to the town and sniff out Lambrecht. Colonel Lorscheder looked surprised, but he eventually agreed to take a chance on his new friend.

Chamberlin telephoned Radecke back in Paris and asked him to arrange for three of his freed jailbirds to travel south. The trio were specifically chosen by Chamberlin for their backgrounds: Estébétéguy had spent a lot of time in Toulouse before the war and Robert Moura and André Girbes were Bordeaux natives. Chamberlin met them at Bordeaux railway station with a selection of passes to get them across the demarcation line and into unoccupied Vichy. Before the gang of four began their journey, Chamberlin gave them a briefing and a pep talk. The next day they crossed into Vichy territory and a different world.

Under Pétain, a coalition of young technocrats, right-wing Catholics and long-time nationalist activists had come together to bring their authoritarian dreams to life among the rubble of defeat. The government espoused regeneration through the Révolution Nationale, which was a paternalism that privileged large families and stopped married women from working in public services; dissolved trade unions and organised workers into horizontal slices of industry; promoted a watered-down version of fascist culture characterised by sports, health and youth groups camping in forests; and enforced a milder version of Nazi anti-Semitism that barred Jews from a number of professions.

Government propaganda posters depicted medieval knights and Napoleonic-era peasants rising from freshly ploughed fields and country churches. Above it all, Pétain floated as leader somewhere between benevolent dictator and hollow figurehead.

Chamberlin and his cronies did not care about Vichy's plans for a new France. They came swimming into Toulouse like a gang of sharks through a shipwreck and hung around the town's cafés and restaurants in search of Lambrecht. Estébétéguy quizzed his underworld friends about the spy until he got an address. When the half-asleep Belgian opened the door of his apartment to a group of men in the middle of the night, Chamberlin beat him unconscious. The gang stole Lambrecht's car and drove back to Bordeaux.

Colonel Lorscheder couldn't believe it when his new French acquaintance opened the boot of the car to reveal Lambrecht lying tied up and desperate inside. Under interrogation the Belgian spy cracked and gave up 600 names of informants, spies and key intelligence sources. Chamberlin was welcomed back to Paris by the Abwehr with open arms.

• • •

The 'One-Two-Two' in rue de Provence was a building with an austere pale grey façade and home to one of the French capital's most expensive and exclusive brothels. Clients could choose to satisfy an infinite number of perversions in one of the establishment's twenty-two themed rooms, which included an Orient Express mock-up cabin that rocked and bounced, a pirate room with a four-poster bed that sprayed the inhabitants with jets of water, an igloo, a barn, a cottage and many more. In the restaurant, the waitresses wore aprons, high heels and nothing else. Before the war, disabled veterans could visit the premises for free. Now the building was full of German officers in Wehrmacht uniform congratulating Henri Chamberlin on his return from Toulouse.

Radecke had organised a party to celebrate Chamberlin's triumph. The building was filled with the sound of popping champagne corks and congratulatory slaps on the back, while pretty girls paid enough to convincingly fake enthusiasm shimmied out of their negligees. Colonel Rudolf refused to attend the soiree, but reluctantly accepted Chamberlin back into the agency.

Once his hangover wore off, Chamberlin had a job waiting for him with Max Stöcklin. Hermann Brandl's Amt Otto purchasing offices were up and running and hungry for anything that French industry had to offer the German war effort. The collapsing economy meant that local businessmen were lining up to offload wagonloads of goods, from carpets to locomotive engines. They were paid in cash, and every shipment that went through the Saint-Ouen docks destined for the Reich bled France a little whiter.

As German fangs sunk deeper into the French neck, a marché noir (black market) quickly proliferated, which grew larger when Vichy formally introduced rationing in September 1940. Criminals made fortunes by supplying sugar, tobacco, bread and anything else that the public couldn't get enough of in the shops. Brandl decided that he wanted a piece of this emerging underground economy but soon discovered that the crooks who operated the system didn't trust foreigners in uniform. A solution arrived with the return of Chamberlin.

By this time Max Stöcklin was now one of the Amt Otto's top men, his door always open to anyone who sold items in bulk and didn't mind the Swiss fiddling the figures to give himself a bigger commission. He installed Chamberlin at a requisitioned shop on rue Tiquetonne to buy food, clothes and furniture from any source, regardless of whether they had been obtained legally or illegally. Two Abwehr men helped out and reported back to Radecke at the Hôtel Lutetia. The one called Maximilian was a short Bavarian with a limp, while Eugene was a former gigolo who joined the service when his looks faded. A Frenchman called Rudy de Mérode delivered bricks of cash every week.

Chamberlin was a quick learner and business boomed. Black marketeers and thieves who might have been reluctant to deal with the Germans had no problems with Monsieur Henri. He was one of them and a fellow Frenchman.

He opened a second office in a requisitioned Freemasonic building on rue Cadet. The opening of other properties followed, including a large space on rue du Faubourg Saint-Antoine that received deliveries of wheat, butter and livestock from Normandy. Chamberlin's freed prison pals did most of the work and made sure to destroy any paperwork that revealed Chamberlin's price gouging. In this way, stock worth 500,000 francs would be sold on to the Germans at the price of 4 million. Everyone involved received their percentage and Monsieur Henri always got the biggest slice. The money came rolling in.

As the business expanded Stöcklin reluctantly accepted that his protégé no longer needed him, and Chamberlin became his own boss. The Frenchman then brought in his own protégé in the form of nephew Paul Clavié, who was one of the few family members that Chamberlin still cared about.

Paul Jean Marie Joseph Clavié was a short, shifty-looking man in his mid-twenties with slicked-back hair and a pencil moustache. Clavié had followed his uncle into the criminal underworld of Paris, but by this time had achieved little aside from a reputation for violence and a nasty case of gonorrhoea, which he was treated for by a Dr Petiot – described by Clavié as 'a physician of the pissoir' – who didn't ask questions.[7]

Other crooks jostled for position in Chamberlin's burgeoning business. The 42-year-old Estébétéguy remained Chamberlin's principal lieutenant and had enough influence to employ his brother Louis as doorman at one of the shops, although other employees regarded the new recruit as being too stupid for even this position. Estébétéguy's former partner Lucien Prévost also became a prominent player. He was a sharp-nosed 34-year-old playboy type with a long neck, the usual slicked-back hair and wore his collar permanently open at a time when only bohemians and artists didn't wear a tie. The defrocked inspector Paul Maillebuau proved himself corrupt enough to be accepted as part of Chamberlin's inner circle. His police background didn't cause any problems; he spoke the same slang and walked the same streets as the rest of the gang. Square-faced Louis 'Eddy' Pagnon acted as Chamberlin's bodyguard and drove his white Bentley.

Having a car during the occupation was an unusual privilege. Only 7,000 private car permits were available to a metropolitan region of 6.7 million people and petrol was even harder to source. Flocks of bicycles filled the Paris roads and flowed around the ever-present Wehrmacht trucks. Designers had already begun working on jupes-culotte divided skirts to allow women to ride bicycles with dignity. The rest of the city took the crowded, irregular buses or crammed onto the Métro, which had whole carriages reserved for German officers and others at the rear for Jews.

The capital was slowly coming back to life, but the ghost of defeat was everywhere in the narrow grey streets that intersected and subdivided before bursting into plazas, boulevards and the wide banks of the Seine, and then threaded together again into more narrow alleys and small flats with sleepy cats in the windows. In the autumn of 1940, the theatres reopened and put on plays by Jean Cocteau, Paul Claudel and other famous names. Music halls and the more risqué shows already struggled to cope with demand.

The Parisians pretended not to notice the Germans all around them, even as the Berlin Philharmonic put on performances at Versailles and military bands oompahed away in parks. In the cabarets the French audiences applauded and laughed extra loud to show that they were not dejected in defeat, merry as a leper's bell.

Banners were hung from the National Assembly and the Eiffel Tower with the message '*DEUTSCHLAND SIEGT AN ALLEN FRONTEN*' ('Germany is victorious on all fronts').

In the winter of 1940 Hitler's troops were still winning as the canals froze and the trains iced up. Supplies of food and fuel began to slow and the population was left cold and hungry. Henri Chamberlin escaped the worst privations when Brandl ordered him to Algeria on a spying mission in December. The Lambrecht operation had impressed some important people who were looking to set up a listening post in Vichy's North African colony. Monsieur Henri left behind the black market for the sparkling blue of the Mediterranean Sea. He was accompanied by his chauffeur Pagnon and a Morse code transmitter.

A deep-cover Abwehr office in Marseille that masqueraded as a travel company from neutral Spain named L'Agence Franco-Espagnole supplied Chamberlin with tickets and fake identity cards. For this expedition he became a businessman called Dolet.

Algeria was dry plateaus and golden deserts, and over the centuries many nations had loved this land intensely. Phoenicians, Romans and Ottomans all claimed Algeria as a tile in their imperial mosaics and in 1830 France joined the list of colonisers. The French carved out irrigation grids and built farms across the hard, arid soil. The capital Algiers expanded into a maze of narrow souks and white-washed villas.

Native Algerians were shoved aside by the influx of French, Italian and Spanish immigrants who would come to be known as Pieds-Noirs. The European arrivals created good lives for themselves. Mornings started with a dose of café au lait and an unfiltered Gauloises Bleu cigarette outside a café under the North African sun before strolling off to a steady job in the shipping businesses, then coming home after a long day to a spacious apartment staffed by Algerian servants, respectful and underpaid. Policemen in blue uniforms blew their whistles and waved their white truncheons, just like back home. It was a life of figs and wine and suntanned limbs.

The Pieds-Noirs had no experience of life under the German occupation and they accepted the compromises of Vichy without much of a struggle. Algerian intelligence services reserved their hostility for local troublemakers, a category that covered everyone from de Gaulle loyalists to Nazi spies. When Chamberlin and Pagnon arrived in Africa they had to be discreet in their search for a suitable spy base.

The pair found a villa named 'Planelas' at Doumia, which sat fifty miles outside of Algiers. Brandl handed over 300,000 francs to purchase the property and boosted the team by adding Chamberlin's nephew Paul Clavié, Abwehr veteran Max Stöcklin who could act as an adviser, a Corsican crook called Venturini and a German radio expert named Gaston Mochler from the University of Stuttgart. By January 1941, the team had bought the villa in Clavié's name, installed the Morse code transmitter and made its first broadcast to Abwehr headquarters in Paris.

After more than a month of smooth running, Brandl was making plans for another champagne celebration at the One-Two-Two in Paris. Then everything fell apart. In March 1941, Pagnon and Venturini became involved in some gold smuggling that put the Algiers police on their trail. Chamberlin was in Marseille when Vichy intelligence kicked in the villa Planelas door and scattered his team. Pagnon and Venturini ended up behind bars.

Venturini was shot by a firing squad, but Abwehr diplomatic efforts meant that Pagnon was transferred to a Paris prison. With the remaining members of the team recalled to the capital, Brandl invited Chamberlin to the Hôtel Lutetia for a talk and intended to hand out some kind of punishment for the operation's failure. But he was unprepared for the tsunami of charm, lies and deflected blame that Monsieur Henri unleashed. The overwhelmed Abwehr boss found himself agreeing to give his French agent another chance.

'If you want me to be useful,' said Chamberlin, 'let me work in Paris. There, I'm in familiar surroundings.'[8]

Brandl agreed to blame Pagnon for the Algiers affair and keep him locked up for a few more months until things calmed down. Talk then moved on to issues concerning Paris police interference in Chamberlin's black market deals. Monsieur Henri laid on the charm thick as country butter and argued that if he was granted German nationality, the authorities would keep out of his business. Brandl agreed and also threw in the rank of hauptmann (captain). Chamberlin left the Hôtel Lutetia as a citizen of the German Reich and an officer in the Wehrmacht. From this point on, he was untouchable.

Chamberlin came out of the Algiers disaster even further ahead when Radecke gifted him a large flat on avenue Pierre-1er-de-Serbie in the upmarket eighth arrondissement to function as a new headquarters for his operation. Under the protection of Chamberlin's German passport, his black market business began bringing in even more money. No one at the Abwehr cared how much cream Chamberlin skimmed off the top for himself as long as he passed plenty on upstairs. Once again life was sweet.

The Germans came down brutally hard on those German citizens who exploited the black market without authorisation. A deserter turned black marketeer found this out in a forest clearing just south of Paris in the spring of 1941. He had a firing squad, a priest and a cheap wooden coffin.

3

PLAYING TO WIN

FAT FLIES SLEPT INSIDE the bullet holes dotted into the ash tree. They lived in two clusters on the trunk, eighteen inches apart, one for the head and one for the heart. Since the start of the occupation this damp forest clearing near Châtenay-Malabry had been used by the Wehrmacht as an execution site for fourteen Frenchmen and a handful of German soldiers who had broken military law. In late May 1941, Hauptmann Ernst Jünger received orders to assemble a fresh firing squad. A German deserter who had made some good money on the black market had been sentenced to death.

Jünger considered faking sickness to get out of the assignment. The 46-year-old had seen enough death over the past three decades. As a teen he escaped the middle-class banality of Heidelberg to join the French Foreign Legion in North Africa. His father had to bribe his jailers to get him out of prison after a desertion attempt.

The young man returned to Germany in time for the First World War and spent four years of close combat as a sturmmann, loping into the enemy trenches armed with gun and hand grenade. At the end of the war he had received seven wounds and his nation's highest award for bravery.

The interwar years saw Jünger search for meaning through the occult, entomology, nationalism, drugs and women. He took long midnight walks through empty streets and wrote obsessively about his experiences in the trenches. As an authoritarian with conservative ideals, Jünger played a minor role in bringing down the Weimar Republic but could not bring himself to support National Socialism. Some interpreted his 1939 novel *Auf den Marmorklippen* (*On the Marble Cliffs*) as an anti-Nazi tract but Jünger claimed that it had a broader symbolism. From his hardline elitist perspective, Hitler and the Nazis looked like left-wing populists.

During the occupation, Jünger was back in uniform, back in France and under orders to execute one of his fellow Germans. He did some light wrestling with his conscience and took up the assignment. The opportunity to watch a man face his own death had a chilly aesthetic appeal to a former front-line soldier whose empathy had been pruned back by years of war and loss. 'I have to confess,' he wrote in his journal, 'it was the spirit of higher curiosity that induced me to accept.'[1]

Two vehicles drove up carrying the prisoner and his guards, a pastor brought along to administer the last rites, a medical officer and gravediggers with spades and a flimsy white coffin. The guards walked the condemned man up to the ash tree. He was young, handsome and wide-eyed, the kind of man a young French woman would happily hide after he deserted his unit. He wore an expensive green silk shirt and grey trousers. Even small players outside of the Amt Otto machine could make good money in the black market.

The collaborationist *L'Œuvre* newspaper, which was based in Paris, told readers that the black market was France's biggest problem. It skated over the role played by the German purchasing markets in birthing the black market in the first place. In 1941 around 15 per cent of French meat and 12 per cent of cereal went straight to the

Reich.[2] Food rationing meant that French civilians were expected to survive on only 1,200 calories a day, which was the lowest of any Western nation.

Things had become so bad that Vichy legalised '*colis familiaux*' (family packages), which were regular food parcels received by those who were lucky enough to have a relative who lived on a farm. The packages kept many from starvation despite the enthusiastic pilfering committed by postal officials. Wider attempts to crack down on the black market failed, and most of the big names involved in the business, like the Lafont gang, had official protection.

The young man in the forest clearing had no one to protect him. Jünger tied a blindfold over his eyes and the medical officer pinned a red tag the size of a tarot card over his heart. The pastor held up a silver crucifix to be kissed by the prisoner and then Jünger barked the order. The rifles cracked and lines of smoke drifted across the clearing. Five bullet holes like drops of rain on the red card, before he sagged and fell to the ground.

When the execution was over Jünger returned to Paris, the city of light and literature that he had come to love for the same reasons that so many others had flocked to the capital for centuries. Notre-Dame, the Louvre, the Eiffel Tower, the bohemian Latin Quarter, the artists of Montmartre, the graves of Balzac and Proust in Père Lachaise cemetery, the white headstone of Baudelaire like a castle turret in Montparnasse, and all the other cultural clichés that never meant anything to Henri Chamberlin and his gangsters as they schemed their way across the metropolis.

A new revenue stream for the gang opened up in 1941 when Brandl introduced them to the Devisenschutzkommando (the Foreign Exchange Protection Commando, known as the DSK), a finance unit that was based in the old Lazard-Frères Bank on rue

Pillet-Will. The DSK had heard about this useful group of criminals in the pay of the Germans and had a mutually profitable operation in mind.

The DSK's official duty was to oversee currency exchanges. Unofficially, its agents grabbed all the cash they could lay their hands on. In the spring of 1941, they went after French gold by imposing an artificially low price on the commodity and funnelling all sales through their books. The tactic backfired when gold sellers began offloading their stock on the black market. The 26,000-strong Paris police showed little enthusiasm for stopping the proliferation of the gold trade, so the DSK enlisted the services of Chamberlin instead.

Monsieur Henri worked out a plan with gang member Robert Gourari, a chinless gold trafficker with thinning hair, known to the underworld as 'Le Pâle' (The Pale). Gourari had spurned his middle-class background and turned to crime after going through a rough patch following his national service. A few months in prison sank him permanently into the underworld of Paris. He developed a talent for fraud and gained himself a pretty young wife in a nice apartment near the centre of Saint-Denis. His friends included Georges Boucheseiche, a hotelier who was well-connected in the criminal milieu.

Things were good for Gourari until the war came along. He was called up and quickly remembered just how much he hated life in uniform. To get out of the situation he shot himself in the arm with a revolver but ended up in a camp for '*indésirables*' in the south of the country. In July 1940, the authorities finally released him into a world of swastika flags and feldgrau. A few months later, Georges Boucheseiche introduced him to a man called Henri Lafont who ran the Amt Otto buying office in rue Tiquetonne. Shortly afterwards, Gourari joined the gang.

The men who sold precious metals in Paris trusted Gourari. He had the right kind of accent and manners and sounded convincing when he pretended to curse the DSK for attempting to corner the market. Under this new arrangement Gourari would make the introductions, members of the gang would pose as buyers and other thugs in the entourage would come hard through the door when the gold appeared, shouting '*Police Allemande!*'[3]

Chamberlin gave his men bogus police identification to flash in the faces of traffickers. Faux policiers (fake policemen) plagued the Occupied Zone during the war. In the hedge maze of overlapping jurisdictions and uncertain loyalties anyone with confidence and a fake identity card could claim to be an authority figure. The fake officers would push their way into businesses and apartments and steal money, jewellery and food while calling it collecting evidence. Wealthy people could be kidnapped under the pretence of an arrest. The scam became so widespread that *L'Œuvre* newspaper ran regular cartoons of law enforcement and burglars confronting each other.

'Imbecile!' says one inspector. 'I'm a fake policeman!'

'Idiot!' replies the criminal. 'I'm a fake burglar!'[4]

Faux policiers came alone, in pairs and in gangs. Other individuals pretended to be fake electric meter readers, gas company officials and even shoe leather inspectors for poor families, who were entitled to free footwear. On occasion, different imposters would collide with one another, as Chamberlin's gang found out when a member of the group named Terrail arranged a gold sale.

'Terrail came to find me and told me that someone called Ricord had some pieces to sell,' said Clavié.

> Terrail made the sale and when Ricord got out the pieces, three of us entered the place like policemen. But then Maillebuau and Ricord recognised each other and we realised that if we were

> doing the fake police routine then Ricord was doing the fake seller, showing some pieces to sell, then, when the moment came to pay, pocketing the pieces and the money.[5]

Following this incident, the thirty-year-old Auguste Joseph Ricord joined the gang. Everybody else who encountered Chamberlin's men got their gold confiscated accompanied by a slap on the wrists and a warning. Those who put up a struggle were dragged off to the Germans. Chamberlin sold the gold on to the DSK, who paid 2,500 francs for a Louis D'Or coin and double that for a Napoléon. This was well below market value, but a lot of money to get for a free bag of dirty yellow disks with beak-nosed men on one side and a coat of arms on the reverse.

Chamberlin was soon overseeing three or four stings a day, each worth tens of thousands of francs at a time when a senior Vichy Contrôle Économique agent employed to enforce food rationing earned 60,000 francs a year and a young French interpreter working for a German intelligence agency regarded his 1,500 francs a month as being a good wage. The Abwehr didn't mind the gang serving two masters. Brandl got a percentage of the DSK cash and was able to mollify Colonel Rudolf with the news that new gang member Jean Sartore had uncovered a smuggling operation in June 1941, which involved a network spanning Paris and the Zone Libre. It specialised in gold, jewellery and helping Jewish refugees escape the Nazi occupation.

Sartore was a balding 35-year-old career criminal of Corsican descent. He had twelve convictions for everything from theft to assault, drunkenness to forgery. He came out of jail at the beginning of 1941 to find all of his friends talking about the new Lafont gang dominating Paris and decided to join up.

One of Sartore's DSK gold scams uncovered a police commissioner running a smuggling route across the demarcation line and Chamberlin passed the details on to the Abwehr. They found out that the commissioner had been robbing the Jews who had used his service to escape the Occupied Zone. He had also murdered a Dutch family to get his hands on their diamonds. The commissioner was sent to a German-run prison for his crimes.

Brandl was impressed by the way Chamberlin handled the smuggler and the gold deals; he gave the Frenchman a new job as black market enforcer. Anyone who crossed the Amt Otto buyers or their friends would have to deal with the gang from avenue Pierre-1er-de-Serbie.

A typical enforcement affair that the gang was involved in concerned a Dutchman called Hendrick Seelen, who kept back 27 million francs from a lead sale that should have gone to the Kriegsmarine. The gang tracked down Seelen and Chamberlin beat him unconscious during an interrogation. The Dutchman spent six months in Cherche-Midi prison, while his friends were forced to scrape together the money to reimburse the German navy. Chamberlin got a percentage of the money that was owed and managed to charm Seelen's 27-year-old mistress Anne-Marie Jeanne Douflos along the way; she fell into his bed and stayed there until the Dutchman's release.

Chamberlin leveraged more advantage from the Seelen affair by covering up some facts that reflected badly on a Kriegsmarine admiral. The man in gold braid was grateful for his efforts and talked about a reward, but Chamberlin just smiled and talked about friendship. 'Now I own the admiral,' he later bragged to his gangsters.

The gang's reputation spread out of the criminal milieu and into the straight world. One day a hamster-faced friend of Clavié called

André Engel turned up at avenue Pierre-1er-de-Serbie looking for a job. Engel was not an established crook, just a young man looking to make easy money in a city blighted by food rationing and blackouts. Chamberlin arranged some driving work as a stand-in for Pagnon, who was still serving time after taking the rap for the Algiers affair; he then promoted Engel to the black market dealings when the chauffeur was out of jail.

Another petty criminal was forced into joining the Lafont crew. In mid-1941 Gourari was doing one of his gold trades with a man named Alexandre Villaplana, which involved some electro-plated lead that Villaplana was passing off as gold. Villaplana was a former international midfielder with commitment and a touch of delicacy in his passes. Well liked by the fans, he was twenty-four years old when he captained France at the 1930 FIFA World Cup in Montevideo, Uruguay. Gambling and race fixing had brought his footballing career to a premature end.

• • •

Alexandre Villaplana grew up in Algiers among the white stone buildings and hard sunlight. He left the colony early in his life thanks to a talent for football. By the age of sixteen he was playing on the mainland for FC de Cette, champions of the Ligue du Sud-Est, and temporarily Frenchified his name to Villaplane. He then moved to nearby rivals SC Nîmois, where he captained the team before a 1929 transfer into the big league with RC Paris. The following year he led the French team to Uruguay for the first ever FIFA World Cup. A photograph of the player from the World Cup depicted a friendly face with brilliantined dark hair that was neatly parted at the right and thinning at the temples. 'This is the most beautiful day of my life,' Villaplana said before the first match in which he captained his country on the world stage.[6]

France won their match, lost the next two, and went out of the competition. The team sailed home from Latin America through a world that was falling apart. The trouble had started in 1929 in New York when share prices tumbled on the stock exchange, which was promptly followed by widespread panic selling. Within weeks economic disaster surged across the nation's financial markets; businesses collapsed and banks closed their doors. The American disease infected economies around the world and killed off a post-war boom that some had believed would last for ever. France held out until 1931, but then started to struggle.

'On street benches and at métro entrances, groups of exhausted and starving young men would be trying not to die,' wrote Breton journalist Morvan Lebesque. 'I don't know how many never came round. I can only say what I saw. In the rue Madame one day I saw a child drop a sweet which someone trod on, then the man behind bent down and picked it up, wiped it and ate it.'[7]

As others drowned in the economic storm, Alexandre Villaplana initially managed to keep himself afloat. In 1932 French football went professional and the money pot that was available grew. Villaplana saw opportunity and quit RC Paris to sign as captain for a struggling team down south called Olympique d'Antibes. He invested in the club and brought along friends from FC de Cette to strengthen the playing line-up. Antibes did well in its first professional season until a late scandal ruined everything. The team had been bribing opponents to lose, and Villaplana was implicated.

The newspapers talked about Villaplana's love of horse racing and gambling, the disreputable characters he hung around down at the racetrack and a strange incident a few years back when he'd been convicted of theft in what the footballer claimed was a misunderstanding. The midfielder avoided punishment and moved on to OGC Nice but his love for football had died. The club fined him for missing training sessions, the fans hated him for lacking spirit and the French national team dropped him. By this time it seemed as though Villaplana only cared about horse racing and living an easy life.

His first coach from FC de Cette arranged a transfer to the second-tier side Hispano-Bastidienne Bordeaux the next year. Villaplana lasted three months until repeat absences led to him being sacked. He had made it apparent that he would rather be at the track with his dubious acquaintances, with his overcoat collar turned up and a wad of cash in his pocket. In 1936 he went to prison for his involvement in race-fixing at tracks in Paris and the Côte d'Azur, after which his wife left and took the kids with her. Life behind bars gave Villaplana's face a sharp cynicism and thinned his hair even further. He had dropped out of respectable life and joined the underworld.

Villaplana and his friend Charles Cazauba were arrested for dealing in stolen goods in the summer that the German tanks rolled into Paris. Cazauba was a thin-lipped bundle of nerves and quivering hands in his late thirties and had been a prominent figure in the pre-war underworld. Friends and police records knew him by one of his many nicknames, which included 'Daix', 'Gros Charles', 'Le Manchot' and 'Charlot le Fébrile' (Feverish Charlie). As a result of five convictions for robbery, dealing in stolen goods and counterfeiting, he had served fourteen years in prison.

The pair escaped during the chaos of the occupation. In August 1940 they were part of a gang that robbed a Jewish-owned warehouse but were rounded up by the police and returned to prison. Villaplana did two months inside and was out on the streets by February 1941 when he sold twenty-five kilos of fake gold bars to

Robert Gourari, who sold them on to the DSK. The Germans were not happy.

Gourari was arrested but then sprung by Chamberlin, who decided to believe that Le Pâle hadn't been part of the scam. DSK agents tracked down Villaplana and offered him the choice of prison or putting his criminal skills to use by working for the man known as Henri Lafont. Villaplana joined the gang and began running gold stings alongside Gourari and Maillebuau and put in a good word for his friend Cazauba, who was still behind bars. Chamberlin used his contacts and charm to get Charlot le Fébrile released and the experienced crook quickly pushed his way into the gang's inner circle.

Villaplana's new boss was a rich man. Chamberlin wore the best clothes cut by expensive tailors at a time when most women made their children's coats by sewing together old blankets, and the shoe leather shortage had Paris streets echoing to a symphony of tapping wooden heels. The skinny teenager who was forced to scavenge dustbins when he was young was now a solid 39-year-old who ate in expensive restaurants such as the Tour d'Argent (the Silver Tower) on quai de la Tournelle, which was full of German officers admiring the view of the streets of Paris. Hauptmann Ernst Jünger visited once and never returned.

'One had the impression that the people sitting up there on high,' wrote Jünger, 'consuming their soles and the famous duck, were looking with diabolical satisfaction, like gargoyles, over the sea of grey roofs which sheltered the hungry. In such times, to eat, and to eat well, gives one a sensation of power.'[8]

Down below and across the Seine, the Louvre had converted its gardens into vegetable plots to feed the starving children in the city. Adults ate boiled nettles and alfalfa horse feed. Those locals who were quick on their feet could catch pigeons in the park, and many turned domestic pets into food behind the blacked-out windows of cramped apartments. Guinea pigs lived in bathtubs until the day they were stewed, after being fattened on handfuls of grass.

High above it all, Monsieur Henri ate his steak and oysters and Canard au Sang in comfort, while the waiters pretended to ignore his table manners.[9] As the final brandy was served, Chamberlin could sit back and think about how far he had come.

Just a year previously, the French government had Chamberlin halfway to a Guiana prison. But now he was a gang boss who controlled warehouses stuffed with black market goods and had bags of gold coins stashed around his upmarket apartment. Money was coming in fast and his only worry was keeping his team of underworld heavyweights loyal to the cause.

Chamberlin's power over the gang came from charisma, intimidation and his carefully guarded access to the Abwehr. He made sure to distance any crooks who posed a threat to his leadership and one of the first of the team to suffer was his most senior lieutenant, Adrien Estébétéguy.

The Basque was too experienced a crook to fully take Monsieur Henri seriously as an underworld godfather. He found himself loaned permanently to the DSK after refusing to help track down a British parachutist in the Zone Libre. Chamberlin didn't need that kind of independent free-thinking.

'For myself,' said Monsieur Henri, 'I don't care whether it's the Krauts or the Chinese, as long as they pay.'[10]

The spy hunt went on without the help of the gang, but Chamberlin could not forgive his old cellmate. Estébétéguy would never rejoin the inner circle, and one day would pay the price.

In June 1941, Germany invaded the Soviet Union and Chamberlin's gang found themselves with new roles as detectives for their fascist bosses. The Abwehr had them on the trail of a gang of former terrorists who couldn't decide if they were loyal to Hitler, Vichy or a free France. The case involved outward protests of loyalty, rumours of hidden arms dumps and an assassination attempt at the heart of collaboration. The Mouvement Social Révolutionnaire had the Germans worried.

4

THE GREAT MISTAKE

A MILITARY BAND WAS playing somewhere behind the disabled old soldiers with empty sleeves, the tricolore flags and crowds leaning over wooden barricades. On 27 August 1941 the first contingent of the Légion des Volontaires Français Contre le Bolchévisme (the Legion of French Volunteers Against Bolshevism, LVF) assembled at a parade ground in Versailles en route to join the German war effort in the East.

A 21-year-old unemployed mechanic with stiff, dark hair and wary eyes called Paul Collette stood among the volunteers. He watched a huddle of saluting dignitaries coming closer. They kept making self-conscious glances towards the camera that was recording everything for a propaganda newsreel. There was the socialist collaborator Marcel Déat with his flat, leering face framed beneath a beret; the career politician Pierre Laval who had skin like greaseproof paper and was in Paris to look for a new route to power after Marshal Pétain kicked him out of his Cabinet; the tall and fat Jacques Doriot of the collaborationist Parti Populaire Français wearing a badly fitting suit; the hawk-nosed diplomat Fernand de Brinon from Vichy; and a gaggle of senior officers in gold braid.

When the group got near the volunteers, Collette stepped forward. He pulled a pistol from his pocket and opened fire.

Two months earlier Hitler had torn up his non-aggression pact with the USSR and declared war. The first bombs of Operation Barbarossa fell on eastern Poland at 3 a.m. on 22 June 1941. Millions of German men, aircraft, tanks, lorries, horses and rubber-wheeled artillery poured into the Soviet empire for a war of ideological extermination. National Socialism versus Communism; Aryan versus Slav; West versus East.

Within a week the Luftwaffe had gained air superiority. Within two weeks the Wehrmacht had taken most of the Baltic States and Belarus and pushed into Ukraine. Over the next six months German troops would advance 600 miles and occupy half a million square miles of Soviet territory.

In France, the invasion was met with astonishment. No one had seen it coming, particularly the Communists who'd spent the last year being ostentatiously neutral in deference to Moscow's pact with Berlin. The underground Communist newspaper *L'Humanité* used up a lot of ink by calling for understanding between French and German workers. '*Ni Pétain, ni de Gaulle*' ('Neither Pétain nor de Gaulle'), was the closest that official party propaganda got to taking a side in the conflict.[1]

Lacking any military capability or sense of organisation, the resistance effort in France so far had been anaemic. Defiance was expressed in private discussion circles, through chalking de Gaulle's Cross of Lorraine on walls and in the publication of an underground newspaper called *Résistance* in Aubervilliers. The French were too numbed by the daily hunger of queues and rationing to fight back. Tuning in to BBC radio in the evening was the closest most citizens got to rebellion. The Germans made little effort to stop such acts of resistance. Across the Channel, even General Charles de Gaulle was complaining that the average French citizen had no interest in taking up arms. Many of those who had joined him in London were recent immigrants or French Jews, who would be in danger if they had returned home. '*Je n'ai que les métèques pour moi*,' De Gaulle reportedly said. 'I have nothing but bloody foreigners on my side.'[2]

Operation Barbarossa changed everything. In August 1941, a Communist cell shot dead a German naval adjutant at the Barbès – Rochechouart Métro station as he boarded a train. The other Germans in the carriage remembered the look of surprise on the man's face as he fell forward with a bullet in his back. As a result, the Wehrmacht authorities executed three French hostages, which led to a downward spiral of assassinations and reprisals.

Communists made up the bulk of the fledgling resistance movement, but not every activist leaned to the left. Paul Collette belonged to Colonel François de la Rocque's Croix-de-Feu, a far-right nationalist movement prominent before the war which had sworn loyalty to Pétain's Révolution Nationale but could not bring itself to collaborate with the Germans.

Collette had been in the navy when the German invasion began, saw action at Dunkerque and made a failed attempt to join de Gaulle in London. His disgust at collaboration metastasised. In 1941 he joined the LVF to gain access to its leadership. The parade at Versailles presented him with an opportunity. Most of his shots went wide but Déat was wounded in the arm and Laval stumbled off clutching his side.

'I've landed a double blow,' said Collette. 'So much the better.'[3]

The shooting took place at a time when Paris was re-inventing itself as a political rival to Vichy. Pre-war nationalists, such as Jacques Doriot's Parti Populaire Français and the war hero Marcel

Bucard's Mouvement Franciste now claimed to be good National Socialists, enthusiastic collaborators and ideologically closer to Germany than Pétain's reactionaries.

Newer groups formed to fight for scraps of Nazi patronage. The capital's streets saw goose-stepping marches by the Mouvement Social Révolutionnaire – remnants of a pre-war rightist terror group called the Cagoule – led by founder Eugène Deloncle, an engineer with a face like a sad pear. The Ligue Française was run by the unbalanced Pierre Constantini, who had declared a one-man war on Britain after Mers-el-Kébir. Marcel Déat's Rassemblement National Populaire (RNP) ran *L'Œuvre* newspaper and was popular with disillusioned socialists who thought collaboration and jackboots were the best way to help the working class.

'Read this text, support de Gaulle if you believe in an English victory,' wrote RNP propaganda chief Jean Fontenoy in *L'Œuvre*. 'Otherwise march with the Rassemblement for collaboration and a profitable peace! But support France and not the cowards!'

Operation Barbarossa offered an opportunity for Paris to demonstrate its loyalty to the Germans. Eugène Deloncle merged his party into Déat's RNP, and persuaded Doriot to support a recruiting campaign for a military unit made up of French volunteers. Vichy gave cautious support to the LVF, but Hitler recoiled at the idea of Frenchmen in feldgrau. The efforts of the Francophile German ambassador Otto Abetz were required to rescue the project.

The LVF founders had fantasised about hundreds of thousands of Frenchmen enlisting. They received 12,000 recruits, who were largely a mix of fascists and misfits and a number of North African immigrants who had been inspired by the anti-Communist rhetoric of the far-right Algerian figure Mohamed El-Maadi. Volunteers queued up at recruiting stations under German banners that bore messages of a united Europe. Fontenoy, who joined the LVF as a lieutenant, described the Legion as being 'composed half of idealists and half of adventurers. One part had participated in the world war, the other could not handle a gun; one part was eighteen years old, and the other was fifty-five.'[4]

The first contingent of recruits had assembled at a Versailles parade ground for inspection by Déat, Laval and the rest. Deloncle had planned a photo opportunity at a nearby railway station where he planned to stiff-arm salute the trains steaming out for Germany. Then Paul Collette stepped out of the ranks and started shooting. A maelstrom of ambulance sirens, running police and panic followed.

No one died. Even Collette's death sentence was commuted by Pétain out of sheer distaste for Laval. The LVF eventually set off to fight in the snowfields of Russia, while Déat convinced himself that the assassination attempt had been masterminded by Deloncle, in an attempt to kill off political rivals as part of an internal coup. Deloncle denied being involved, but no one listened. He split from the RNP in October 1941, taking his followers with him, and re-established the Mouvement Social Révolutionnaire.

The two factions had been incompatible from the start. The Mouvement Social Révolutionnaire was unshakeably right-wing, its tracks leading back through the ideological snow to nineteenth-century monarchism, whereas Déat was a socialist and former government minister trying to win the benefits of collaboration for the left.

Germany let the two sides fight it out but became concerned by rumours that Deloncle had arms dumps hidden across the country created before the war during his time as head of the Cagoule terror group. The veteran politician René Marx Dormoy had recently been assassinated while under house arrest in the Zone Libre. The Germans suspected Deloncle's men had been responsible. No one in the occupation authorities liked the idea of Frenchmen, no matter how far-right their politics, having a private supply of bombs and guns.

The situation got more twisted after one night in early October 1941 when a rogue Schutzstaffel (SS) officer helped Mouvement Social Révolutionnaire militants blow up seven Paris synagogues. The Wehrmacht authorities reclassified the party as being '*Geduldigte*' (tolerated), rather than '*Genehmigte*' (authorised) like other collaborationist parties, but some suspected the bombings were all part of Heinrich Himmler's plan to expand his power into the west.[5]

At the end of the year, the Abwehr launched an official investigation into the Mouvement Social Révolutionnaire and Henri Chamberlin received a telephone call. Despite the Algiers disaster some members of the Abwehr still believed he had potential as a spy. It helped that gang members Paul Maillebuau and Lucien Prévost had recently helped round up a resistance group run by a businessman called Jacques Paul Kellner out of his warehouse. The pair had found a Morse code transmitter hidden in an office and German troops swept in and arrested Kellner's relatives and associates, some of whom were executed.

Chamberlin accepted the Mouvement Social Révolutionnaire assignment, but reluctantly. Truffling for resistance groups and investigating collaborators would distract him from focusing on his growing empire. Chamberlin's gang had scraped out a niche in the Paris underworld, full of gold and Amt Otto cash, and they were ruling it from a new headquarters in the upmarket heart of occupied Paris where they lived like aristocrats.

• • •

No. 93 rue Lauriston was four storeys of high ceilings and huge salons, with a grey and beige block façade and a discreet walled garden out back. The cellar windows peered out on to the pavement from under an arched stone eyebrow. Abwehr officers presented the mansion to Chamberlin in late 1941 when his black marketeering exploits outgrew the apartment in avenue Pierre-1er-de-Serbie. The original owner, a Jewish-American of Polish origin, had fled France after the German invasion and wasn't coming back any time soon.

Chamberlin took over an expansive bedroom and sitting room on the second floor and a few other gang members moved in above on the top floor. The surrounding sixteenth arrondissement was home to the machinery of occupation, which included the Wehrmacht's Hôtel Majestic on avenue Kléber and Himmler's counterintelligence Sicherheitsdienst (SD) unit at 84 avenue Foch. A short walk away in neighbouring arrondissements were the Abwehr's Hôtel Lutetia, the Eiffel Tower and the Champs-Élysées.

The move to rue Lauriston triggered a new recruitment drive for the gang. Most of the enrolment work was done by the pimps Auguste Jeunet, better known to the underworld as Cajac, and Henri Tanguy, who was an old friend of Chamberlin. The new arrivals were stick-up men, hijackers, card-sharps and burglars. Some were professionals in the art of violence. René Mâle, better known as 'Riri l'Américain', was a charismatic thirty-year-old with a big chin and tousled hair, who was never without his revolver and a wallet thick with bank notes. Mâle liked to boast about his energetic sex life and penis the size of a horse's leg, but always went home to a small, plain girlfriend who never smiled. 'She is the one person in the world that I'm afraid of,' said Mâle.[6]

As the gang grew, important figures in the Paris underworld began to approach Chamberlin to pay their respects, arrange protection and settle disputes; he was even asked to preside over criminal tribunals. Monsieur Henri would hear evidence from all sides, weigh up the evidence, and invariably fine the richest party and take a percentage for himself. More tithing came from the brothel and gambling businesses that paid protection to the gang through Auguste Ricord. The owner of the One-Two-Two contacted Chamberlin when some gangsters tried to muscle in on the legendary brothel. Monsieur Henri took care of it.

Another protection racket covered restaurants that bought their food on the black market. One bistro owner who refused to pay the gang for their security efforts had his premises raided. Diners dived under the tables as Chamberlin led his men through the door, shouting about espionage and British spies. One gangster produced some Gaullist leaflets that he claimed to have found on the floor; another groped a girl who was trying to hide under a table; and a third emptied a carafe of water over a woman who had fainted.

Events took a surreal turn when Alexandre Villaplana spotted cinema actor Jules Auguste Muraire, better known as Raimu, sitting at a table and approached him for his autograph. Raimu was a big football fan and requested Villaplana's autograph in return, then asked him to pay for a bottle of champagne which had been spilled as the gang crashed through the restaurant. Villaplana handed over a thick wad of cash with a flourish.

The bistro owner was dragged back to rue Lauriston. When he demanded to speak to the prefect of police, Chamberlin dialled the number himself and handed over the phone. The prefect apologised but advised him to cooperate with anyone working for the Abwehr. The restaurateur emptied his pockets and agreed to pay the gang every week.

The police could do little to stop Chamberlin and his cronies. On

13 December 1941, a police inspector who was posing as a gold seller got caught up in a sting. His attempt to arrest everyone failed when Chamberlin's faux policiers dragged him off to their headquarters to face their angry boss. 'You're going to Cherche-Midi prison,' said Monsieur Henri, 'because you're making a lot of trouble and it's my men who have to deal with the consequences.'[7]

The policeman spent the night in a cell before a DSK man released him the next morning with a brusque apology. On 15 December, police colleagues got their revenge by picking up a gang member called Marcel Carrier on the Champs-Élysées black market outlet he operated alongside Roger Tissier. Carrier had barely been put behind bars when a German officer and two soldiers arrived to demand his release. The gangster walked free and the German officer tore up the arrest warrant, theatrically dropping the pieces on the floor. The inspectors involved in the arrest went into hiding for a few weeks.

As Chamberlin's influence in Paris grew, his relationship with Abwehr command became increasingly strained. By this time Radecke was annoying him, with his Germanic assumptions of superiority, which required Chamberlin to beg and grovel each time the gang needed passes or car permits. For Chamberlin, the Mouvement Social Révolutionnaire investigation was a pointless distraction from making money. He sent Maillebuau undercover to infiltrate Deloncle's RNP rivals, but began looking for a different patron among the occupation authorities.

He found one in senior Gestapo man, Sturmbannführer Karl Bömelburg. They first met at a celebratory dinner organised by the Abwehr when the gang moved into rue Lauriston. The party was full of champagne, good food and vases of the white orchids that Chamberlin loved so much and now could finally afford, even at occupation prices. The conversation over dinner touched on how Operation Barbarossa had overturned the crab bucket of competing German agencies in Paris and had led to chaos as various organisations attempted to assert themselves. Bömelburg was too polite to emphasise how much his power had increased at the same time as the Abwehr's dimmed.

Karl Bömelburg was from a bourgeois family that ran its own bakery business. He studied in France before the First World War but returned home to fight for the fatherland and earned himself the Iron Cross as a non-commissioned officer. When the war ended Bömelburg set up a sweet shop in Berlin, married his wife and had a son. The small but prosperous business was derailed by the world-wide slump that followed the Wall Street Crash and Hitler and his National Socialists seemed to have the answer to solve Bömelburg's problems. He joined the Sturmabteilung (SA), but spotted the potential for power in Heinrich Himmler's SS and was wearing their black uniform when the Nazis took power.

A few years later he joined the Gestapo as a low-level clerk in the anti-Communist section. The Geheime Staatspolizei (known to everyone as the Gestapo) had begun as an amalgamation of various Prussian police squads. A bureaucratic power struggle meant that it was absorbed into the empire of SS chief Heinrich Himmler and became a gang of men in black leather overcoats who specialised in cracking down on dissent at home and abroad.

Bömelburg's fluent French helped him climb the Gestapo career ladder and he became a specialist on German leftists living in Paris. His superiors promoted him to kriminalkomissar, then to head of the Berlin unit's anti-Communist section, then official liaison with the French police during King George VI's state visit to Paris. The French never trusted Bömelburg and soon expelled him, but he returned during the occupation and took particular pleasure in establishing his headquarters in the former Sûreté Nationale headquarters at 11 rue des Saussaies.

Initially, the Gestapo had limited powers in France. Its activities in Eastern Europe had become notorious enough that the army refused to allow the agency more than a minimal presence in the West. Adolf Hitler was flush enough with his recent victories to agree.

France was under the control of the Wehrmacht, which structured its administration like a layer cake. On top was the Oberkommando der Wehrmacht (the High Command of the Armed Forces), which was effectively run by Hitler. The next layer down was the Oberbefehlshaber des Heeres (the German Army High Command) of General Walther von Brauchitsch, a square-headed professional soldier who was rarely in Paris and often out of France. Below Von Brauchitsch the real power lay in the hands of the Militärbefehlshaber in Frankreich (the Military Commander in France) General Otto von Stülpnagel, who was based at the Hôtel Majestic. Paris had another, lower, layer in the form of Generalleutnant Ernst Schaumburg, the Kommandant von Gross-Paris (the Commander of Greater Paris).

The different layers of power fought among themselves, with the backstabbing made worse by political meddling from Otto Abetz's German embassy and frequent interventions by various people in Berlin with their own agendas. The quarrelling factions were united only in their determination to keep Himmler out of France. That unity began to weaken when resistance activities ramped up after Operation Barbarossa was launched and German soldiers started dying.

This new wave of resistance saw the Feldkommandant of Nantes assassinated; bomb-making instruction manuals circulated; and the reprisal shootings of hostages. The Communist-led Francs-Tireurs et Partisans Français (the French Snipers and Partisans) derailed trains and sabotaged factories. In Paris, '*V pour Victoire*' and pro-Gaullist Cross of Lorraine graffiti was being chalked on the walls faster than the Germans could wash them off.

Bömelburg convinced the generals at the Hôtel Majestic that his men could restore internal order. The Wehrmacht reluctantly granted permission for the Gestapo to organise intelligence networks, promote anti-Communist drives, kick in doors and arrest French citizens. Turf wars soon broke out between Abwehr chiefs and the Gestapo agents who were trespassing on their territory. At the rue Lauriston housewarming, everyone put on their best smiles as they chatted over the champagne and foie gras, but the tension was obvious.

Chamberlin noted how the power had shifted and kept in contact with Bömelburg after the party. He sent daily hampers of food and wine to the Gestapo chief's villa in the boulevard Victor-Hugo. He escorted Bömelburg's student son around the city when he visited from Berlin, and dutifully supplied him with money, jewellery and a night at the One-Two-Two brothel.

Bömelburg appreciated the generosity, but he had explicit orders from Berlin not to employ any local auxiliaries at that time. Monsieur Henri remained stuck with Radecke and Brandl and their Mouvement Social Révolutionnaire investigation. He filed away rumours about the fifty-something Bömelburg's supposed bisexuality for future use.

In April 1942, a man calling himself Faure visited rue Lauriston with a report on the Mouvement Social Révolutionnaire and its Cagoule forebears. He had been sent by Brandl, who thought that Faure's unique skill set could help Chamberlin's operation.

The visitor's real name was Pierre Bonny. Eight years earlier he had been the most famous police inspector in France, but that was before a conman called 'Handsome Sacha' who had important friends and a gun was cornered in the mountains and Bonny's life fell apart.

5

ROTTING FROM THE HEAD DOWNWARDS

IN JANUARY 1934, ALEXANDRE Stavisky was found dying in a pool of blood in a chalet at the Chamonix ski resort near Mont Blanc. The policemen had heard a shot and broke down the bedroom door to find him lying on the bed in a navy blue shirt and trousers with a Browning 6.35 automatic in his hand and blood running black out of his nose and down his face. The hand with the gun was still shaking. France's most wanted man had apparently committed suicide.

The newspapers didn't believe it. Publications for the left and the right of the political spectrum believed that the suicide was a cover-up orchestrated by men in high places. Far-right royalists writing in *Action Française* and the Communists behind *L'Humanité* all claimed that Stavisky had been murdered.

Smooth manners and a talent for playing on other people's greed had taken Handsome Sacha from life as a Jewish Ukrainian immigrant working in a soup factory to prosperity as a wealthy businessman. He built a fraudulent empire selling worthless shares and bought off anyone who threatened to expose him. His scheme worked until 1927 when the police finally managed to get criminal charges to stick after 'emeralds' that he was using as collateral turned out to be green glass. The proceedings dragged out for seven years before Stavisky realised he was going to prison and made a run for the Swiss border.

The Stavisky affair should have been just another scandal with political overtones, just like the gossip that had circulated in Paris about Louis-Théodore Lyon, a well-connected restaurant owner in the capital who had somehow avoided jail when a laboratory on his property exploded and coated the rue St Honoré with heroin. The French assumed rich and powerful men could not be trusted, and they were rarely surprised. The *Rire* magazine ran a cartoon of a man in a dinner jacket addressing his domestic staff: 'Tonight we shall be entertaining a minister and two deputies ... Count the silverware.'[1]

Something about Stavisky's death tipped the scales. It caused a political scandal that brought down two successive Prime Ministers, almost caused a coup and left fifteen people dead after a February 1934 riot. Many more people had their lives ruined and one was Inspector Pierre Bonny of the rue des Saussaies. At the time, he was the best-known policeman in Paris.

Bonny was born in Bordeaux in 1895 to a farming family. When growing up he decided that he wanted something more from life than watching plough horses carve up fields and was working his way into a promising clerking career when the First World War changed everything. He had been in the army for ten months when German soldiers captured him at the Battle of the Somme. Bonny spent the rest of the war in a prison camp, during which time he occupied himself by writing long letters back home, venting his hatred for his captors.

'What a beautiful day it will be, Mamma, when we will be masters of the dirty Boche and shall see them screaming and flattened under the feet of France, of "petite France", always great and eternal. I hope to be at the party that day.'[2]

When he returned home with his horizons significantly widened, he joined the police force and showed enough talent to become a detective with the Paris Sûreté. He was a tall, dark and lean man of the left back then, sharp-witted and good at his job. He had a particular talent for cracking fraud and blackmail cases. While serving in the police force a jeweller tried to chloroform him during an undercover sting; an Italian counterfeiting gang that he helped capture got paraded in front of the cameras; and he allegedly played a role in getting Pope Pius XI to condemn the royalist anti-Semites of Action Française. The newspapers starting calling him 'Le Premier Flic' (France's top cop) and running his photograph, which usually captured him wearing a fedora with a dark band and an expensive overcoat, with a smear of moustache on his upper lip and dark hair scraped down either side of a straight white parting.

Bonny was never infallible. He couldn't escape ridicule in the spring of 1930 when he claimed American actress Jeanette MacDonald had been murdered by Princess Marie-Jose of Belgium in Nice. The Hollywood star promptly turned up alive, but the inspector decided that the resurrected MacDonald must be an imposter and burst into her box at the theatre demanding to see some intimate birthmarks. The actress slapped him in the face.

Bonny had a wife and young son and a standard of living that made some of his colleagues suspicious. He dressed well, took frequent holidays, had his own car and rented an expensive apartment on the boulevard Pereire. Police investigations raised suspicions that Bonny had been involved in the blackmailing of criminals and high-rollers who had been caught with prostitutes.

He claimed innocence and blamed far-right Paris police prefect

Jean Chiappe for persecuting him. Nothing was ever proved, and Bonny became an inspector just in time to jump into the Stavisky affair when things began to heat up.

Four days after the police found Stavisky's body, Bonny interviewed the conman's wife Arlette. She gave up the names of powerful men who'd known her husband and remembered him talking warmly of Chiappe. In reality the connection was flimsier than she believed, but Bonny grabbed the chance to humiliate his rival. He sent the information to government ministers and they dismissed Chiappe. However, Bonny was also then suspended in retaliation by right-wing politicians, who claimed the inspector was part of a government conspiracy to cover up Stavisky's crimes. Bonny tried to claw his way back into the police force by tracking down Stavisky's cheque books, which were rumoured to contain the key that unlocked the case. As he looked, the government fell.

On 6 February 1934, over 40,000 nationalists and a few Communists gathered in the Place de la Concorde to defy the city's new police prefect. The Obelisk of Luxor stood in the centre of the square like the style on a sundial among the surging crowd. As slogans were shouted, the crowd surged forward and smashed down barriers before clashing with the police. A riot erupted that lasted through the evening.

The government was on the brink of collapsing, but no right-wing leader would risk plunging the country into civil war and the violence burned itself out. Fifteen demonstrators were killed and hundreds were injured. In the aftermath of the riot, the government resigned and was replaced by a largely ineffective coalition. Two years later a left-wing backlash brought the Front Populaire to power on a promise to sweep away corruption. By this time Bonny was a convicted criminal.

Bonny had got hold of the Stavisky chequebooks when long-time informant Georges Hainnaux turned up drunk at his door with them one evening. Hainnaux was a Foreign Legion deserter, former boxer and pimp who'd been Stavisky's bodyguard for a few months. The affair made him famous and notorious enough to briefly date the famous American-born singer Josephine Baker and acquire the nickname of 'Jo-la-Terreur' from Belgian crime writer Georges Simenon. Bonny treated him as a loyal informant, but in a world of paranoia and conspiracies some thought it significant that the man Hainnaux chose to ghost-write his autobiography was the far-right journalist Maurice-Yvan Sicard.

After locating the chequebooks, Bonny was reinstated but the documents soon proved to be less significant than was expected and the inspector's change of fortune was temporary. In the aftermath of the riots there was a widespread hunt for scapegoats. Bonny was given six months in Santé prison for extortion on charges arranged by Chiappe's friends; lost a libel case against far-right weekly *Gringoire*; was falsely accused of murdering a peripheral figure in the Stavisky affair; got a three-year suspended sentence for corruption, relating to earlier investigations; was roasted in the press by hard-line Catholic figures such as Philippe Henriot; and got kicked out of the Sûreté.

Bonny's police career was over and his name became shorthand for corrupt policemen and urban sleaze. Soon, Stavisky and Bonny would become symbolically entwined in the imagination of the far right with the leftist Front Populaire government and its Socialist Prime Minister Léon Blum. The disgraced Bonny became a hate figure to the gathering wave of fascism in France.

• • •

Léon Blum was a former lawyer with integrity, a bushy moustache and a comb-over. In June 1936 he became Prime Minister of France. The right accused him of riding the red horse of revolution but Blum's Front Populaire government was less radical than it seemed. He publicly dispelled rumours about a Marxist coup and persuaded workers not to go through with a general strike. His position on French imperialism even seemed to ape that of conservatives.

'It is the right and even the duty of superior races,' he said, 'to attract those who have not arrived at the same degree of culture and to call them to the progress realised thanks to the efforts of sciences and industry.'[3]

Blum's most extreme measures were the introduction of a forty-hour working week and bans on some far-right groups. Action Française managed to stay alive in the shadows of French politics and the Croix-de-Feu reinvented itself as the Parti Social Français with an unconvincing attachment to the democratic process. The right continued to see Bolshevik revolution and Jewish conspiracy in everything that Blum did.

'Your arrival in office, Monsieur le Président du Conseil, is incontestably a historic date,' sneered the one-legged, one-eyed war veteran Xavier Vallat. 'For the first time this old Gallic-Roman country will be governed by a Jew. To govern this peasant nation of France it is better to have someone whose origins, no matter how modest, spring from our soil than to have a subtle Talmudist.'[4]

Vallat and others argued that the real France could be found out in the countryside. A France with photographs of dead men in uniform on kitchen walls, busy masses in village churches, grandmothers who made jam in glass pots, war memorials in town squares, farmers who blamed Jews for price gouging. Blum could never be part of this version of France.

The right frequently brought up the Stavisky affair in the same breath that they cursed Blum. Pierre Bonny could never escape the past. As the Front Populaire struggled on, Bonny got a job as a private detective and supplemented his income by writing for leftist newspapers such as *L'Œuvre*. His friends helped him out financially, but times had become tough for the former policeman. He spent time as a fisherman in Cap Ferret, south-west France.

The former inspector remained politically on the left. He did some investigative work into Eugène Deloncle's Cagoule, the rightist terror group, which had been created after the Place de la Concorde riot by disillusioned Action Française militants. The monarchists had been at the centre of the fighting, but leader Charles Maurras refused to support attempts to bring down the government. On the night of the riot, the veteran monarchist was cornered in his office by youthful supporters and he refused to commit himself. 'I don't like people to lose their self-control,' he said.[5]

Defections began soon after, which led to the founding of Deloncle's Comité Secret d'Action Révolutionnaire (Secret Committee for Revolutionary Action). Enemies nicknamed the group the Cagoule, and imagined its members wearing hoods as they prowled the city at night. The committee launched a terror campaign that assassinated the exiled Italian anti-fascist Rosselli brothers, bombed the rue de Presbourg in Paris killing two policemen and left a young woman dead in a Paris Métro carriage with a stiletto in her neck.

Security was never good and by 1937 the Cagoule leadership had been rounded up by the police. Bonny wrote articles in leftist newspapers claiming that he had a played a role in bringing down the group, helped by information from Jo-la-Terreur. The authorities denied that he had been involved and the right-wing dredged up the Stavisky affair once again to discredit his claims.

By the end of the 1930s, with war on the horizon, Bonny was just another former celebrity whose time had passed. In the summer of 1939 his name was mentioned in connection with the alleged unmasking of a German spy network by Jewish groups, but the authorities took no action on the information and rightist newspapers took the line that Bonny's involvement proved that the network had probably never existed.

'We have made this little policeman a symbol of everything the Sûreté Nationale has done,' protested his lawyer Philippe Lamour. 'He has been thrown to the wolves by a public eager for scandal, who want a new instalment of their real-life crime novel every morning. Bonny is the "pantomime villain" that they like to hiss.'[6]

The war began on 1 September 1939, but it was over for France by the following June. The country had been shipwrecked on the German coast, and the survivors were clutching at wooden splinters with seawater in their mouths. Bonny had been in Paris working as secretary at an aircraft company when the German tanks arrived. His path to rue Lauriston came through Jean Guélin, a well-connected and crooked lawyer who he had known for a few years.

Guélin came from a minor political family that had links to the entourage of former Vichy minister Pierre Laval. The lawyer opened his own Amt Otto bureau in boulevard Malesherbes and made good money buying up factory machinery and locomotives and selling them on to the Germans.

In early 1942, Guélin arranged a meeting between Bonny and Brandl with the idea of getting his policeman friend some work as an Abwehr agent. Bonny was too notorious for this to be feasible, but Brandl saw the advantage that could come from inserting a disciplined, experienced investigator into Chamberlin's criminal chaos.

Bonny's time spying on far-right groups had given him an insight into Deloncle and the Mouvement Social Révolutionnaire. The Abwehr asked him to prepare a report on the party and take it to rue Lauriston. Bonny thought about the offer, his leftist beliefs and a promising career snuffed out by conspiracy and libel.

In March, a play entitled *Les Pirates des Paris* had opened at the Théâtre l'Ambigu-Comique. The politically charged drama was written by fascist theatre critic Alain Laubreaux under a pseudonym and was set during the Stavisky affair. 'For the first time we have a play where a Jew is called a Jew,' said Laubreaux, 'and where the Jew stands out clearly against the background of a regime of filth and decadence.'[7]

The play closed inside a month but reminded Bonny that his past would never be forgotten. The Abwehr offered him a chance to rejoin the establishment, even if it now spoke German. He wrote the report for Brandl.

In April 1942, he arrived at rue Lauriston to find the place empty except for Chamberlin's secretary Edmond Delehaye, a diabetic with a face like a skull. Delehaye handed over 20,000 francs for the report and told Bonny to return later for a personal meeting with Monsieur Henri. When they finally met, Chamberlin's charisma and towering physical presence overwhelmed the former police inspector who had spent a long time floundering among the city's poor, disgraced and hungry.

Bonny later provided the following description of his first encounter with Chamberlin:

> He was a sadistic hedonist. He emanated at that time a sort of fluid of vice and malice, which was difficult to resist. That may be the reason for his success with women. Despite being almost

illiterate, he was clever, cunning, treacherous … what he had in mind could not be refused.[8]

Chamberlin immediately saw the usefulness of having a former inspector with a specific set of skills, experience and contacts on his side. He flattered Bonny, talked about a decent salary and an Abwehr card and argued that it was stupid for French people to starve when there was ripe fruit hanging from the tree to be picked under the occupation. Within a week Bonny had a desk at rue Lauriston and began shaping the gang into a professional organisation that had filing cabinets, kept receipts and wrote up operational reports.

By this time, the gang consisted of the kind of men that Bonny had made his name arresting: the violent Sartore, the slick Prévost, greedy Gourari, amoral Clavié, Tissier, Carrier, Moura the pimp, shaky Cazauba, Villaplana the footballer, Jeunet, Ricord, Engel, 'Gros' Charles Fels, former theatre decorator Alex Bowing, one-time Foreign Legionnaire Eugène Slovenski, Keller, Estébétéguy, who had been assigned to the DSK but was still socialising with gang members, and Pagnon, who had recently been released from prison after serving his time for the Algeria affair.

Other individuals worked for the gang in gold stings and through the Amt Otto business, including Riri l'Américain, François le Mauvais and Armand le Fou. Most members of the crew understood Bonny in the same way they had Maillebuau and kept their distance. He was in the same game but on a different team.

'Some are small-time crooks,' he told his wife and son later. 'OK, I'm fine with that. At least with them I have no history and they obey without question.'[9]

Bonny was a hard-working professional, the polar opposite to his new boss. When the inspector asked for the gang's records,

Chamberlin pulled out a bundle of papers from inside his shirt that were covered in a barely readable scrawl.

Monsieur Henri preferred to drink champagne, cavort with influential people and show off his orchids rather than do paperwork. There were long evenings spent in restaurants and nightclubs then back to rue Lauriston, with curfews broken in the blackout, women tumbling giggling out of cars and men in expensive suits with a cigarette burning carelessly between their fingers, the gramophone blaring. Chamberlin had grown accustomed to mixing business with pleasure, and in recent months he had met some very strange and some very important people.

6

[illegible]

IN OCCUPIED PARIS, it wasn't hard for German soldiers to pick up local women. [illegible]

[illegible]

[illegible]

6

GREEN FRUIT

IN OCCUPIED PARIS IT wasn't hard for German soldiers to pick up local women. The men in feldgrau packed out the tourist districts to drink beer and watch the women of Paris parade past. Rich ladies in fat fur coats and netted hats, girls in bobby socks and polka dots; the colour red was in fashion that year.

Senior officers with polite manners and haughty good looks could get themselves a celebrity. Coco Chanel drifted through the Hôtel Ritz with her German baron boyfriend from the Abwehr; the actress Arletty was seen around town with a Luftwaffe officer; the American expat Florence Gould held regular artistic salons where she did her best to seduce Hauptmann Ernst Jünger away from his wife and mistress.

Other ranks of German military men walked out with the girls who served food and cleaned their lodgings.[1] A smile could lead to a joke delivered in bad French, and then a date. The writer Simone de Beauvoir thought such women 'tarty' as they clung tight to their uniformed men in cafés during the bright cold days of spring 1942 when the swastika flags hung red, white and black down the Champs-Élysées and the new daily newspaper *Pariser Zeitung* was stacked on wire racks at the kiosks.

Affairs between occupier and occupied were loving, lustful and often mercenary. The occupying Germans received blocks of theatre tickets for every performance, had their own cinemas, private Métro carriages and dined in exclusive restaurants. In a time of hunger, it was easy to sleep with someone who bought you a decent meal. Food and sex were commoditised and exchanged.

A Vichy decree graded most Paris restaurants into categories 'A' to 'D' and set appropriate prices according to the grading. Eighteen francs for a meal at the lowest-quality establishment and fifty francs for one in the highest, both places serving up dishes of boiled vegetables accompanied by watery wine. Additional restaurant categories that were invisible to most Parisians served food that was good enough to appear on the menu as 'pre-war' quality. The more exclusive the restaurant, the more likely it was to buy its produce on the black market. Diners ignored the lawbreaking and tucked in, while ordinary Parisians drifted past the windows outside like fish behind aquarium glass.

'I don't want the French to set foot there,' said Reichsmarschall Hermann Göring. 'The excellent cuisine in Maxim's should be reserved for us. Three or four of these places for German soldiers and officers, that's fine, but nothing for the French.'[2]

Despite his complaints, Göring sometimes had to share his dining experiences with well-placed collaborators. Pierre Laval could be seen in Maxim's celebrating his triumphant return to Vichy as Chief of the Government. He had defeated rival Admiral François Darlan with some light backstabbing. At another table Robert Brasillach held court. The journalist was out of prison and had become editor of the hardcore collaborationist newspaper *Je Suis Partout*; he would frequently speak with relish about the domination of France by strong German forces. And on other nights, Henri Chamberlin and his men might make an appearance.

The gang would enter dressed in their fancy clothes and accompanied by girls from the cabaret, prostitutes from a Maison Close brothel, strippers, madams, would-be singers who sounded like third-rate Edith Piafs and chorus girls who could have been a big star if only they had talent. The waiters would bow as they entered and lead them to a good table.

Chamberlin liked to dine with second-rate actresses who were past their prime, such as the hard-drinking femme fatale Ginette Leclerc and her close friend Milly Mathis, who was born to play the role of the nagging mother-in-law. Chamberlin had watched them in black and white on the big screen back when he was a nobody and now he had them on his arm. They were more than happy to spend time with a man who had money in his pockets and drove around in a white Bentley. The trio would eat expensive meals together, with black market meat disguised on the bill as 'apéritifs', then tip big and leave to join the social whirl.

The music hall maestro Loulou Presle owned a nightclub that was popular with the film and theatre crowd. *Vedette* magazine raved about the club: 'Loulou Presle finally advances smiling, the eye keen under the sharp curls of blonde hair. Immediately, we find ourselves celebrating the spirit of Paris. Cheerful couplets, light fantasy and frivolous rhythms alternating in sparkling malice.'[3]

At Loulou's place, Chamberlin would look out for a Spanish dancer called Esméralda squeezing through the crowds to his table. On a good night she would have a young friend of hers trailing behind. Chamberlin had used his Abwehr contacts to free Esméralda's American husband after a round-up following the Japanese attack on Pearl Harbor. She repaid the debt by pimping out her music hall friends to Monsieur Henri.

Anne Jean-Claude was a nineteen-year-old when the war began

and a dancer '*acrobatique*' at the Bal Tabarin cabaret on rue Victor-Massé in the sixteenth arrondissement. The place was known for half-naked girls and drunken Germans firing off champagne corks like an artillery barrage.

Anne had ambitions towards making her name in legitimate theatre and dreamed of becoming a director. She was pretty, hungry and full of energy. Esméralda suggested Anne spend time with a man she named as Henri Lafont who could help her career. The dancer was initially reluctant:

'I am too young,' said Anne.

'He likes green fruit,' said Esméralda.

'Not experienced.'

'He's a swordsman.'

'It scares me that I don't know much.'

'It will please him.'[4]

A meeting was arranged. Chamberlin liked the young dancer and took her to a nightclub and then to bed. She got 40,000 francs for the evening and soon she was making regular visits to rue Lauriston. When Chamberlin was absent, Anne slept with other gangsters, usually Prévost or Cazauba. Monsieur Henri was not the jealous type.

Anne Jean-Claude lasted longer than most girlfriends and was a regular at the Saturday night parties that Chamberlin threw in rue Lauriston. Brandl and Radecke were always there, drinking and talking business. Max Stöcklin would sweep in late with his circle of White Russian émigrés and Belgian barons. Chamberlin played the affable host, slapping backs, lighting cigarettes and stroking the petals on his orchids.

The lights of rue Lauriston attracted some unusual nocturnal insects. One was Violette Morris, a famous swimmer, boxer, football manager and all-around athlete, who took shot-put gold at the 1922 Women's World Games in Monte Carlo. Morris claimed to have cut off her breasts so that she could fit better into a racing car and the press believed her. She lived to win. 'Anything a man can do, Violette can do, too!' proclaimed the promoters' slogan.[5]

Those who knew her from the famous lesbian bar Le Monocle, a dimly lit cellar on rue Edgar Quinet, thought that Morris had a double mastectomy to better fit her masculine self-image. She dressed in men's clothes, smoked a cigar and had a thing for sunken-eyed blondes with rag-doll arms.

'There is nothing, to my knowledge, unseemly about male clothing,' she said. 'I am bound only by my professional obligations and, as long as the laws of the French Republic do not prevent me, nothing and nobody can forbid me to dress in a way that you will agree, is always decent.'[6]

She was born Emilie Paule Marie Violette Morris in 1893 to a bourgeois Paris family. Her father was an army officer with a gambling problem and her mother came from an important Middle Eastern family. Violette also had an elder sister, a brother who died young and a Jewish grandmother.

As a motorcyclist for the Red Cross during the First World War she discovered the joys of driving fast and wearing a uniform. She continued to dress in men's clothes when the war ended, opened an automobile accessories shop at 6 rue Roger-Bacon in Paris and pursued a sporting career.

In 1926 the Fédération des Sociétés Féminines Sportives suspended her for giving a football team performance-enhancing drugs. Morris turned racing driver and the following year won the Bol d'Or automobile 24-hour endurance race in a BNC car that looked like a tin can on wheels. Her court case against the Fédération failed thanks to gossip about predatory lesbian behaviour in the locker room and her bisexuality outside of it. Newspapers let everyone know that Morris was having an intense affair with Raoul Paoli, a hulking Corsican boxer.

The next decade saw her move to the political right. She went bankrupt in July 1931, as a victim of the recession and living the high life. Someone involved in the downfall of her shop was Jewish, which fed Violette's growing anti-Semitism, despite her grandmother's background. There were rumours that she had become an agent for Heinrich Himmler's Sicherheitsdienst (SD) intelligence agency, but nothing was ever proved.

In 1937 Morris shot dead a man on her houseboat. She was acquitted on the grounds of self-defence and soon after opened a garage and began to mix with an avant-garde Paris set that included the filmmaker Jean Cocteau. When the war came, Morris watched France fall without any sense of regret.

'We live in a country made rotten by money and scandals,' she said, 'governed by phrasemongers, schemers and cowards. This land of little people is not worthy of survival. One day, its decline will lead its people to the ranks of slavery but me, if I'm still here, I will not become a slave. Believe me, it's not in my temperament.'[7]

Morris was another washed-up celebrity like Bonny and Villaplana who discovered that the German occupation offered a road back to the high life. The Luftwaffe requisitioned her garage and kept her on as a driver. She did some black marketeering on the side and joined the Abwehr's Service Léopold, a gang of collaborators who infiltrated resistance groups under their Belgian leader Jean Édouard Léopold van de Casteele.

Morris's entry into rue Lauriston social circles was made possible by her boyfriend Georges Hainnaux, who had been Bonny's informant in the Stavisky affair. She came for the champagne, the food, the music and stayed for the verbal sparring with Chamberlin and the other gangsters. Neither side was sure how they felt about the other and the chat was spiky and tense.

For all her individuality, Morris wasn't the most unusual guest to attend the Saturday night parties at rue Lauriston. That honour went to a Bulgarian mystic who liked underage girls and magic wands.

• • •

Mikhaël Ivanov was a long-haired cult leader who read palms at rue Lauriston while talking about world peace and the healing power of the sun. He grew up Bulgarian under the rule of the Ottoman Empire in what is now North Macedonia.

His family was in the coal business, first in a remote village and later in Varna. Ivanov's father died young, which meant the boy had to balance school with jobs working at iron foundries to support his family. He later talked about how he discovered yoga, the biographies of saints and the magical properties of fire while still a teenager, and then became Peter Deunov's favourite disciple in the Universal White Brotherhood.

The brotherhood was a New Age cult that mixed elements of Christianity, theosophy, Rudolf Steiner's anthroposophy and occultism. Methodist priest Deunov had created the movement in the 1920s near Sofia. His followers learned about palmistry, numerology, the healing power of colours, sun worship, astrology, theories that humanity was descended from the extinct races of Atlantis and Lemuria, and Deunov's own concept of progressive racial reincarnation in which every suitably enlightened ethnic group eventually comes back as white.

Ivanov was a long-faced 37-year-old schoolteacher with neat white teeth by the time he left for Paris in July 1937 to visit the World Fair with some letters of introduction to exile Bulgarians in the capital. He loved the city enough to stay and lecture about Universal White Brotherhood beliefs, first to Bulgarian émigrés and then to French audiences. He claimed that Deunov had given him the job of establishing the movement in France, although other disciples back in Bulgaria disagreed.

By the start of the Second World War Ivanov had established a small following of spiritually engaged middle-class French women who were impressed by his talk about astrology and were enthusiastic about open-air gymnastic routines set to music. However, occupied France had little time for esoteric groups. The police stamped out the Freemasons and pursued other occult groups that it described as being subversive. As a result, Ivanov lowered his public profile and focused on delivering talks at the homes of his sympathisers.

In early 1942 some followers of the movement obtained a villa in Sèvres, in the western suburb of Paris, as the basis for a commune where they could sit at the feet of their Bulgarian guru. By this time Ivanov was living off donations and playing the role of the simple holy man. 'He was always natural, humble, unpretentious and sometimes seemingly ignorant, and this astonished me very much,' described one follower at the time.[8]

Rue Lauriston saw a different side of Mikhaël Ivanov. There he was a dirty-minded materialist, fond of money and talking about '*divino-sexualles*', which were exercises that involved young girls. When teenagers were hard to get, Ivanov brought along the striking Marga d'Andurain, who also went by the name Jeanne Clérisse. She had been a double agent in the Middle East, watched her aristocratic husband die in mysterious circumstances, married a camel driver in a failed attempt to see Mecca then poisoned him to avoid a divorce, was pardoned by King Ibn Saud, and all before returning to Paris to get involved in black marketeering and dealing opium.

The relationship between Ivanov and d'Andurain puzzled outsiders. They had little in common outside some shared business interests. She was cynical and ruthless and once tried to persuade her own son to attack an old lady with a clawhammer to get her jewellery. He preferred magic wands and the occult powers of a sacred pentacle formed by crawling over naked female companions. 'I work for France,' Ivanov told the gang. 'I am pure. For me, the sexual act is essentially pure.'[9]

Most gangsters sneered at such sentiments, but the Bulgarian's spiritualist theories impressed Paul Clavié. This was an unlikely connection as Chamberlin's unstable nephew could usually be found at rue Lauriston parties telling cronies about his adventures on the streets of Paris. The latest story detailed how an inspector had stopped Clavié on 30 March 1942 as he was driving through the city centre. The officer drew attention to some overdue fines and other minor offences. The policeman perched on the car's running board and instructed Clavié to drive to the station. 'I'm not going to obey you,' said Clavié, 'and you're going to come with me, you're going to see what this will get you.'[10]

He drove off with the policeman still balanced on the running board and banging at the window with his pistol. Clavié stopped outside his parents' house and took his own gun from the car for a stand-off in the street. The pair shouted at each other to surrender. The policeman fired two shots into the ground to intimidate Clavié, but it didn't work. A German patrol arrived, consulted both men and took the policeman away. He was warned to leave Clavié alone.

'We'll make you understand with bullets in the head,' said a Wehrmacht officer. 'We don't only shoot Jewish hostages.' A week later, Clavié hit and killed a pedestrian with his car. He parked his car outside 93 rue Lauriston with a crumpled bumper and bloodstains on its doors; death didn't bother his conscience much.

'If you can steal then you can kill,' Clavié said. 'Because you have to kill in order to steal.'[11]

The police put him under observation, but they couldn't touch Henri Chamberlin's nephew. Inside rue Lauriston, Clavié would drink and joke with Engel and the boys, while waiting for the exotic dancer Anne Jean-Claude to finish with Ivanov and go perch on Monsieur Henri's lap. Then Clavié would sit with the Bulgarian for hours to discuss fortune telling, paneurythmics and the future of humanity.

'I was an anarchist before I met Ivanov,' Clavié said at the time. 'Since I've met him, I'm no longer one. I was a beast. Now I'm no more than half a beast.'[12]

Pierre Bonny would sometimes stick around to have his fortune read by the Bulgarian, but he would rarely spend long at the parties. The former inspector preferred to head home to his wife and teenage son for some regular bourgeois life and a good night's sleep. The next morning, he would have a clear head when Pagnon arrived in a white Bentley to drive him to work for the continued reorganisation of Chamberlin's messy hierarchy.

Under Bonny's regime every member of the gang got a file and a photograph tucked away in a filing cabinet. His days were spent clacking away on a typewriter, scribbling notes in margins and organising receipts and signatures, all legacies of Bonny's time in the police force. The gangsters called themselves 'the Carlingue', which was underworld slang for a crime family. Bonny preferred 'the Service', as it sounded more professional.

He was usually the only member who was around in the first half of the day, directing domestic staff and typing up reports. Business for the rest of the group began just before noon when Chamberlin wandered out of his bedroom to examine the flowers for signs of wilting and briefly chatted about business with Bonny. Then the pair would proceed downstairs for lunch with the inner circle of gangsters, which included Sartore, Prévost, Cazauba and others. Chamberlin would hand out assignments and talk about whatever was on his mind.

A wobbly sense of professionalism had entered the gang's operations. Attempts to con the Germans with fake gold sales and electroplated iron bars, such as the Villaplana and Gourari scam, were now slapped down hard by the boss. 'You're stupidly depleting our supply of trust and credit with the Germans,' said Chamberlin at one meeting.[13]

Less important gang members were formalised into teams run by members of the inner circle, while a closer eye was kept on independent crooks who ran their own scams, to ensure that a regular 10 per cent was kicked back to Chamberlin. Any underworld figure who crossed paths with the Carlingue on joint ventures paid a tithe, and all the while Bonny recorded the figures in neat columns.

As the gang got richer, they invested their money in nightclubs and cabarets and apartments with high ceilings and gilded walls. Auguste Ricord took a share in the L'Heure Bleue cabaret, which was managed by Roger Duchesne, who was a dark, sleek cinema actor who had become close to Chamberlin. Robert Moura had an interest in Le Petit Chapiteau cabaret with Garcia de la Palma, a Corsican hero of the First World War who sold alcohol in bulk to the Germans and secretly worked for the resistance. Charles Cazauba bought l'Hôtel de Nice in rue Victor-Massé. Bonny's friend Jean Guélin became the director of the Théâtre Édouard VII and the restaurant-café Zardas on the rue de Sèze. When a leaseholder caused trouble, Guélin denounced him to Abwehr contacts as a Gaullist and watched on as the man was dragged off to an internment camp.

Chamberlin had no interest in real estate or investment. The early days that he spent in poverty had left him with a complicated relationship to wealth. 'He didn't like money,' Bonny said. 'He didn't need it, and spent it without caring.'[14]

However much Chamberlin and his gang spent, the money continued to roll into rue Lauriston as German forces advanced. By the summer of 1942 Nazi forces were driving through North Africa and digging in close to Moscow, while their Japanese allies had taken Singapore and the Dutch East Indies.

In Paris, Chamberlin's empire was big and getting bigger. The expansion came at a price. His gang would have to join the forces of law and order.

PART II

FROM THE ABWEHR TO THE GESTAPO

7

THE BIG SCORE

THE CRÉDIT INDUSTRIEL ET COMMERCIAL headquarters on rue de la Victoire had a façade of pale coffee-coloured stone and old iron grillwork. On an afternoon in February 1941, a black front-wheel drive Citroën sat outside the bank with the engine running. Six cylinders, four doors, licence plate 1031 W1.

It was a cold wintry afternoon with too much damp in the air. Three bank guards in thick, blue uniforms turned into the road wheeling a trolley piled with canvas sacks. The sacks contained close to 4 million francs from a nearby Crédit Industriel et Commercial branch. An old leather satchel slung over one of the guard's shoulders held another 21 million in treasury bonds. None of the three men had guns. The Germans wouldn't allow them to carry weapons.

A few concierges along the rue de la Victoire gave the Citroën curious looks. They decided that it must have had something to do with a lorry driver and his assistant unloading boxes from their own vehicle nearby.

The guards were getting close to the front doors of Crédit Industriel et Commercial at No. 66 when four men came out of the Citroën fast and grabbed at the trolley. The road was full of shouting and threats of violence. A guard named Henrì Guérin refused to let go of the cash-filled satchels. The concierge across the road at No. 65 heard four shots and peered outside to see a man in a marine-blue overcoat with a gun in his hand and Guérin sat on the road in a puddle of blood, looking amazed.

Another guard ran for the bank entrance and four more shots brought him down. The third guard backed away with his hands up while the lorry driver and his assistant froze in place. The thieves piled the sacks into the Citroën boot as office workers in overlooking buildings threw inkpots out of the windows at them. Smashed glass and puddles of ink were all over the road as the car peeled away, chased by bank employees. The Citroën outdistanced them and shot through the Paris afternoon like a fire arrow, before disappearing somewhere near the avenue du Bois-de-Boulogne.

The robbers had got away with 3.75 million francs. One security guard was dead and another badly wounded. The furious Germans demanded that Paris police find the criminals. Witnesses of the crime sat around smoky police stations and flipped through books of black and white mug shots. It was endless photographic miles of unsmiling and unshaven men in suits, their shirts buttoned to the neck and ties confiscated, some of veteran criminals among them with their eyes squeezed shut to make life harder for police.

The investigation eliminated the lorry driver and his assistant, but then the leads dried up. The police finally hit on something when one witness lingered over a distinctive mug shot, which depicted a heavily built tough guy with light-coloured hair pomaded back from a face that was about as friendly as a butcher's slab. Small black eyes, with a razor cut for a mouth, but with something handsome about him. The witness tapped the photograph; this was one of the robbers.

The man in the picture was Abel Danos. To members of underworld Paris, he was known as Le Mammouth.

Abel Paul Guillaume Danos was born in 1904 to a poor family in an Haute-Garome village. His father was a stonemason who liked to drink and couldn't control his temper; there were two older sisters and a brother. Danos should have joined the family business of moulding stone blocks into pleasing shapes, but he preferred the easy life. It helped that he did not care much about consequences or other people.

Danos turned to burglary around Dijon and began breaking into houses on Sunday mornings while the owners were at mass. On other days of the week he would pose as a gas inspector and fake his way past gullible householders. His family could not understand how Abel had turned out the way he did. In one report on his early activities, a police inspector described Danos as 'a killer, a cold-blooded criminal, a strange person, and to a certain extent a mystery. Lazy, possessed by some kind of inner demon, he turned to theft … mostly for fun.'[1]

Danos stood 5ft 7in tall, which was average height for the time, but was built like a circus strongman. He picked up a handful of nicknames early on, such 'Le Sanguinaire' (The Bloodthirsty) and 'Le Bel Abel' (Handsome Abel), but the one that stuck was Le Mammouth.

Abel liked engines, motors and stealing cars. He raced his motorbike professionally when he wasn't in prison. He won a gold medal in the Concours de la litre d'Essence de Chanteloup; came thirty-sixth in the Grand Prix de France in Montargis. He made it onto the cover of *Moto Revue 1923*.

Later, Danos did his national service in the Bataillons d'Afrique (Bat d'Af), a unit for troublemakers who were forced to sweat under the Tunisian sun. After he left the forces, he returned to Dijon to steal more cars with a friend named André Jolivot. He progressed on to robbing businesses, which led to more arrests and more prison time.

Danos had a girlfriend called Simone Bouladour, who had dark bouffant hair and a full face. She was only seventeen when the pair met. As one female friend described: 'Abel didn't like grandmas, you know. He was drawn to pretty, young women, brunettes preferably.'[2]

When the Second World War came Danos was called back to the Bat d'Af and endured further boredom, route marches and ditch digging. After the authorities connected him to a strongbox theft, Danos deserted. He was lying low in Dijon when an altercation with some soldiers went wrong and the gendarmes discovered his pockets were full of fake identification cards and a gun. He went to prison under someone else's name.

On 15 June 1940, with the Germans approaching fast, the wardens in Dijon opened the gates and let the prisoners escape. Danos took his girlfriend Simone up to Paris and hid under another fake name. He connected with contacts Joseph Rocca-Sera, Emile Buisson and Jean-Michel Chaves, all of whom knew how to make a living on the black market.

Rocca-Sera was a Corsican crook with a twitchy trigger finger, known to his friends as 'Jeannot le Corse' and a key figure in the pre-war cocaine trade. Buisson was a man with a sharp nose and dark hair, who had served in the army during the Rif War in Morocco and made enough cash in the underworld to open a brothel in Shanghai. He lost it all and returned to France just in time to watch the German tanks arrive. Chaves went by 'Nez de Braise' (Glowing Nose) because his beak lit up a scarlet colour when he drank. He had an alcohol problem, a prostitute girlfriend from Marseille called Dany la Brune, and a bad reputation among other crooks. There were widespread rumours that he had been informing for the police, but Danos, Buisson and Rocca-Sera found his thuggish brutality useful enough to ignore the gossip.

The four men daydreamed about escaping to America, that paradise across the Atlantic for a generation of French crooks who spent their youths watching Hollywood movies full of skyscrapers, money and Tommy guns. Danos and his friends needed a big score to secure them passage on a liner to New York and a new life. Someone tipped them off about a bank in rue de la Victoire that had large cash deliveries.

They hit the Crédit Industriel et Commercial and got away clean but didn't realise that they had missed 21 million francs in a satchel that one of the guards was carrying until the newspaper headlines the next day. The gang hid out in Marseille after the robbery while they waited for the police search to cool down. Danos was spending his share and enjoying life when some men in plain clothes stuck a gun in his ribs and pushed him into the back seat of a car. He was preparing for another prison term when the men identified themselves as members of the local Deuxième Bureau, the secret service of the French state. Not everyone in Vichy worshipped the Germans. The men who picked up Danos turned out to belong to a secret resistance ring inside the system.

In an anonymous office, Danos was introduced to a spymaster who wore a hat low over his suspicious, pudgy face. The man needed crooks that were prepared to use their skills for a free France: sometimes things had to be stolen and sometimes people had to be killed. Danos could be a patriot and accept this offer or choose to be a fool and rot in prison. He accepted.

In July, the network sent him to murder a Paris-based Abwehr agent who lived in a block at the square du Vivarais. Danos brought along Sera and Buisson, but couldn't call on the talents of Chaves, who was on an alcoholic spree. The murder plot failed to go anywhere after the gangsters saw German soldiers with submachine guns guarding the entrance to the target agent's building and their newly acquired sense of patriotism melted away like spring snow.

Danos and Buisson rescued something from the mission by faking their way inside disguised as decorators and stealing a suitcase of documents from the man's room. The trio's resistance career ended soon after when Danos got himself arrested for having fake papers, Serra was landed in jail for another robbery and Buisson finally got picked up for his involvement in the Crédit Industriel et Commercial job.

The Deuxième Bureau network either lacked the power or did not have the inclination to free the men and they remained in prison. A bitter Danos felt as if he had been abandoned. The gossip going around his cellblock in Fresnes claimed that the Germans released men that they could use. He wrote a letter to the Gestapo.

> I was arrested for an affair of which I am wholly innocent … I came to Paris to meet you through a friend who has been in your service for a long time because I had in my possession a list of a huge organisation working against you … I would like to meet you to explain my situation.[3]

The letter intrigued Himmler's secret police enough for Karl Bömelburg to visit Danos, but nothing came of the interrogation. Danos refused to hand over the names of his resistance contacts without a guarantee of freedom that the sceptical German would not provide. A second letter that was sent to the Gestapo went unanswered so Le Mammouth started working on an alternative plan.

On the evening of 22 March 1942, Danos went over the wall at

Fresnes using a window in the infirmary and a rope, while his girlfriend Simone waited patiently outside as the getaway driver. The couple hid at the apartment of old friend André Jolivot near the Métro La Chapelle and waited out the manhunt.

Jolivot had a sideline selling fake ration tickets bought from Charles Cazauba, the shaky sideman of the Carlingue. A meeting was arranged in May 1942 at a smoke-filled, alcoholic cellar bar where Cazauba often hung out with fellow gang members Moura and Villaplana to play long sessions of the card game Belote. Danos shouldered his way through the crowd with his collar turned up and Jolivot made the introductions. Cazauba casually pointed out other notable faces in the bar with his quivering hands: in that corner are the fellow collaborators, here are the politically apathetic and over there are the crooks like Joseph Soro known as Jo Catch, René 'Le Petit' Gottelans and Frantz 'Le Gitan' Puech who belonged to resistance groups. Regardless of their political affiliation, everyone drank and did business together.

Danos asked Cazauba for help and gilded his story with lies about being involved with a Corsican team that had robbed the Marseille-Blancarde gold train before the war. Cazauba thought things over and told Danos not to worry about the police any more. He could join the Carlingue.

Le Mammouth would be signing up with a gang that had recently branched from affiliation with the Abwehr to the Gestapo. An internal Nazi power struggle, Pierre Bonny's handsome godson and some North African male prostitutes had pushed the gang up the collaborationist ranks. Monsieur Henri's men were now official German policemen working for the Nazi Reich.

• • •

Sleek, dark and handsome as a film star, Jean-Damien Lascaux was tied to a chair in a cellar for the second time since the war had begun. He was a bad spy.

The married 22-year-old father of one had been a small-time militant in Eugène Deloncle's Mouvement Social Révolutionnaire until money troubles had forced him to accept 6,000 francs from a Gestapo agent as part of a mission to infiltrate the Parti Social Français (PSF). Colonel François de la Rocque's far-right party appeared outwardly loyal to Vichy, but the Germans suspected that the group was involved in the resistance. The PSF was banned in the Occupied Zone and Gestapo agents chased the party underground.

Lascaux joined the PSF Paris section and reported back names and any juicy gossip to his Gestapo contact. However, sloppy spycraft alerted the party's internal security, which led to Lascaux getting locked up in a cellar to be interrogated and beaten. He secured his release by agreeing to feed the Germans false information, but the amateur spy failed once again when his Gestapo contact discovered the deception and marked him for death.

An assassination attempt sent Lascaux on the run in the south of France, but he failed to secure passage to North Africa and reluctantly returned to Paris. It was at this point that Lascaux's family recommended that he contact his godfather Pierre Bonny at 93 rue Lauriston.

Lascaux's godfather had been busy gathering intelligence on Deloncle's activities for the Abwehr. He had seeded spies throughout the Mouvement Social Révolutionnaire, including Deloncle's own chauffeur and a former Cagoule killer called Huguet. Carlingue member Maillebuau remained undercover in the rival RNP, although his habit of dipping into the petty cash box would soon see him kicked out of the party. Bonny spared an afternoon for a drink with his godson. After hearing about Lascaux's predicament, all Bonny could offer was more spy work and a return to Deloncle's Mouvement Social Révolutionnaire as an agent for rue Lauriston. Burned-out and poor and with nowhere else to turn, Lascaux could see no other option than to accept his godfather's proposal.

Lascaux successfully wormed his way into high-ranking circles near Deloncle before his luck went sour again and he found himself tied to another chair in a cellar with another group of internal security thugs beating the truth out of him. One guard was Jacques Labussière, a fascist militant two years younger than his prisoner. In the periodic breaks from the interrogation, the two men were left alone in a room full of cigarette smoke and the smell of blood and sweat. An unlikely friendship developed.

Lascaux pleaded with his captor and promised rewards and a brighter future in exchange for just one telephone call to his godfather. Labussière was feeling disillusioned with the Mouvement Social Révolutionnaire over recent hints that Deloncle was turning against the Germans and agreed to help.

A few hours later Chamberlin and Prévost arrived at the cellar in a white Bentley to pick up the battered Lascaux and his new ally. Monsieur Henri's arrival sent a warning to the Mouvement Social Révolutionnaire that Lascaux was now under rue Lauriston protection. Any threat of retaliation evaporated in May 1942 when Deloncle was kicked out of his own party after factionalism led to a coup that deposed him. The Mouvement Social Révolutionnaire rejoined the RNP, and Deloncle sulked off into the political wilderness.

Lascaux, Labussière and a few other younger gang members got put to work on a chicken farm outside Paris that had been bought by Chamberlin. Their duties involved running the farm and keeping it tidy. Monsieur Henri had gifted the property to Karl Bömelburg, who was rumoured to enjoy having handsome young men around when his wife was safely in Berlin. Chamberlin hoped this gesture would persuade the Gestapo chief to recruit the Carlingue into what was rapidly becoming the most powerful agency in occupied France.

The Abwehr and its Wehrmacht masters had been significantly weakened in February 1942 when General Otto von Stülpnagel resigned as Militärbefehlshaber in Frankreich after suffering a nervous breakdown. Close to 500 hostages had been executed since Operation Barbarossa in revenge for resistance attacks and Von Stülpnagel could not take the pressure of following orders from Berlin that he thought were misguided. His patrician and less scrupulous cousin Carl-Heinrich von Stülpnagel replaced him but inherited a less powerful empire.

Berlin had taken the changeover as an opportunity to expand Himmler's foothold in France. The blond and deceptively jovial-looking Höherer SS-und Polizeiführer Carl Oberg arrived as head of German and French police in the Occupied Zone. 'It's no longer a question of leaving the security of our armies just to the military,' said senior SS figure Reinhard Heydrich. 'It requires specialists.'[4]

Paris had seen seventeen bomb attacks during December and January. More would follow. Oberg believed in terror to stop resistance and ordered more hostages to be executed for every attack. Eighty-eight men would be shot in four and a half hours at Mont Valérien by a firing squad that refused to carry out the orders without schnapps and cigarettes. Another forty-six were executed a few weeks later. The Germans secretly buried the cremated ashes in the cemeteries of Paris, while locals would leave flowers at any freshly dug grave they came across.

Oberg's security reorganisation left the Abwehr at the bottom of the occupying pyramid, looking up at an alphabet soup of SS agencies that included the SD and Geheime Feldpolizei (GFP). Above them all sat the Gestapo.

Chamberlin had been keeping polite pressure on Bömelburg by lavishing him with meals and favours for almost a year. By now Gestapo patronage was more desirable than ever for the gang. When Lascaux and Labussière's time spent on the farm failed to have any effect, Monsieur Henri remembered the rumours about Bömelburg's sexuality and took a more direct approach. He selected some North African male prostitutes from the groups who hung around Pigalle.

Bonny typed their names in a file and sent the young men off to Bömelburg's villa, ostensibly as bodyguards to keep their new friend safe from the resistance. Chamberlin gave each one a pep talk before they left.

'No tricks, Mohammed,' said Chamberlin, showing his pistol. 'You can shove a length into this old Kraut fag but don't take anything, don't even nick a swastika, or I'll comb the hair under your fez with a bullet.'[5]

Regardless of whether the men acted as bodyguards or if the Carlingue had misinterpreted the Gestapo chief's sexuality, they elicited a positive response. Bömelburg made the case to Berlin and Chamberlin's men joined the first wave of local auxiliaries taken on by the Gestapo. In the summer of 1942 Chamberlin was officially inducted as agent BOE 43 and given the power to recruit fellow gangsters. He was among the first of around 2,000 French Abwehr agents who crossed over to the Gestapo across France.

Chamberlin's inner circle and a favoured few received yellow identity cards with Nazi eagle stamps. Not even German soldiers could arrest the gang now. Gestapo men Emile Hess and Willy

Kharlof joined the gang as observers but their official loyalty to the Reich was quickly dissolved by the ready supply of alcohol, money and women. The two were soon just as corrupt as the gangsters around them.

Despite the change of loyalties, the Carlingue continued to run its Amt Otto bureaus and DSK gold stings. There was too much money around for Brandl and Radecke to cut the cord.

Abel Danos was one of the few newcomers who was deemed important enough to get a Gestapo card. He had made a good impression; Sartore and Jeunet worked with Le Mammouth before the war and Villaplana had also heard good things about him from mutual friends. Chamberlin offered his friendship and protection. 'Tell him to telephone me if something happens,' the Carlingue boss told Cazauba after monitoring Danos's progress.[6]

Danos became close to two other recent arrivals, both veterans of the Bat d'Af. Jo Attia was built like a rhino and had a taste for tattoos and boxing. He grew up in a poor family in Brittany to a Breton mother and a Tunisian father who died in the trenches during the First World War. Attia had more muscles than teeth and ran away from home young, served some time in prison for theft, dabbled in a little boxing and took on jobs as a hard man of the underworld. He did his national service in the late 1930s with the Bat d'Af, in a unit made up of troublemakers and bad attitudes.

Attia was demobilised after the German victory and spent some time in Marseille before heading up to Paris on fake papers to join his mother. In the capital he returned to a life of crime and served a short jail sentence for theft. He was just out of prison in 1942 as the spring was starting when he bumped into Pierre Loutrel – known as 'La Valise' (The Suitcase) – at L'Heure Bleue nightclub in Pigalle. The pair had served in the Bat d'Af together.

Loutrel was in his mid-twenties and had a smooth lozenge of a face topped with neatly groomed dark hair and eyes that were as emotionless as a shark's. He had a spark of madness in his brain and had ditched his well-off family ten years earlier in search of adventure with the merchant navy. He did not get far before a drunken fight saw him thrown off the ship and into prison. The criminal world eventually led him to the Carlingue. In L'Heure Bleue he invited Attia to take on a role in Charles Cazauba's team.

Danos did his own recruitment by bringing in his old partner in crime Jean-Michel Chaves, who had recently reappeared. The alcoholic Nez de Braise was soon earning 10,000 francs a month selling fake ration cards and Swiss watches that had been smuggled over the border. This was big money, but such an income had become necessary; the cost of living in Paris had jumped 65 per cent between August 1939 and the summer of 1942.[7]

All of these characters did their time in the rue Lauriston daily grind, which consisted of theft and robbery and protection rackets. One gangster who arrived around this time, and worked with Villaplana and a friend of Clavié called Louis Haré, explained the daily routine for gang members:

> In the car we made the rounds of six bars in Pigalle and Blanche. Each time the same scenario. The car stopped outside the bar. Villaplana got out first and we followed. We entered the bar. The barman served us each a drink and slid an envelope in front of Villaplana. The drinks are downed in one: we leave for a new bar where we go through the same scene. Silent all the time.
>
> At the end of the afternoon, return to rue Lauriston. A tall guy with glasses, slim, a southerner [Delehaye], welcomes us into the office, opens the envelopes, counts the money. My two

> companions receive their cut: 2,000 francs. I'm just a newcomer so I get half: a thousand francs. I'm happy.[8]

Danos loved his newfound power as a Gestapo man and immediately abused it. When a traffic policeman stopped him in the middle of the night, Le Mammouth waved a revolver in his face and drove off. The Paris police had identified him as being an escaped prisoner, but they could do nothing, Danos was affiliated with the Gestapo; he was untouchable.

Danos, Chaves, Attia and Loutrel all hung around together. The four men floated in a sea of alcohol and easy money and shared anecdotes about their exploits until La Valise's obsessive refusal to respect authority annoyed Chamberlin enough to offload him as bodyguard onto a friend of the Carlingue. Joseph Joinovici was a plump, Jewish scrap metal merchant who worked for the Nazis.

8

REVERSE OF THE MAP

THE VÉLODROME D'HIVER (VÉL D'HIV) was an amphitheatre of hanging lights, two tiers of spectators, netting, smoke and drop handlebar bikes doing endless circuits. Back in the glory days between the wars, crowds queued for hours to watch cyclists in jerseys and flat caps race each other around the 250 metres of banked wooden track. No one seemed to care that team bosses fixed the results and all the riders were wired on cocaine and brandy. On a good day, 20,000 people crammed themselves into this amphitheatre on the Seine to cheer their heroes.

Later, the central bowl grew into a roller-skating rink and the venue diversified into boxing competitions and other sporting spectacles. Attendance fell in the hungry years of the depression and by the end of the 1930s the place was empty except for some ice hockey games and the occasional political rally. Business was still slow in July 1942 when the Germans confiscated the keys and turned the sporting arena into part of the final solution to the Jewish question.

Anti-Semitism was branded on the heart of National Socialism. Hitler's racial scientists saw Jews as the eternal enemy, grappling with Aryans for supremacy since the dawn of time, hiding behind Communism and Capitalism and Freemasonry. Jews brought darkness to the Aryan's light; destroyed what superior races had built;

and lied where others told the truth. Within months of taking power, the Nazis sacked all Jewish civil servants and began a boycott of Jewish businesses. The 1935 Nuremberg Laws prevented Jews from marrying Aryans. In the same year, the first concentration camps opened, and the noose began to tighten.

The Second World War offered fresh territory for the Nazis to test out their Manichean race theories. The Jewish population in France had grown from 80,000 at the turn of the century to 300,000 in 1939, most of the new arrivals being refugees fleeing the Nazis.[1] The occupation of France forced them back in front of the hunter's gun.

In September 1940, the Germans ordered all Jews outside the Zone Libre to register with their local police station. Jewish businesses were sold off cheap through the introduction of '*Arisierung*' (Aryanisation), although French bureaucracy meant that sales were slow, either as a result of passive resistance or incompetence. Jewish employees were sacked or removed from public sight.

The next year the Germans arrested 3,700 foreign Jewish men who were living in Paris and held them as hostages against future resistance sabotage. Many French Jews attempted to escape to Vichy or overseas. The Paris telephone directory that was published in December 1941 listed only 477 Lévys and 170 Blochs; before the Germans had taken the city, there had been 747 and 270 entries under those names respectively.

The invasion of the Soviet Union radicalised the German machinery of repression. A January 1942 conference of senior Nazi officials at a villa in the Berlin suburb of Wannsee established the formal measures to deport Europe's Jewish population into occupied Poland for forced slavery or the gas chambers. Men, women and children were stripped naked and shot and their bodies were dumped into pits. Propaganda newsreels concealed the horror with talk of resettlement and humane prison camps.

In the spring of 1942, the Jews of Paris were ordered to surrender all radios and bicycles. Their telephones were disconnected and the use of public boxes or phones in cafés was forbidden. Communication among the Jewish community was reduced to the use of pre-printed postcards with stock phrases like 'The ____ family is well' or '____ need food ____ money'.[2] Jews were forbidden from entering parks, museums and other public spaces. '*Parc à Jeux. Reserve aux Enfants. Interdit pour Juif,*' read the signs outside the children's playgrounds. Only for children. Forbidden for Jews.

Jewish children could still attend school and receive, like all French pupils, vitamin tablets and the allegedly healthy Biscuits Pétain. The free biscuits were hard and tasted bad. Schoolboys would glue the tough crumbs to windows and watch birds smack their beaks against the glass.

All Jews in the Occupied Zone wore a yellow cloth star on their coats. In the Zone Libre, the Vichy government refused to impose the wearing of stars but fired Jews from jobs in government and education. Any Pétainist resistance to anti-Semitism, if it ever existed, vanished when Pierre Laval returned to power and convinced the cabinet that sacrificing outsiders could save the lives of French Jews. On 16 and 17 July 1942, police forces loyal to Vichy but following German orders rounded up 13,000 foreign Jewish men, women and children across the Occupied Zone.

In Paris, the arrested were held at the Vél d'Hiv. The place soon became crammed beyond capacity. Toilets overflowed and families fought over floor space as the police pushed more people in through the doors. There were hysterical breakdowns and suicides. Soon the crowds were loaded on to buses to Drancy and then on to trains destined for Auschwitz. Back in Paris, the abandoned apartments gaped empty. Dogs howled for their departed owners and cats slinked off into the city in search of food. Those Jews who escaped the round-up lived in constant fear and wondered when the next mob of policemen would seal off the streets.

A few Catholic bishops objected to the measures. Some Parisians watched coaches full of children crying for their mothers pass through the capital's streets and felt sadness or guilt at all the tiny hands pressed against glass.

Not every Jew in occupied Paris lived in fear. The forty-year-old Joseph Joinovici was a cheerful businessman with eyes dark as knot holes in an oak plank. Shortly after the Vél d'Hiv round-up, the office of Reichsführer-SS Heinrich Himmler officially announced that Joinovici was not Jewish. He was too useful.

Joinovici was born in Kishinev, then the capital of the Bessarabian Governorate in the Tsarist Empire and now the capital of Moldova, Chişinău. Almost half of the population of the large, modern town were recent Jewish arrivals from the provinces who were looking for a better life. The rapid demographic change inflamed local anti-Semitism, and Joinovici was still only a baby when the murder of a young Ukrainian boy incited a pogrom that ripped apart the Jewish district of the city. Forty-nine people died, with Joinovici's parents among them. More pogroms followed, which prompted many Jews to flee to America to escape the mobs.

The Russian Revolution of 1917 killed the Tsar of Russia, put Bolsheviks in the Kremlin and passed Bessarabia to Romania. A few years later a young Joinovici decided to quit his job as a locksmith and follow his relatives abroad. He left his wife Hava Schwartz behind, but only managed to get as far as France when the local police arrested him for visa issues. The police eventually lost interest but Joinovici no longer had a taste for travel and settled down in Clichy, north-west Paris. He started as a locksmith, then established a scrap metal business with a Jewish Pole, who would be the first of many partners over the years to be squeezed dry and abandoned by Joinovici.

Business went well and soon Joinovici brought his wife and brother Mordhar over to Paris. The brothers formed Les Établissements Joinovici Frères and turned it into one of the biggest scrap metal dealerships in the country. The business survived the slump of the early 1930s and kept making money thanks to friends in strange places. Files held by the Paris police noted that a number of informants believed that Joinovici had contacts within the Belgian Communist Party; others claimed that he had provided assistance to the Abwehr, a German agency that seemed less committed to anti-Semitism than the rest of the Nazi machine. The police concluded that he was a 'notorious fence' with underworld connections.[3]

When the Germans took Paris, Joinovici smelled profit and swam against the stream of fleeing Jewish refugees to visit the capital. Joinovici discovered his warehouses had been requisitioned and watched Wehrmacht soldiers changing guard at dawn and dusk in the Place de la Concorde. A bribe to the police provided a certificate that declared him as being an Orthodox Christian. 'Joinovici, son of Isaac' became 'Joinovici, son of Ivan'.[4]

The cover wasn't strong but Joinovici had chutzpah to spare. He approached the occupation authorities, spread some money around and became a supplier of scrap metal through his newly established Société Joinovici et Compagnie.

Joinovici set about rebuilding his business empire. On 17 January 1941 alone, the Germans ordered 100 tonnes of copper and forty-five tonnes of bronze, and Joinovici was able to deliver. However, the local police weren't happy with Joinovici's new business model and arrested him in September for black marketeering, which led to a few months spent in jail. After his release, both Vichy and the more ideologically committed German agencies began investigating Joinovici's racial background, but lack of paperwork made a definitive conclusion impossible. In the following spring a fellow scrap dealer, a Jewish Pole called Krasnik who was hiding behind the name Louis Nivelle, introduced Joinovici to an Abwehr subordinate of Hermann Brandl. Soon Joinovici had a near monopoly on the supply of metal to the Amt Otto. An impressed Brandl handed over a certificate, which declared that Joinovici was officially in German service: 'All French and German agencies must help him in the execution of his missions,' read the header on his paperwork.[5]

Joinovici was one of a select group exempted by the Nazis from their racial laws for political or economic reasons. Others included the Arabic Grand Mufti of Jerusalem, cancer expert Dr Otto Warburg, Japanese emissaries and Romanian-born Comédie-Française actor Jean Yonnel, who regularly got a standing ovation from Paris audiences for wearing a yellow star on stage.

Some Jews were allowed to operate behind false identities if it suited the Germans. The Russian-born Michel Szkolnikoff made millions in Paris by producing uniforms for the Kriegsmarine. A Jewish friend of Eddy Pagnon called Albert Modiano made smaller sums selling metals to the Amt Otto. A prominent member of a Russian gang of collaborators known as 'Gestapo Géorgienne' was a Crimean Jew, who posed as an Iranian. Other Jews simply bought their way out. At least 400 Dutch Jews paid over 35 million Swiss francs to escape an internment camp in the Netherlands.

In the overlapping circles of collaboration, it was inevitable that Joinovici would encounter Henri Chamberlin, and it was Radecke of the Abwehr who introduced the pair. Eventually, a meal at 93 rue Lauriston was organised, with every surface covered in flowers chosen by Monsieur Henri, and this led to more regular meetings. The two men became black market business colleagues and an edgy friendship was born.

Joinovici remained in a permanent state of jovial obsequiousness around the Carlingue boss. Chamberlin had grown into a godfather figure in Paris, spending his days holding court at rue Lauriston and being driven in a white Bentley across town to lunch with Gestapo heads, senior Abwehr agents and DSK contacts. The days in which he had played a central role in gold stings and black marketeering were behind him. Chamberlin bragged: 'Personally I don't like to accompany my men in these kinds of operations. I give them precise instructions and they carry them out themselves.'[6]

Occasionally a juicy target pulled Chamberlin out of rue Lauriston. Adrien Estébétéguy – who Chamberlin now described as 'a crook in which I had only relative confidence' – contacted him to talk about a rich old lady who was looking to sell a stash of gold.[7] She believed that Chamberlin was a trustworthy member of the black market and would talk only to him. Monsieur Henri turned on the charm, arranged the deal and then confiscated 1 million francs worth of gold.

'The poor lady was completely shocked,' he later explained. 'She didn't understand anything. I quickly realised she wasn't involved in any big kind of operations and told her: "You're free to go."' As she left the building, she muttered that Chamberlin had ruined her life as she went out the door. Two days later she gassed herself in a kitchen oven. 'I felt that day a terrible sadness,' remarked Chamberlin.[8]

Joinovici pretended to believe in Chamberlin's regret at the old woman's death. It was part of their wary meeting of minds. Both men were the same age, had been marginalised in society, became rich thanks to the Germans and had two children they no longer saw. Joinovici's wife and daughters lived separately after he took up with his secretary Lucie Bernard – a figure who was so disliked in the scrap business that she was known as 'Lucie-Fer'. Chamberlin hadn't seen his own children for years but had recently instructed a lawyer from Marseille to begin the process of tracking them down.

Despite the similarities between the two men and their shared love of socialising, Joinovici was never allowed into the rue Lauriston inner circle. Monsieur Henri never quite trusted him. 'When I look deep into his eyes,' said Chamberlin, 'I see his teeth.'[9]

Those fears were well-founded. Since 1941 Joinovici had been funding a resistance group called Turma-Vengeance through a nephew who lived in La Rochelle. When the Germans uncovered the network, Joinovici escaped detection and looked for other groups to finance.

Some members of the police force in Paris had resistance plans and were in need of money. Joinovici was happy to help. He balanced his books by continuing to orbit the man he knew as Henri Lafont and looked on as his new friend developed links to men operating at the highest levels of Pétain's government. One was Jean Luchaire, a horse-faced seducer with slicked-back hair and a shifty smile, who thought that siding with the Nazis would bring about peace.

• • •

The defining moment of Jean Luchaire's life came at the age of thirteen when he volunteered in an Uriage-les-Bains hospital for the war wounded. He would always remember the mutilated men, ceaseless crying at night and empty beds in the morning.

Luchaire was a Frenchman brought up in Italy whose family had returned home to help the war effort against the Kaiser. His experiences in Uriage-les-Bains turned him against war for good and towards Franco-German friendship. He became a left-leaning pacifist and deciding to work as a journalist when he left school.

As a tyro reporter, Luchaire reported on the usual mix of stories from the interwar years, such as the daily life of diplomats, the suicide of a comedian, White Russian exiles, refugees in Syria and boxing matches. Occasionally he got a byline. In 1927, Luchaire founded his own newspaper entitled *Notre Temps* to spread his anti-war message. Two years later he followed this with a pacifist manifesto called *Une Génération Réaliste*. 'I knew Jean Luchaire in 1924,' said anti-fascist novelist Julien Green. 'He was a sincere and kind man!'[10]

Luchaire lived a bohemian life in Montparnasse with his wife, four children, a love of luxury and an army of mistresses. As the Second World War approached, *Notre Temps* was struggling and Luchaire took money from anyone who could keep it afloat. He received subsidies from the Socialist politician Joseph Paul-Boncour as well as the Communist Party. His commitment to peace through a Franco-German alliance saw him attending youth camps in the early 1930s where he encountered a young Francophile drawing instructor called Otto Abetz.

The pair became close and Abetz ended up marrying Luchaire's secretary at *Notre Temps*. The friendship drew the Frenchman away from his leftist roots and far enough right to believe that the Nazis wanted peace. But the invasion in 1940 destroyed all that. During the first days of occupation, Luchaire found himself emotionally shell-shocked in Vichy, but regained his sense of mission when Pierre Laval sent him to Paris with instructions to become a press baron and spread Pétainist propaganda. Like many former leftists, Luchaire joined Déat's RNP and collaboration replaced pacifism as his political northern star.

Around the same time, his friend Otto Abetz had become German ambassador to France. Luchaire was soon spending his days and nights among collaborationist café society of alcoholic journalists, washed-up celebrities, adventuresses and bed-hoppers and all the crooks and marginal figures who were pushing their way into the limelight of occupation.

Luchaire started up the Club de la Presse to bring together collaborationist journalists once a week between 5 and 7 p.m. in a smoky room for gossip and chat over real coffee and red wine, and a lecture on the correct line to take about the Nazi war effort. He also set up companies to buy black market goods for the Germans. Luchaire's messy and decadent personal lifestyle earned him the nickname of 'Louche Herr'. It was a short step to the inhabitants of 93 rue Lauriston.

Luchaire's invitation was brokered by a business contact who had shared a Toulouse cell with Monsieur Henri fifteen years earlier. Lionel de Wiet was a distinguished-looking man with a wobbly hint of jowls and pale blond hair that was swept back from his forehead. He liked to talk of his adventures in a rich rolling voice, claiming to have been a lieutenant in the Spahis cavalry regiment during the First World War and to have been decorated with the Croix de Guerre medal for bravery, but it was all lies.

De Wiet was born in June 1899 to a good family in Constantinople where his father worked as a French diplomat. However, after discovering cocaine he rapidly went off the rails and found himself in prison for pretending to be a war hero. This early disgrace didn't stop him marrying a rich divorcée and former hairdresser named Maddy Pabion. The couple had two children, and de Wiet built a small business empire from his wife's finances.

De Wiet supplied coal and contraband to the Spanish Republicans through front companies, but never cared much about politics. He ran businesses with impressive names which traded on the fringes of legality, including the Society Anglo-French and Spanish Commercial Union, the Société Française des Carburants and others. The businessman served more time in prison for fraud before drifting back into the fringes of respectable high society.

Jean Luchaire had covered de Wiet's trial for impersonating a Spahis officer back in the 1920s, but the pair did not meet until the late 1930s when they formed an unsuccessful film production company named Centrazur. When the war arrived, Luchaire encouraged de Wiet to set up the Société Européenne de Fournitures Industrielles et Commerciales (SEFIC) and to do business with the Nazis.

By 1941 de Wiet had secured a deal with the Kriegsmarine to supply 6,000 tonnes of paint for 140 million francs. As the money came rolling in, de Wiet funnelled some of it into Jean Luchaire's new pro-Nazi newspaper named *Les Nouveaux Temps*. In return, members of Luchaire's family received high-paying jobs in SEFIC.

Late in the year something went wrong and de Wiet was arrested.

Luchaire and Abetz were unable to help him out. The jowly businessman reached out to an old jailbird friend who had been doing well for himself in the black market. Henri Chamberlin was happy to intervene. In February 1942 he used his Abwehr contacts to spring de Wiet and then lent him 2 million francs to get SEFIC operational again.

This turned out to be a good investment; Chamberlin got his money back within a few weeks. Soon de Wiet was richer than ever from supplying materials to the Amt Otto and wine to the Waffen-SS.

Jean Luchaire had become aware of the Carlingue's growing power through de Wiet's gossip and some disapproving reports from Abetz, who disliked the idea of gangsters benefitting from collaboration. Laval's clique in Vichy looked over the reports, saw an opportunity and urged Luchaire to make contact. The press baron began socialising with Chamberlin and the others in their nightly rounds of the One-Two-Two, the Fanfan and the Tanagra. Luchaire was usually accompanied by Georges Prade, a corrupt municipal council of the fifteenth arrondissement, and Bonny's friend Jean Guélin.

Despite the connection, Bonny didn't like Luchaire. He saw the press man as a wolf who played the part of a docile lamb, who would politely listen and smile and always get more than he gave. Bonny warned Chamberlin about the man, but his advice went unheeded. Monsieur Henri enjoyed charming company and appreciated the fact that Luchaire's contacts with Laval and his entourage opened up connections to the highest powers in Vichy. Chamberlin let it be known that he was happy to do favours for Pétain's government: they only had to ask.

Over the drinks and nightclub noise, Luchaire liked to tell the story of how a resistance group had once tried to murder him. At a party earlier in the year allegedly a girl had flirted her way into offering him a poison diluted in soda water. 'No thanks,' said the oblivious Luchaire. 'I take my whisky straight.'[11]

The press baron only realised how close he had come to death when the party was over. Chamberlin laughed at the story, and then assigned Jeunet as bodyguard.

'Very special, nice looking, the perfect pimp,' Luchaire said.[12]

Joseph Joinovici watched the power play and deals from the sidelines and requested some bodyguards of his own from Chamberlin, although he was more concerned about anti-Semites coming after him than the resistance. Monsieur Henri tried to reassure him that the SS paperwork certifying Joinovici as not being Jewish was enough and told his friend that he was being paranoid.

'Don't worry,' said Chamberlin. 'You've got a ticket from the Fritzes. Without you where are they going to get all those non-ferrous metals you deliver to them by the tonne? They won't cause trouble just because the rabbi cut a slice of ham off you.'[13]

Joinovici insisted on protection and Chamberlin assigned him Louis Seiche and Georges Boucheseiche as bodyguards. The pair were soon joined by the insubordinate Pierre Loutrel and Henri Fefeu, who was better known as 'Riton le Tatoué', a grim-faced thirty-something covered in tattoos from his time in the Bat d'Af.

As 1942 rolled on, Chamberlin was making friends with rich businessmen, press barons and powerful men in Vichy. He would gain even more influence after a senior SS figure made a serious mistake over the arrest of a French duke and came to the Carlingue for help. The power balance between rue Lauriston and the Germans would never be the same.

9

NIGHT AND FOG

THE CREST OF THE Duchy of Ayen was a blood-red shield slashed upper left to lower right by a gold band. It stood for two hundred years of nobility. In the middle of the night in late 1942, the door to the cell that held the 6th Duke of Ayen opened and a group of men stood silhouetted against the light from the corridor outside. The duke crossed himself and prepared to die.

The 1st Duke of Ayen earned his coat of arms by accompanying Louis XV across the battlefield in his role as Marshal of France. Subsequent dukes dodged the revolutionary guillotine to become historians, soldiers and men who lived for pleasure. In 1942, the 6th Duke of Ayen was Jean Maurice Paul Jules de Noailles, a 48-year-old world pigeon-shooting champion.

Noailles had beautiful manners, a wife and two children and no apparent interest in anything except gunning down small birds. On 28 January 1942, he had disappeared from the streets of Paris. German officers denied knowing anything when his wife came begging for information. They suggested the reason for his disappearance could be gambling debts, a demanding mistress or the Allied bombs that were by this time falling regularly across the city. An air raid on the Renault complex in the working-class Boulogne-Billancourt district had killed over 400 people. Solange Marie Christine Louise de Labriffe refused to believe that the Germans weren't involved.

She was right. Her husband had vanished under 'Nacht und Nebel' (Night and Fog), a kidnapping operation organised by Berlin to bypass international laws on detainees. Nazi officials borrowed the term 'Night and Fog' from Wagner's *Das Rheingold* to add a sense of romanticism to piss-stinking cells and the firing squad.

'These measures will have a deterrent effect,' said the paperwork explaining the decree, 'because A. The prisoners will vanish without a trace, B. No information may be given as to their whereabouts or their fate.'[1]

Nacht und Nebel demoralised the resistance and offered plausible deniability when the Swiss Red Cross came to lecture Nazi officials about human rights. Anyone arrested under the measure was to be executed within eight days or deported to a concentration camp for head shaving, a striped uniform and forced labour in the German war machine. Neither happened to the Duke of Ayen. He stayed in his Paris prison cell at 84 avenue Foch for almost a year, waiting to find out what the Germans wanted from him.

A guard who took bribes allowed the duke to smuggle letters out to his wife. She wept tears of joy that her husband was alive and took the case to Vichy. Marshal Pétain, who could not resist a well-born lady, wrote back a concerned letter: 'You cannot imagine, Madame, how much I sympathise with your misfortune. I pray to God nothing happens to your husband.'[2]

Vichy diplomats raised the issue through contacts close to Heinrich Himmler. Requests for information trickled down the Nazi hierarchy and arrived on the Paris desk of Standartenführer Helmut Knochen. As a subordinate of Höherer SS-und Polizeiführer Carl Oberg, Knochen was the SS man in charge of security in northern

France and Belgium. The Gestapo, the SD and other intelligence agencies took their orders from him.

Knochen was a slim and blond man in his thirties with a degree in History and English. He had quit a teaching career in 1932 to join the Nazi Party, then joined the SS where he raced up the ranks like a lightning bolt. Senior officers saw a significant future for Knochen and did not want the botched arrest of a French aristocrat derailing his brilliant career. In early November 1942 he invited a French Gestapo agent who had a reputation for efficiency to his office to discuss the matter.

Henri Chamberlin arrived at 84 avenue Foch with its warren of offices and cells and pneumatic tubes that carried messages all over Paris in sealed cylinders. Up in his third-floor office, Knochen outlined the mission: 'I have a prisoner that you need to take into the unoccupied zone,' he said, 'and, once there, liquidate him.'[3]

The duke had been picked up by agents of the GFP back when their organisation still worked as a secret police force for the Wehrmacht, but the power reshuffle in 1942 had brought them and their prisoners under SS control. Soon after, the duke had been moved into a new cell and forgotten about. None of the case paperwork explained why he had not been executed or deported and no one could remember who ordered the arrest. The closest Knochen's investigation got to an explanation were rumours that the duke's mistress shared her favours with a lovesick German officer who wanted his rival off the scene.

The result was a bureaucratic mess that reflected badly on Knochen. He decided to erase the problem without telling Berlin. Henri Chamberlin got the job.

Contract killing was a new act for the circus at rue Lauriston. The gang's main business remained black marketeering and protection rackets, with a recently acquired sideline into looting abandoned Jewish apartments for the Dienststelle Westen. The Dienststelle was an anarchic outfit that was barely legal even by Nazi standards and operated under the command of Oberfeldfüher Baron Kurt von Behr, a hollow-cheeked aristocrat and former German Red Cross chief with a stare cold enough to flash-freeze a forest fire.

The Dienststelle Westen had spun off from the larger Einsatzstab Reichsleiter Rosenberg, which stole artistic treasures from across occupied Europe in the name of cultural research. Von Behr was more interested in the everyday items that were gathering dust in Jewish apartments left empty after the first round-ups in Paris. Von Behr's men would break in and cart off furniture, paintings, jewellery, pianos and clothes. The German's wife made herself notorious by sorting through the packing crates to select the best items for herself; the remaining booty furnished administration offices in the occupied East.

Rue Lauriston became involved in the practice when Von Behr needed extra manpower and asked Gestapo contacts for reliable locals. Soon Chamberlin's men were swarming over the wreckage of Jewish Paris like cockroaches.

When the Dienststelle Westen ran out of warehouse space, Chamberlin offered up 40 rue Lauriston, which was a block of apartments and shops just down the road from gang headquarters. At the time Lionel de Wiet also used parts of the building for his black market activities. His man on the scene was Oliver Allard, the son of a Belgian businessman who owned a correspondence school. De Wiet tried to keep the place secret from his fellow crooks, but word got out in early 1942 when Allard was arrested for selling inferior-quality paper, tissues and chocolate to the Amt Otto.

Chamberlin helped the Belgian wriggle off the hook for this

misdemeanour and for other problems with the DSK, and then called in the favour. As a result, de Wiet could do nothing when Eddy Pagnon was sent to take possession of the storage space. A guard who was on duty on the day described what happened: 'One time I saw a man I didn't know and to who I refused access. The guy worried me so I told de Wiet who said to me that he was acting for Henri and he could do whatever he wanted because he was the boss.'[4]

In one of the many coincidences that layered collaborationist Paris, the building in rue Lauriston was sometimes visited by Captain Ernst Jünger, executioner of deserters and black marketeers. He came to visit the dark-eyed Umm-El-Banine Asadullayeva, a writer from Azerbaijan whose well-connected family had fled the Bolsheviks after the First World War. Two divorces had moved her from Constantinople to Paris where she lived in an apartment block on rue Lauriston, which had a view of the water tower on rue Copernic over a cluster of princess trees bright with mauve-coloured flowers.

Banine met Jünger through a mutual friend after her first novel *Nami* was published by Gallimard in 1942. Jünger visited her apartment for strong coffee and literary solace after he returned from a grim tour of the Eastern Front that autumn.

The war against the Soviets was nothing but murderous cold, technological backwardness and casual jokes among officers about killing prisoners. The best hotel in Kiev had no running water. Colleagues passed on rumours that poison gas was being used to kill Jews. Jünger spent four months among frozen corpses, collapsing front lines and a disillusioned officer corps. He read Rimbaud and Gogol and thought about an age of romantic chivalry that had been wiped out by the mechanisation of war and society, while suffering from intense headaches.

Jünger returned to Paris with a changed perspective on life and felt guilt at the sight of Jewish people wearing yellow stars on their coats. He sat with Banine in her rue Lauriston apartment and talked about literature and wartime gossip over tiny cups of thick Turkish coffee. On the street below, Chamberlin's lorries unloaded their loot. 'The so-called Security Service here seems to have allied itself with French criminals', Jünger wrote in his journal, 'in order to extort rich Frenchmen.'[5]

Jünger would not have been surprised to hear that Chamberlin had agreed to execute the Duke of Ayen. No one would. Paris already believed that the Carlingue boss had no qualms about murder and had even killed one of his own men.

• • •

A story was doing the rounds of Pigalle and Montmartre, shared in the bars, brothels and the gambling houses, and passed from gangster to crook and pimp to prostitute. The details were different every time.

Roger Tissier had been found drunk in a small bar on rue Damrémont at 2 a.m., or possibly in a mansion on rue de Villejust. Chamberlin, Cazauba, Danos and Tissier's friend Carrier had walked in and found him, or perhaps it was Prévost and not Carrier. Tissier didn't see them, but the barman or other witness did and immediately excused themselves.

'Roger!' called Chamberlin.[6]

Tissier was one of the original criminals that Chamberlin had freed from Fresnes. He was a hefty man in his forties with little in the way of bravery. The Vichy Deuxième Bureau had got its hands on him and turned the crook into an informer. Chamberlin found out and called a council of war at rue Lauriston where he argued for the death penalty. His inner circle agreed.

Tissier sat on a seat in a drunken stupor and as he turned to face the man who had shouted his name, Chamberlin shot him three times. Cazauba and Carrier carried the body into a black Citroën parked up outside, or perhaps Cazauba and Danos loaded it into the trunk of a white Bentley. Tissier's corpse was dismembered and scattered in the woods, never to be found.

By the winter of 1942, the story was all over the city. Pierre Bonny pieced together the highlights from dark jokes made by other gang members. When he asked the boss about the rumours, Chamberlin shook his head and dismissed the whole idea. 'Pure invention,' he said.[7]

Rue Lauriston secretary Delehaye explained that Tissier had just disappeared one day and no one in the gang knew where he had gone. Bonny didn't believe him, but some underworld cynics suspected the whole story might have been a piece of opportunistic fiction spread by Chamberlin to intimidate anyone who was planning on betraying him. Certainly, a few Carlingue members were already playing a double game. 'I knew it, I couldn't trust anyone,' said Chamberlin. 'They had in my ranks some people who worked for British Intelligence and the Deuxième Bureau.'[8]

The Tissier affair, regardless of whether it was true or not, failed to frighten off other informers. François Suzzoni and two other Corsican career crooks regularly passed information to Vichy's Deuxième Bureau about Lafont and his gang. Alexandre Villaplana told a resistance contact anything he heard about German agents infiltrating the Zone Libre, as the result of blackmail over a gold deal that had gone wrong. Jo Attia had his own friends in the resistance and already regretted passing on information that had allowed the Germans to arrest fifteen members of a resistance network when he first joined the Carlingue.

Chamberlin never realised that Suzzoni, Attia and the others were helping his enemies. Instead, he wrongly suspected that Pagnon the chauffeur was 'wearing a hat', which was underworld slang for talking to the police. Monsieur Henri flitted between raging at the chauffeur for betraying him and then awarding him huge pay rises as some kind of apology. Pagnon's 12,000 francs a month barely covered the fits of temper, the constant bullying and the fatigue of waiting at the wheel all night while Chamberlin visited girlfriends and German officers.

This all seemed especially unjust to Pagnon when his boss continued to be friends with Jean Rossi, the full-faced but good-looking owner of the bar Le Chapiteau, who regularly hosted Chamberlin and the gang. Rossi had known connections to the resistance and ran a spying operation against drunk German soldiers at the L'Abbaye de Thélème bar. Chamberlin knew which side Rossi had chosen, but he did nothing about it.

In this double-crossing world of spies and informers and the disappeared, killing a French aristocrat seemed to be a good career move for Chamberlin. When the cell door swung open, Knochen gave the duke a cover story about being released to the Vichy authorities. They escorted him out of the building and into a white Bentley that was waiting in the street.

Knochen's murder plan went immediately wrong. Chamberlin had never met a real aristocrat and decided that he wanted to get the most out of the experience. The domestic staff at rue Lauriston prepared a huge meal for the duke up on the first floor that consisted of hors-d'œuvres, expensive meat, a bottle of Meursault 1928 and two bottles of Eyquem. Abel Danos served the food on silver plates as Chamberlin made conversation with his guest.

The duke impressed everyone with his well-spoken, calm exterior and his casually disdainful attitude towards death born from two centuries of aristocratic inbreeding. Chamberlin still intended to kill him, but over dessert the duke strategically mentioned that he had successfully smuggled letters out of prison to his wife. Knochen's plan for a secret liquidation would never work if the dead man could be traced to avenue Foch. As a result, Chamberlin immediately dropped the idea of a forest execution but decided to keep this new information to himself while he waited to see what advantage might be able to develop from the situation.

The gang moved their guest around safe houses in Paris. His first stop was a requisitioned three-room apartment near the Trocadéro that had recently been vacated by Cazauba. Pagnon served as guard. After a few days, the duke was transferred into the care of Danos, whose apartment was not known to the Germans. Chamberlin ordered both men to stay indoors.

Danos hated being stuck inside the apartment all day. He preferred to spend his afternoons at the One-Two-Two brothel with Clavié and Villaplana, popping open magnums of champagne and groping the girls. By this time, he still had a longstanding girlfriend in the bouffant-haired Simone Bouladour and had recently also picked up another love interest; Rose Hélène Maltat's parents worked as concierges a few doors down in rue Lauriston.

After a week of being cooped up, Le Mammouth sneaked the duke out to the Bois de Saint-Cucufa for some target practice. They both enjoyed the adventure, but within a few days Danos was begging his boss to cut him loose so he could spend some time with his new lady friend. Chamberlin agreed and sounded out pre-war friend Lucien Guitard to take on guard duty. He discovered too late that the new recruit worked a sideline job with the Gestapo and immediately informed his other bosses about the duke's existence.

A ringing telephone woke Monsieur Henri the next morning. On the other end was Danos, shouting about men hammering on his front door. Chamberlin told him to shoot anyone who tried to enter, and quickly drove over to find that the building was sealed off by a crowd of soldiers in feldgrau. He moved on to avenue Foch and found a furious Knochen waving a pistol around in his office.

Chamberlin explained about the duke's letters and used his charm to calm the situation down. The SS chief put the pistol away, grudgingly thanked the gangster and pretended not to notice when Monsieur Henri took credit for saving his career. In the aftermath, the duke was transferred to a prison camp and then on to a concentration camp. Knochen battled with Berlin over who should take responsibility for the affair before both sides agreed to blame the mess on SS underlings.

After this episode, the power subtext between rue Lauriston and the occupation authorities had permanently changed. Chamberlin immediately understood this shift and within a few weeks was abusing it.

Chamberlin's men Sartore and Jeunet had recently ended up in hospital after being knifed by a pimp from the Montmartre underworld, who was known only as Phono. On 18 November 1942, Chaves identified the attacker as Henri Tanguy and made a telephone call from a bar on rue d'Aboukir.

Chamberlin and Tanguy were friends from way back. In the late 1930s they were close enough for Chamberlin to arrive unannounced at Tanguy's house and stay on for two weeks, during which time he drank anything that had a cork in it and entertained the pimp and his prostitute girlfriend with his elaborate anecdotes. 'He made us scream with laughter at his stories of crooks,' Tanguy's girlfriend remembered, 'which he told in his falsetto voice.'[9]

During the occupation, Tanguy operated on the fringes of the Carlingue and recruited fresh gang members for cash, but he was too independent to subordinate himself completely to an old friend like Monsieur Henri. Then came the mysterious fight with Sartore and Jeunet. Chamberlin set out to make an example of anyone who crossed the Carlingue, and his old friend Tanguy was no exception. The pimp ended up bleeding out on the steps of the Métro Strasbourg – Saint-Denis with bullets in his back.

Sartore returned to the gang when his wounds healed but Jeunet disappeared from the scene. Getting a knife in the face had killed his appetite for collaboration with the Nazis. He moved into a Florentine villa on the coast somewhere between Cannes and Nice and started up a prostitution network with a sideline in distributing fake ration vouchers. He cut all contact with the gang.

Back in Paris, Bonny typed up a report which claimed Henri Tanguy had been a resistance operative and how the shooting had been justified. Bömelburg doubted this version of events, but Chamberlin had plenty of leverage after the Duke of Ayen affair. The complicated and confused nature of the murder closed down the possibility of any investigation, but the German advised the Carlingue boss get out of town for a while.

A trip to Biarritz on behalf of the Amt Otto offered Chamberlin the chance to combine business with pleasure. For company, he brought along a beautiful blonde Russian émigré countess whose manicured fingernails had been all over the Parisian black market in recent months. The street urchin who had once found his meals in dustbins was now sleeping with aristocratic women who had titles, pearls and morphine addictions.

10

TOUT VA TRÈS BIEN, MADAME LA MARQUISE

COUNTESS MARA TCHERNICHEV-BEZOBRAZOV WAS the second child of a Muscovite count and could barely remember her homeland. Her last view of Russia came at four years old from the deck of a ship steaming away from a Crimean port as the Bolsheviks came over the hills. Cossacks with tears running through their beards shot beloved horses on the quayside as the last Tsarist holdout collapsed after years of revolution and civil war. It was the end of empire and of everything the Russian aristocracy knew.

In 1922, Mara and her family washed up in Marseille before moving on to Paris. Her father abandoned the family when their last Russian jewels had been pawned and left his wife to bring up two children on her own. Mara's mother got a job at the diamond exchange in rue Cadet and made enough to give her children a decent education at a local Russian-language school. White Russian exiles had become familiar figures in Paris, where they were known for their good manners and conspiracies but were rarely taken seriously by the French. 'They were tall and handsome and splendid,' said fashion designer Coco Chanel, 'but behind it all – nothing: just vodka and the void.'[1]

Mara had an adventurous nature, blonde hair and a model's

poise. Whatever plans her mother had for Mara's future failed to stick and at seventeen years old, the young woman turned up on the Côte d'Azur as an extra in the film *Les Aventures du Roi Pausole*. A short career modelling for Chanel followed, then a stretch living with a gay Russian painter to deter the suspicions of his traditionalist family. More film roles followed for Mara whenever one of her rich lovers had the money to play producer, until she moved in with a professional gambler from Romania. One night, as her lover was transfixed by the steel ball rattling around the amphitheatre of a roulette wheel, she left him and walked away with a man called Henri Garascu. He was another Romanian, widely known in France as Henri Garat, heart-throb actor and singer.

When Mara took off with Garat, he was already deep into a long decline of gambling, cocaine, women and debt. His first marriage had just collapsed when the Russian blonde with the smiling eyes walked into his life. She was broke and he was famous. They married in 1939 and sailed for Rio de Janeiro a year later to escape the invading Germans.

Brazilian high society was a technicolour whirl of cocktail parties and lounging on the beach with the exiled King Carol of Romania. A giant sculpture of Christ looked on from above with welcoming arms. Garat was less famous in Latin America than he was back home, and it wasn't hard for a local Brazilian industrialist to steal Mara away. The actor sailed for France after threatening divorce.

Mara planned to wait out the war with her new boyfriend in the sun, but everything changed a few months later when a letter arrived from Garat claiming her mother was seriously ill. Mara struggled back into France via the Spanish border but found her mother perfectly healthy and Garat begging for another chance. The fake letter failed to force a reconciliation and the divorce was signed.

Countess Mara moved into a cramped apartment with long-time friend Michel Chirkov and his old, paralysed nanny. She still had some money, a few remaining choice pieces of jewellery and a taste for luxury. An acquaintance called Serge Landchevsky saw that Mara possessed a sharp business brain under her blonde curls and invited her to join a gang of Russian exiles who were selling alcohol to the Amt Otto.

A disappointed German report on local morale at the time described most Parisians as 'cool, hesitant, and negative' towards the occupying forces.[2] However, the Russian émigré community was different. Many Russians in Paris cheered on the Nazi invasion of the USSR, in hope that the Germans could bring an end to Bolshevism and allow them to return to their ancestral estates. They had no problem doing business with the men in feldgrau. Landchevsky introduced Mara to his Swiss boss, a man called Max Stöcklin.

After the Algiers debacle, Stöcklin had reinvented himself as Guy Max. He managed an Amt Otto black market office from the fourth floor of 1 rue Lord Byron, where the gold lettering on the door declared that the place was home to a company that manufactured electric cars. Inside the office, a team of rackety Belgian aristocrats and exiled Russian gentry strolled around counting thick wads of francs.

Stöcklin saw potential in Tchernichev-Bezobrazov. There were many women who bought and sold goods for the Germans and made a successful business out of it. Well-known faces included Genia Rosenthalis, who everyone knew as Madame Dubail; Madame Gere from Austria; the German Clara Peter; and Suzanne Henrio who ran a firm that had been stolen from its Jewish owners. Their activities annoyed the more chauvinist black marketeers such as Gaston Ansart, who ran several Amt Otto fronts and a German buying concern called Primetex. He had no time for them. 'I banned entry into Primetex for women,' said a disgruntled Ansart. 'The great majority of suppliers were women.'[3]

However, Stöcklin was more broad-minded. Soon Tchernichev-Bezobrazov had her own Amt Otto office that sold wine, brandy and more to the Germans. A secretary called Zina Afrossimova and a poodle called Dingo accompanied her everywhere. The office was furnished with pieces that had been taken from requisitioned Jewish homes.

Towards the end of 1942 Stöcklin took the countess to a Saturday night party at rue Lauriston. The gramophone was blaring, the champagne was flowing and the Russian was impressed to see celebrities among the other guests; it was the winter that everybody came to see Henri Chamberlin.

As one cynical partygoer observed: 'Every Saturday there was a reception in the grand salon. A crowd of people were there. I remember Maurice Chevalier … Oh, he went there very innocently, like all the celebrities.'[4]

The actor and singer Maurice Chevalier was as smooth as a silk scarf. He was talented enough to have made it big in Hollywood before the war, but French enough to remain a local hero. His 1925 hit song 'Valentine' was still being crooned across Paris when the Second World War came along. Chevalier possessed property in the Zone Libre but had problems crossing the demarcation line once the occupation began. A show-business friend suggested that he approach a man named Lafont based out of rue Lauriston.

A meeting was arranged, which led Chamberlin to make a call and obtain a border pass. In return, Chevalier attended a dinner in his honour at rue Lauriston. Later, Chamberlin attended a charity event for French prisoners-of-war still in German hands that had been organised by Chevalier and held at the Théâtre des Ambassadeurs. He made an ostentatious donation of 1 million francs. Chevalier was grateful but kept his distance; the singer had performed in some occupation revues that had been ambiguous enough to get himself a reputation as a collaborator but was hiding a Jewish family down in the Zone Libre.

Other Parisians visited rue Lauriston just to eat. Collaboration and resistance meant nothing to hungry people facing a table piled high with food. Cheese came from Madame Prince's shop at 84 rue Lauriston and was bought in bulk for cash. Fresh bread and cakes came from Coulon's bakery on avenue Montagine, which also satisfied Chamberlin's sweet tooth, a legacy of years spent starving on the streets. Sometimes the gangsters used ration cards and sometimes not; no one ever asked questions.

A North African butcher supplied the gang with meat. In September 1941 he and his two sons had been arrested by the Germans after a gold deal went wrong. His friends contacted Chamberlin and begged him to help. Chamberlin had the men released and played the generous godfather by refusing to accept any payment. The butcher supplied meat for free to rue Lauriston from then on.

Monsieur Henri was playing the charming host at one of his soirees when Tchernichev-Bezobrazov walked in the door and introduced herself as 'Comtesse Garat', because no Frenchman ever pronounced her maiden name correctly. She had an Austrian SS boyfriend called Hans Leimer waiting at home for her in an apartment near the Trocadéro, but Henri Chamberlin stormed into her life that night like a force of nature, and they became lovers within days. She laughed off Leimer's suspicious questions asked in broken French.

Soon after, Chamberlin could be seen in the Paris nightclubs with

Countess Mara on his arm. They talked about black marketeering and gossip and he regaled her with unbelievable stories about gangsters that made her laugh. It was cocktails, seductive company and one of Chamberlin's men with a gun in his pocket keeping an eye on the door. The countess's cosmopolitan sophistication smoothed down some of Chamberlin's rougher edges. He removed Anne Jean-Claude and the rest of Esméralda's dancer friends with their dramas from his life.

After Anne Jean-Claude decided that she had aspirations to become a theatre director, Chamberlin had recently bankrolled a production of George Bernard Shaw's *Pygmalion*. The show closed in days. 'This theatre is stupid,' declared Anne, blaming the venue for the show flopping.[5]

Anne wanted to try again, but Chamberlin had lost interest. She decided to hire another theatre on credit but couldn't pay the actors' salaries as opening night approached. To raise funds, she acquired some fake gold coins from Cazauba and gave them to her new boyfriend, who was a student called Montejoye. The student arranged faux policiers gold deals and pulled out a blank firing prop pistol when the money appeared. Unfortunately for Montejoye, one buyer was an undercover German policeman with a real gun.

The student was deported to the camps and Anne was arrested. Chamberlin called in a favour and had her freed. The Gestapo man who had arrested Anne took her to dinner the day that she was released.

'A crazy woman who thinks she's a good actress,' said Chamberlin to his cronies.[6]

Shortly after Anne's run-in with the Gestapo came the Duke of Ayen affair and the Tanguy shooting. Chamberlin left town and took Countess Mara along with him.

• • •

Before the war, Biarritz was a beachside playground where aristocrats threw their money away in casinos and cheated on their spouses in overpriced hotel suites. On a good day minor royalty could be seen promenading along La Grande Plage. During the occupation, the shops were empty and the streets full of sandbags, swastika flags and goose-stepping German troops.

Chamberlin arrived in town with Mara at his side. He had a mission from the Abwehr to set up an Amt Otto office that could process clothing smuggled in from over the nearby Spanish border. Radecke came along to take care of the paperwork; Lionel de Wiet brought members of his wife's family to serve as office staff; and Cazauba and Prévost were there to make contacts across the border.

The group took over a sprawl of requisitioned villas in the old town. They spent their days drinking in the Carlton Hôtel, an arc of shimmering pink Belle Époque overlooking the foaming breakers of the Bay of Biscay. Mara's boyfriend, the SS man Hans Leimer, had invited himself along but failed to notice her disappearing into Chamberlin's bedroom in the afternoons.

Cazauba and Prévost made contact with a gang of Basque smugglers who drove lorries through the mountains and into France at night. A corrupt Spanish diplomat called Alvares Muñoz helped smooth out any issues at the border. The smuggling route brought in clothes by the tonne and quickly started making a lot of money.

After a few weeks in the sun, the group left the buying office to run itself and returned to Paris. Chamberlin's passion for Tchernichev-Bezobrazov had already cooled and been replaced by a close friendship. He gifted her some black market storage space in *3bis* place des États-Unis, which was a four-storey building that

Radecke had requisitioned early on in the occupation. In exchange she introduced him to Princess Sofia Hazrakoff, a bisexual Russian morphine addict, who arranged threesomes for Monsieur Henri with a parade of her aristocratic French lovers.

Even Chamberlin was surprised by the debauchery of the upper classes. One after another, women with titles and pedigrees fell into his bed, including a duchess, a countess and many others. The Marquise d'Austerlitz taught him to ride horses but things quickly soured between them until the gangster was describing her to cronies as 'a crazy woman and a bitch'.[7]

During one party at rue Lauriston, Violette Morris added up all the aristocratic titles Chamberlin had slept with and remarked: 'All you need is a Grand Duchess, an Archduchess, a Queen and an Empress. But there, friend, the frontiers are closed.'[8]

Chamberlin's new high-society friends advised him on how to live the good life. The gangster began appreciating fine wines, more subtle foods and graceful living. His friends helped him furnish rue Lauriston with exotic furniture: sphinx-legged chairs, claw-footed tables and curling chaise-longues. They introduced him to art. Chamberlin paid 1 million francs for a Rodin bronze at a gala of the Union des Artistes. However, he couldn't see the attraction of anything that was more modern and hated Picasso. 'It's shit,' he said. 'Even his Blue Period is just a bluff.'[9]

When the aristocratic well ran dry, Chamberlin moved on to celebrities. Dita Parlo was a statuesque German actress with hair the colour of vanilla ice cream. Born Grethe Gerda Kornstädt in Pomerania, she made her mark in silent melodramas, such as the 1928 *Heimkehr* (*Homecoming*), before crossing borders and sound technology to appear in Jean Renoir's French anti-war classic *La Grande Illusion*. She had a frustrating time in Hollywood during the late 1930s, which included being promised a role in Orson Welles's aborted version of *Heart of Darkness*, then returned to Germany before the war.

In Paris during the occupation, she met Henri Chamberlin and fell for his charm. She understood how much American gangster films such as *Angels with Dirty Faces* and *Little Caesar* and the French noir *Le Quai des Brumes* (*Port of Shadows*) meant to the man who'd sat watching them in a darkened cinema before the war. Chamberlin's favourite kind of film told the story of a character who came from the gutter and clawed out their own territory and gained money, power and respect, before paying for it all in a storm of bullets in the final act.

Gangster fashion from the American movies was all over rue Lauriston. Everyone wore suits with silk scarves around their necks and Borsalino hats pulled down low over their eyes. Even Bonny took to wearing black ties with a black shirt and glasses with smoked lenses.

Dita Parlo didn't stick around for long but continued to inform for the gang and sleep with Radecke's brother-in-law, who also worked for the Abwehr. Chamberlin moved on to other women. There was Carmen Palma, who was a German Jew with an effective fake identity card, and an African-American singer known only as Kay, who hid behind an Irish passport and made a living singing 'Night and Day' and 'The Man I Love' to Wehrmacht soldiers. However, all of these love interests were just temporary diversions. Nothing could distract Chamberlin from running his burgeoning business empire.

As Christmas 1942 approached, a former gang member telephoned rue Lauriston with information that could make Chamberlin a lot of money. Jules Minard was a petty crook who had been roaming the fringes of the criminal milieu and who had recently been kicked out by his wife. One night he ran into a drunk Abel Danos in the

Mitzi, a bar on the boulevard des Batignolles. Danos introduced him to Chamberlin, who was bar-crawling up to Le Chapiteau with a crowd of his cronies. Minard made a good impression and was invited along to rue Lauriston for a follow-up meeting. 'You know the address,' said Chamberlin over a cocktail. 'It's open to everyone and I'm not a dog.'[10]

Minard received a few weeks of training for his new duties, but it turned out that he wasn't much of a gangster. One day Pierre Bonny called him into the office. 'Bonny said to me: "Minard, we don't need you here. There are too many people. You could, perhaps, be useful elsewhere. Stay alert to what's going on, keep your eyes and ears open. And if you hear something of use to the Service, don't hesitate."'[11]

Minard then went to see Chamberlin and the boss gave him a few kind words and a fistful of cash and escorted him out. Minard returned to a life of petty crime and an operation selling black market cigarettes. As Christmas approached and the freezing rain began to fall, he heard a Swiss trafficker boasting about a stash of pre-war cigarettes that were hidden somewhere in Paris. Someone connected to the American embassy had trusted the Swiss with a few crates as they fled the country after the USA was dragged into the war following Pearl Harbor.

Minard made a telephone call. Chamberlin, Clavié, Haré and an associate named Meningault came racing down the rue des Siants-Pères in a white Bentley to grab the Swiss black marketeer with the big mouth. After a few intense hours in rue Lauriston he cracked and gave up the location of the cigarette stash.

On 24 December 1942, Chamberlin and his men uncovered 150 cartons of cigarettes that were stacked in a wooden crate marked as being property of the '*Ambassade des États-Unis*'. The gang were congratulating themselves on an easy Christmas score when Clavié levered open another crate, burrowed through the packing straw and came up with a shining soup tureen. The other boxes contained serving spoons, plates and cutlery. The gang had stumbled across the American embassy's antique silverware.

Radecke sold the haul on to some Paris antique dealers for tens of millions of francs. Chamberlin kept most of the money, but made sure to spread enough around to keep everyone happy.

Chamberlin enjoyed Christmas in 1942 and things were looking good in his gangster paradise, but the seismograph needle was starting to twitch. As the year ended, the German forces were crumbling in North Africa, being pushed back in the East and spreading themselves too thin across France. The resistance movement was getting stronger and bolder with every passing day.

Bömelburg decided that it was time for the inhabitants of rue Lauriston to pay Germany back for all the money and the power they had enjoyed over the last two years. Chamberlin's men were about to be enlisted to join the Gestapo crackdown on the resistance, with dawn raids, prison cells and batons. Not everyone in the gang liked the idea.

11

THOSE DAMNED AND FALLEN

THE LECTURERS AT THE orthopaedic medical school had not seen Émile Marongin for a while. The short, skinny student preferred to spend his days drinking in the crowded bars of the Latin Quarter. Marongin was happy sitting at a wooden table with a glass of red wine in his hand and a few cigarettes paced to last the day, with chatter all around him. It was more fun than studying medicine.

In late 1942, Marongin met Dr Lukaszek, a Polish émigré physician who was taking a break from inspecting prostitutes for disease at L'Hôpital Saint-Louis. He bought Marongin a drink and flattered him by showing an interest in the life of a failing student.

Marongin had been born in Italy but moved to France as a youngster and became a French citizen. After being called up when the Second World War began, he was wounded in May 1940 and did his convalescence in Marseille. While hobbling around the port city he became friends with a man called Jean who was angry enough at the Germans to talk about forming a resistance group. Marongin didn't care much about politics and decided to leave Jean to his plotting and return to Paris to enrol at medical school.

Lukaszek listened carefully to Marongin's chatter and asked him a lot of questions. To anyone a little more astute, the Polish doctor's motives would have been obvious: he had a secret life working for the Gestapo.

Nazi ideology placed Slavs one small step above Jews on the racial totem pole. The best that a Pole like Lukaszek could hope for in occupied Eastern Europe was a life of slavery and starvation. In Paris, he found Gestapo agents who were pragmatic enough to see his potential as a spy. They assigned him to infiltrate resistance-minded student groups. Lukaszek did the job well and collected bounties with every arrest that was made. He met Marongin on a trawl through the Montmartre bars and detected the existence of some useful moral ambiguity in his new friend. They shared drinks and a meal and talked about money and self-preservation in occupied Paris. Lukaszek warned him not to believe what the BBC said about the reversal of German military fortunes.

There was a lot not to believe. In the autumn of 1942, the British Eighth Army had turned back Rommel's advance into North Africa at the battle of El Alamein. A few months later, the Soviets encircled General Friedrich Paulus's frozen Sixth Army at Stalingrad, and in Algeria former Vichy loyalist Admiral François Darlan struck a deal with the Allies that handed them North Africa. The politicians back home struggled to explain Darlan's treachery. Huge propaganda posters appeared on the Paris Métro: 'Who stole our North Africa? Roosevelt. Who inspired him? The Jew.'[1]

Darlan had changed sides partly as an act of revenge for being pushed out of power by Pierre Laval. He remained loyal to Pétain and believed that France could be liberated without giving up the ideological programme of Révolution Nationale. The Allies allowed Darlan to form a new regime in Algiers that opposed the Germans, while claiming secret support from men in Vichy. An angry de Gaulle tried to have the admiral removed from power, but the Allies refused.

Losing North Africa spooked the German occupiers. On 11 November, German troops moved into the Zone Libre renaming it Zone Sud and extended their rule over France down to the Mediterranean. French sailors sank what was left of their fleet to keep it out of Nazi hands. The tiny Armistice Army in Vichy briefly considered fighting back before being disbanded. Pétain remained head of state, but this position meant even less than it had before. Collaborationist journalists gave their best excuses.

'So that France may live,' wrote Robert Brasillach in the newspaper *Je Suis Partout*, 'France and Germany desire the unity of our countries and the unity of the West; we must want these conditions ourselves.'[2]

Darlan's hopes of brokering a deal between Vichy and the Allies ended on Christmas Eve when a young monarchist called Fernand Bonnier de La Chapelle shot him dead as part of a failed plot to put the Count of Paris on the throne. De Gaulle's men swept away the remains of Darlan's neo-Pétainist regime and took over. Vichy minister Pierre Pucheu defected to Algeria soon afterwards and found himself sentenced to death by the Gaullists that he had hoped to join. No mercy would be shown in France's civil war.

Within a month of Darlan's death, resistance groups on mainland France received a manpower boost that energised the struggle. German pressure had forced Vichy to introduce the Service du Travail Obligatoire (Obligatory Work Service) in an effort to conscript young Frenchmen for factory work in the Reich. The conscription drive was immediately unpopular. Vichy propaganda posters depicting serious-faced French workers operating German machinery were vandalised with chalk nooses.

French youth preferred to join the resistance rather than move to Germany and work for the Reich. The expanding anti-collaboration groups unified themselves into the Mouvements Unis de Résistance, with the Armée Secrète as its armed wing. Attacks on German troops began to increase. Grenades were rolled down cinema aisles during the newsreels showing heroic blond men roaming around the ruins of Slavic villages. A bomb exploded in a Légion des Volontaires Français recruiting office, and isolated Wehrmacht soldiers were ambushed in the suburbs.

By this time, Nazi intelligence reports were noting that the majority of French believed that Germany would lose the war. Factory labourers worked insolently slowly; the wheels of bureaucracy moved as if they were bogged down in treacle; and German soldiers in the capital had to wait longer and received ruder treatment. German engineers erected a concrete bunker near the Hôtel Majestic for von Stülpnagel and his staff to use in the event of an uprising.

'Today Germany no longer has very many friends,' said a Nazi district commander in Paris.[3]

The government at Vichy could no longer rely on its police force to fight the resistance and formed the paramilitary Milice Française under former Cagoule terrorist Joseph Darnand. The Milice would keep order in what used to be the Zone Libre. In the north, the Gestapo would lead the fight against the resistance. In early 1943 Bömelburg summoned Henri Chamberlin; he wanted the men from rue Lauriston fighting on the front line.

Chamberlin's faith that Germany would be victorious remained absolute. He had recently moved his children up to Paris to share in the good life after a Marseille-based lawyer discovered them living with his ex-wife Rebecchi, now remarried, in southern France. Chamberlin gave her a new villa in exchange for custodial rights over the children and waited for the train to arrive from the south at the Gare de Lyon with a posse of men. The gang stood chain-smoking cigarettes among the platforms, steam and dirty glass. When the train pulled into the station, the Marseille lawyer stepped out of a first-class sleeping compartment alone. 'Where are my kids?' Chamberlin demanded.

The advocate explained that they were travelling in third class to save on the ticket fares. Chamberlin beat the lawyer to the ground and had to be dragged off by his men. Two policemen attempted to intervene but were waved away by a Gestapo identity card. When Chamberlin embraced his children after they alighted from the train, he still had blood on his knuckles.

'My brother [Pierre] was a bit sulky,' remembered Henriette, then eleven years old.

> I was a little frightened by this giant who kissed me with passion. From this moment passed between us a mysterious current, an irresistible attraction, the discovery to a powerful degree, respectively of filial and paternal love. I was overwhelmed by the radiance of this colossus, and from that moment I devoted to him a violent and exclusive affection.[4]

The children lived in an expensive apartment on rue des Belles-Feuilles, near the Champs-Élysées. Chamberlin hired domestic staff and instated Anne-Marie Jeanne Douflos as a governess for the children. The former girlfriend of Dutch black marketeer Seelen had reached out to Chamberlin and the two had formed what both described as a 'platonic' relationship. Eddy Pagnon delivered crates of fruit to the apartment daily, at a time when the average Parisian was queuing three hours to buy two apples. The children played among Old Master paintings, three Louis XV commodes, a selection of Louis XIII chairs and a bureau that bore a portrait of

Madame de Staël. 'Who is this chick?' Chamberlin asked, peering at the oval miniature.[5]

He enrolled his children at a Catholic school and made sure to pay attention to their studies and their homework, which usually meant asking Bonny to look over it. He tried hard to be around for meals and bedtimes. For Chamberlin, life was sweet and complete, and he didn't want to believe that the Nazi new order was crumbling at its foundations. He agreed to coordinate with Bömelburg and go after the resistance.

As Chamberlin crawled deeper into the belly of the German beast, the passage behind him closed. In the spring of 1943, Hermann Göring ordered an end to the black market across occupied Europe. A report had established that buying goods on the marché noir hampered the war effort rather than helping it. The corrupt anarchy of the Amt Otto was swept aside and replaced by a ruthlessly planned economy. The Carlingue was forced to shut its warehouses. Radecke burned the files and blocked any enquiries by responding with official-sounding statements about security.

The Vichy authorities could finally go after the marché noir without the Germans holding them back. They identified 379,405 cases of black marketeering, with 45 per cent caught by the anti-black market agents of the Contrôle Économique, 35 per cent by the Gendarmerie and the rest by other police forces, including the Répression des Fraudes in Paris and the Police Économique.[6] Around 1,185 black marketeers who tried to continue exploiting the system ended up in prison, including a surprised Max Stöcklin – the man who first introduced Chamberlin to the Abwehr – who must have thought that his German security connections would protect him. Friends managed to spring him, but the message had been received: the marché noir was finished.

Chamberlin gathered the members of his inner circle at rue Lauriston and informed them about Bömelburg's new orders. No one seemed to object, Danos just shrugged. A meeting with the rest of the gang was less straightforward. Many of the peripheral players began to peel away.

As one gang member left rue Lauriston for the last time, he warned Chamberlin:

> Be careful, or you'll be in the shit. As long as we're making big money, I'm with you. If we're tumbling those fags from high society then I'm in. If we're getting rich, I'm on board. Where I pick up my marbles and go home is when we're hunting for Jews, Communists and Gaullists. Because that, Henri, is not our onions.[7]

The departing crook was not the only member who disapproved of the gang's new direction. Pierre Bonny could hide the black marketeering, protection rackets and gold sales in the dark corners of his conscience, but hunting down French patriots was too much.

• • •

One day in early 1943, Jacques Bonny took advantage of his parents' absence from their apartment. He invited over some of his school friends to sit around smoking and listening to the gramophone. They talked about the war and girls.

A key rattled in the front door and Jacques's father stormed in, ordered his school friends out and disappeared into his office. After a few long minutes of silence, Jacques peered around the doorframe to see his father sitting at the desk with his head in hands.

'I was hoping that your mother would be here,' Bonny said

without looking up, 'because I have some news that, deep down, would probably make her rather happy. I've packed it all in. It's too much like police business, this thing. You understand.'[8]

Going after resistance members was a step too far for the former police inspector, a war veteran who still regarded himself as a man of the left. He had signed a resignation letter and left rue Lauriston for ever. Later that evening he had a long conversation with his wife Blanchette. She approved of his decision but worried about what they would do for money. The next day she arranged to take up dance lessons with Chamberlin's old friend, the Spanish cabaret star Esméralda, in the hope of becoming a choreographer or teacher. After a few more days, Pagnon appeared at the door to the apartment explaining that Monsieur Henri needed to see Bonny immediately.

Bonny returned to rue Lauriston and the two men talked in the office on the first floor with its windows overlooking the street below. Bonny refused to come back, but Chamberlin just smiled and turned on the charm.

His subordinate remained obsessed with clearing his name over the Stavisky affair. Chamberlin sympathised and promised to help track down the individuals who had set up his former second in command. He then got out the brandy and began talking about money. At 5,000 francs a month, Bonny was one of the few at rue Lauriston on a regular salary, but he had been frozen out of the percentages that were enjoyed by the rest of the gang when they received a windfall. Chamberlin said that he would double the money and promised gifts from future scores.

Bonny struggled against Chamberlin's charisma. He protested that the gang was undisciplined and untrustworthy. The gangsters were constantly brawling and stealing from one another. Chamberlin agreed to introduce a system of fines for infractions: 5,000 francs for a fight that did not result in bloodshed; 7,000 for one that did; and various penalties for other crimes. He promised that the Carlingue would become 'the Service', an efficient private police force charged with helping to maintain law and order in Paris. Bonny gave in and pushed his conscience into a closet and locked the door. His wife pretended that she was glad.

The first signs of the new regime arrived when Chamberlin began insisting on polite language being used among his men. Some interpreted this as being a sarcastic barb at Bonny's sensibilities. 'It was hilarious,' remarked one gangster, 'to see Big Arm Jojo making salaams to Georges the Armenian, or Nez de Braise exchanging amens with Hirbes la Rigole.'[9]

Carlingue members were less happy when Delehaye began totting up the fines for those who had broken the rules. Maillebuau had to pay 7,000 francs; while Danos owed close to 32,000 francs. Inner-circle member Lucien Prévost was fined 25,000 francs. Behind Prévost's sporty playboy front lurked a vicious temper. He had recently taken care of a crook who wanted a bigger slice of a Paul Clavié scam; the two drove out into the countryside to retrieve the man's share of the cash and Prévost returned alone. A few days later, a corpse washed up in a stream, bloated and full of bullet holes.

Soon after Bonny's return, Émile Marongin arrived at rue Lauriston. The medical student was naive and money-hungry enough to believe Lukaszek's assurances that the Germans would win the war. He agreed to do some detective work for the Gestapo at rue des Saussaies and Bömelburg handed him some cash and an ID card and then sent him across town to see Monsieur Lafont in the sixteenth arrondissement.

Bonny became Marongin's handler at rue Lauriston, noting reports, making operation plans and creating a card file. The medical student leveraged his earlier friendship with Jean into membership of a resistance circle in Lyons. Cazauba, Sartore, Danos, Chaves and a handful of German non-commissioned officers drove to the city and came in through the door with guns in their hands. Twelve prisoners were arrested and thrown into Gestapo cells. Another raid on a circle in Paris led by a former deputy called Paul Appel led to further arrests, but the information turned out to be rotten and the Gestapo was forced to release the prisoners. Marongin promised his boss that he would do better.

Chamberlin started to enjoy himself in his role as spymaster. He had plans for a network of informants spread across France. Gang member Jean Leroy was sent down to the resistance heartland of Limoges with orders to set up a listening post and pass back any information he could glean about local networks, parachute drops and anti-German activities.

Leroy was a friend of Danos and was known on the streets as 'Le Flingue' (The Gun) or 'Le Chevrotine' (The Buckshot). He had a love of firearms and an anger that burned out of control. In Limoges he set up a small team and managed to successfully plant a man called André Lewin into a resistance group. Not long after, the Limoges Gestapo conducted a raid on the group and two young men were executed, with another seven sent to the camps.

After initial successes, the weekly reports from Limoges slowed, and then stopped completely. Chamberlin investigated and found that Leroy had become hungry for power and had established himself as a godfather figure in the town. He was now giving his best information directly to the local Gestapo. This looked like treason from Paris and Chamberlin assembled a council of war in rue Lauriston that included Bonny, Maillebuau, Clavié, Cazauba, Prévost, Danos and Chaves. Bonny laid out the facts.

'Jean Leroy wants to undermine the authority of the Service by seeking the protection of the Limoges Gestapo.'

'Criminal duplicity,' said Maillebuau.

'We saved this bastard,' said Clavié, 'and now he's out to get us.'

'He's a shit,' said Cazauba. 'We have to bump him off.'[10]

During the exchange, Danos kept quiet and Bonny quietly accepted the death sentence. The next day, Jean-Michel Chaves walked into 93 rue Lauriston after lunch and headed up to the office. Bonny handed him a typewritten sheet of yellow paper without looking up from his desk. The paper stated: 'Jean Leroy – 13 rue du Cadran – Limoges – Eliminate.'[11]

Chaves headed down to Limoges to carry out the order. He met Leroy for lunch in a restaurant and handed over a brick of money, but it took a few glasses of wine and some more cognacs before the suspicious Leroy relaxed. When he started talking about his plans for the future, Chaves allowed himself a smile. After lunch, the pair took Leroy's car for a drive to his lodgings just outside the town.

When the car reached a cold and bleak part of the winter countryside, Chaves told Leroy to pull over. He took out a gun and Leroy immediately realised what was going on: 'You're not going to do anything to me?' he said. 'You're not going to do this?'[12]

Chaves shot him six times with a pistol and then dragged the body out of the car and onto the grass. He took back the brick of money from Leroy's pocket, before sawing off the gangster's head and putting it in a hat box after it had drained of blood. Chaves took the package back to Chamberlin in Paris. 'I knew that it would please the boss,' he said later.[13]

Soon after the contract killing, Chaves was knifed in Paris. Danos was escorting the mother of his lover Rose Hélène Maltat back home late one night when a car rolled up next to them and Chaves fell out of the door. Madame Maltat later explained the experience: 'One evening when [Danos] brought me back to rue Lauriston, a car stopped with its headlights on. It belonged to Michel Chaves, who was wounded inside. A knife cut to the femoral, not brilliant. Abel got him to a hospital.'[14]

Chaves survived the knifing but refused to identify the attackers. The underworld code of silence led to rumours that Leroy's friends had ordered the attack, while others blamed the attempted murder on the resistance. The truth was probably some kind of criminal feud. Chaves had always made enemies easily; even Violette Morris had once punched him at a rue Lauriston party.

Chamberlin would have pressed Chaves to tell him the truth, but he was busy trying to save his former lover from spending the rest of her life in jail. In March 1943, Mara Tchernichev-Bezobrazov and her SS lover Hans Leimer had been thrown into Fresnes for helping a friend to leave the country.

Hélène Ostrowski was a pre-war friend of Tchernichev-Bezobrazov. She had married into a rich Jewish family with a successful jewellery business. Her husband had already fled into the Zone Sud, but Ostrowski was left trapped in Paris. Tchernichev-Bezobrazov and Leimer drove her down to Spain and arranged for a border crossing to Portugal. German agents in Lisbon uncovered the plan and had Tchernichev-Bezobrazov and her boyfriend arrested.

Chamberlin was still friendly enough with the countess for her to call in a favour. He began by removing papers and jewellery from her apartment for safekeeping at rue Lauriston, then made a few telephone calls which secured the release of the couple. Chamberlin agreed to act as guarantor for their future good conduct. The Gestapo transferred Leimer to the provinces and expelled Tchernichev-Bezobrazov from her warehouse at *3bis* place des États-Unis.

Knochen had the building converted into prisoner holding cells to be used in the fight against the resistance.

The Carlingue was playing its part in the Gestapo battle plan when Adrien Estébétéguy made the mistake of robbing the wrong people. Chamberlin's anger sent his former cellmate running off to a man with a broken moral compass and a ratline to South America.

12

HALF A FLAMING SUN

THE MAN IN THE back room of the barbershop had a face as cheerful as the hangman's rope. Dr Eugène's hair was pomaded back in waves over a creased forehead and crazed eyes. The man could have passed for a villain pacing the boards of a nineteenth-century melodrama, waiting to drop arsenic into the citron pressé of an innocent heroine.

Eugène rubbed his hands together and talked business. The owner of the barbershop on rue des Mathurins, with its cracked floor tiles and paint flaking off the woodwork, allowed him to use the back room for meetings that required discretion. A grubby curtain shielded the doorway from curious customers.

It was Adrien Estébétéguy who had arranged the meeting; he was trying to find a way out of France. He had a suitcase, a lot of money and was accompanied by a girl with cat-like eyes.

Estébétéguy was born at Bayonne in French Basque country and started his criminal career young by deserting the army during the First World War. While everyone else was fighting at the front he robbed houses in his hometown with a gang that included his younger brother Louis.

Adrien had too much of a temper to stay out of prison. In May 1918, a homeowner who fought back as Adrien carried off his possessions was shot at and beaten. A judge gave Estébétéguy eight years behind bars. The prisoner spent his time inside covering his body in tattoos and returned to crime the moment that the prison gates opened.

By the late 1930s Estébétéguy was involved in a fraudulent scheme that involved fake British pound notes. The money entered France via an arms dealer named Félix Fusco, who supplied the Cagoule terror group with guns and seemed to have received the forgeries from officials in Nazi Germany looking to destabilise their European neighbour. Estébétéguy helped distribute the counterfeit notes and as a result was arrested in 1938 but managed to stay out of prison. He teamed up with a friend of Fusco's called Lucien Prévost to defraud a businessman in a complicated scam that involved a stash of gold and a fake charity for Jewish refugees. Once again, the police swooped in and both men ended up in Fresnes prison until Estébétéguy's old colleague Henri Chamberlin sprung them at the start of the occupation to become founder members of the Carlingue.

Estébétéguy worked the black market and moved in with his 35-year-old former typist girlfriend Gisèle Rossmy, who had dreams of being a show business star in the cabarets. She landed a comedy role under the name Gine Volna in Maurice Poggi's *La Revue des Deux Anes*, but playing 'Third Angel' in the prologue wasn't the kind of role that led to stardom. A crook like Estébétéguy seemed to offer a chance at something better.

He lavished her with money and jewellery but beat her when he was drunk and cut off all contact she had with her family. The couple moved from apartment to apartment, throwing noisy parties and getting evicted as they went. They eventually found some stability in rue Lemercier, calling themselves the Dumartins.

Estébétéguy was sidelined into DSK gold deals by Chamberlin early on in the rue Lauriston story, and a faction within the inner circle made sure that he stayed there. One of the gang's ringleaders Cazauba saw him as a rival and fed Chamberlin a steady diet of gossip about Adrien being disloyal and pocketing sums of money. The Basque denied everything, but even his former partner Prévost looked distant when they ran into each other at gang hangouts such as Le Chapiteau bar.

By the summer of 1942, Estébétéguy was boiling with jealousy at the money that his Carlingue colleagues were making and refusing to share with him. He decided to start robbing houses out in the provinces with his friend Joseph Réocreux, who was a brute of a man known to all as 'Jo le Boxeur'. After a few jobs Réocreux got sloppy and soon had the police on his trail. Underworld friends advised that Réocreux arrange a meeting with a Dr Eugène, who could smuggle people out to South America. The plan seemed plausible; the Argentinian embassy in Paris sold visas to those people who had the right connections. Réocreux packed his suitcase and disappeared. Estébétéguy continued with his small-time crime but filed away the doctor's details for future use.

On 14 December 1942, Estébétéguy joined with Charles Lombard and some others in a raid on a Dordogne farmhouse. The owner was hiding a rich Jewish couple named Saada. Estébétéguy forced his way in, waving a Gestapo card. Lombard began slapping Gilbert Saada around the face and shouting some nonsense about a radio transmitter. Another raider found a strongbox and a key. The gang left with Saada but dumped him in the countryside, scared but alive. The strongbox contained $2,300 in gold dollar coins, $530 in gold Louis D'Ors, $7,000 in cash and 500,000 francs. A massive score.

Somebody on the inside talked about the robbery. By the New Year,

Estébétéguy and Lombard's names were all over the collaborationist press. Using the Gestapo name for unauthorised crime annoyed the Germans. Chamberlin was furious enough to inform rue des Saussaies that Estébétéguy was no longer a Carlingue member. He spread the word to the gang that anyone who brought him back to rue Lauriston would get a fat reward.

Estébétéguy didn't want to stick around to see what kind of reception his former cellmate had planned. Chamberlin's old friend Tanguy was already dead, Tissier was missing and presumed murdered and in March 1943 the gang leader had Jo Attia deported to a concentration camp.

Attia had been doing well for himself; Cazauba had expanded the fake ration card operation into a secret print shop and sent his team drifting through Paris to offload the ration documents at fifteen francs a set. Attia was a good salesman and made decent money, but he could smell German defeat coming. He reached out to the Réseau Centurie, a resistance network headed up by Gilbert Renault. The hard-right former banker and film producer had refused to follow his Action Française colleagues into collaboration and fought the Germans under the name Colonel Rémy.

A few months into 1943 and Chamberlin uncovered the double game that Attia was playing. Gestapo agents picked him up and brought him to rue Lauriston. 'I'm going to shoot you,' said Chamberlin, 'you little shit.'[1]

Abel Danos protested the decision and an inner-circle council of war convened to debate Attia's punishment. Danos persuaded them to send Attia to a German concentration camp called Mauthausen. Pierre Loutrel quit the Carlingue in disgust at the treatment of his friend and joined a gang of Frenchmen under René Launay who worked for the SD.

Estébétéguy had no intention of ending up in a camp like Attia and reached out to Dr Eugène. Contact was made and money handed over; the doctor required 25,000 francs to guarantee the safe passage of each individual.

By this time, Paris had become a knotted maze of entwined escape routes used by downed airmen, escaped prisoners, desperate Jews and anybody else who needed to leave the country. A typical escape might include one night in the hay of a barn, two nights in a sleeping car, one night of silent sleeplessness in a disused maid's room, then a change of clothes, the receipt of fake documents and a border crossing. The Comet and Pat O'Leary escape lines snaked across the Pyrenees into neutral Spain. The Shelburne line ran from Brittany to Plymouth via high-speed Royal Navy boats. Other lines headed north to Brussels or south to Marseille. Eugène's South American route was an exotic addition to a variety of options for anyone wishing to escape the occupation.

Estébétéguy was not leaving France alone. Alongside his girlfriend Gisèle Rossmy – whom he had persuaded to abandon the city of her dreams – Estébétéguy was accompanied by a handsome 44-year-old pimp called Piereschi, who had a criminal record that stretched back to the First World War for arms trafficking and jailbreak. Piereschi had 800,000 francs in his luggage and plans to open a brothel in Argentina with his girlfriend Joséphine-Aimée Grippay, known as 'Paulette la Chinoise'.

The two gangsters decided to swap girlfriends for the trip to prevent a double cross, sewed money and gold into their clothes and packed their suitcases. It was 9 a.m. on the last Saturday of March in 1943 when Estébétéguy and Paulette la Chinoise met Eugène at the rue des Mathurins barbershop. Black bags drooped beneath Eugène's eyes like slashed rubber tyres. He rubbed his hands together.

Estébétéguy and Paulette followed the doctor out into the street. They headed west towards the Place de L'Étoile and vanished into the crowd. No one ever saw them again. The next day Piereschi and Rossmy also disappeared from Paris. Soon after, Dr Eugène showed his barbershop friend a 100-franc note that had been torn in half through a drawn-on flaming sun. His men working the ratline had sent it back to indicate that Estébétéguy and his friends had arrived in Argentina. News of the escape quickly spread, and Chamberlin raged at the damage that had been done to his criminal reputation by the affair.

All the rumours and gossip stirring in the underworld alerted the Gestapo. Its agents began to take an interest in 25 rue des Mathurins.

• • •

The barbershop had a good location near the glittering shopping emporiums of Galeries Lafayette and Printemps. Bonny's lawyer friend Jean Guélin didn't mind spending the April of 1943 hanging around the area and dropping heavy hints about the need for a long holiday in South America, hoping to find out more about the mysterious Dr Eugène.

By this point, Guélin was living in a luxury flat that had been confiscated from an imprisoned businessman and was working for the Gestapo. He reported to a former butcher with a crew-cut called Dr Robert Jodkum who ran the IV–B4, which was the Jewish affairs department of the Gestapo. Guélin submitted a progress report on his investigation into Eugène's operation:

> The long and fastidious investigation which I have made shows that this network is organised in a remarkable fashion and takes

> infinite precautions to avoid crossover or communication between adjacent cells in the network's hierarchy. It would be interesting to be able to organise surveillance all along the railway trajectory to the frontier and discover the method of crossing the border. Members of a foreign embassy are certainly collaborating in the furnishing of false passports.[2]

His efforts to burrow deeper into the barbershop scene failed when his questioning made the owner Raoul Fourrier suspicious enough to deny any knowledge of Eugène. The Gestapo replaced Guélin with Yvan Dreyfus, a round-faced wealthy Jewish businessman from Lyon who had been arrested when attempting to join de Gaulle in London. Guélin had been recommended to his wife as someone who could help. The lawyer gouged her for over 4 million francs, which he split with Jodkum, and got Yvan Dreyfus out of prison and back on the street. Before the cell door was opened, Dreyfus was bullied into signing some compromising documents and in early May 1943 the Germans called in the favour. Dreyfus was to infiltrate Dr Eugène's network with the help of Guélin and report back to the Gestapo.

'Dreyfus asked [Fourrier] if he could obtain a passport for him,' reported Guélin, 'and Fourrier escorted him into a neighbouring room, where in the shadow between the curtains, I saw a rather tall man who spoke with them.'[3]

On 20 May 1943, Dreyfus arrived at the barbershop with a suitcase and a tail of Gestapo agents who were ready to pounce before he got anywhere near Argentina. The tall man behind the curtain was Dr Eugène and he escorted Dreyfus down the Champs-Élysées. The agents then lost the two men as they entered a Métro station. Dreyfus submerged into the ratline and would never resurface.

An angry Jodkum started to arrange a second infiltration when another Gestapo organisation stumbled on the barbershop network and messed up his plans. Sub-office IV–E3 dealt with military security and counterintelligence in occupied territory; it had heard rumours about German deserters escaping to South America rather than return to the fighting on the Eastern Front. On 21 May a gang of IV–E3 agents stormed Fourrier's barbershop and arrested everyone inside while the shaving soap was still frothy on their faces.

Dr Eugène was absent but agents tracked him down and made the arrest at his home in 66 rue de Caumartin. Jodkum immediately annexed the investigation from IV–E3 and took custody of the prisoners. Eugène, Fourrier, a friend named René Nézondet and a theatrical make-up artist called Edmond Pintard were rotated through damp prison cells while Jodkum squeezed them for information.

The interrogators discovered that Dr Eugène's real name was Marcel André Henri Félix Petiot. He was a 46-year-old doctor and violent lunatic.

Petiot grew up in Burgundy with a middle-class family who realised that there was something desperately wrong with him from an early age. He was expelled from schools for shooting guns, propositioning female classmates and stealing, and only dodged criminal charges for theft after psychiatrists judged that he was mentally ill. Petiot joined the army in 1916, was wounded and gassed on the front and had a breakdown.

Behind the lines he stole from supply sheds and army comrades until he was sent to jail and then on to a psychiatric hospital. When he was sent back to the front in 1918, he shot himself in the foot and returned to hospital; eventually he was discharged with a disability pension for his mental illness.

In civilian life, Petiot joined an education system that was established for veterans and to everyone's surprise he went on to qualify as a doctor. He settled in Villeneuve-sur-Yonne, got married and kept up a respectable front while performing illegal abortions, avoiding tax and stealing from his patients. He was a kleptomaniac and was briefly treated for the condition; his own brother even insisted on searching him whenever the doctor left after a visit.

Despite the fact that one of his young mistresses mysteriously disappeared after she threatened to talk to his wife, the locals liked Petiot enough to elect him mayor of Villeneuve-sur-Yonne. He eventually moved to Paris to avoid criminal charges that would not go away and set up a new practice, helped along by lies about his cutting-edge medical knowledge and fake certificates on the office walls. Before long, Petiot became known as someone who would treat sexually transmitted diseases; before the war, Chamberlin's nephew Paul Clavié had even paid him a visit.

When the Germans rolled into the city, Petiot found a new niche for himself by prescribing morphine to desperate addicts. Soon he faced more criminal charges, but his court case about the oversupply of narcotics collapsed when important witnesses disappeared or died of overdoses. Petiot then struck up a new lucrative business supplying fake medical certificates to young men who wanted to escape forced labour in Germany.

Petiot liked to tell his friends stories about his involvement in resistance activities and the deaths of a number of Germans. Most of his tales were grandiose lies, but he did pass on scraps of information that had been gleaned from patients to an American intelligence operation, although none of it proved to be useful. In 1942 he announced that a ratline from France to South America had been created. He enlisted Raoul Fourrier and Edmond Pintard to identify new clients and gave them a slice of the profits for their trouble, and everyone involved started making a lot of money.

A recruiter who escaped the barbershop raid was Rudolphina Kahan, a tall bleached-blonde Jewish woman in her forties, who had fake identity documents and no morals and made her livelihood on the fringes of the black market. Alternately claiming to be Romanian or Austrian, she helped fellow Jews escape or informed on them, whichever paid more. She charged three families for an introduction to the mysterious Dr Eugène who could get them out of the country. In the crowded world of collaboration, she could also be found attending parties at rue Lauriston and dropping hints to Chamberlin about a medical man called Eugène smuggling Jews out of the country.

Monsieur Henri apparently showed no great interest: 'I have a lot of Jewish friends', he said, 'who are very good to me and did me some good turns. I've never had anything against the Jews. They're brave people, perhaps even more generous and nice than the rest.'[4]

After the arrest, the Germans could get nothing out of Petiot. The doctor only opened his mouth to shout abuse at his captors and the investigation soon fell apart. It was discovered that his friend Nézondet had nothing to do with the escape network and he was released early; Fourrier and Pintard were only in it for the money and had no knowledge of the ratline's inner workings. Jodkum began to wonder if the whole operation was just some kind of scam to squeeze money from the desperate. With no evidence or confession with which to lay a charge, he released the prisoners and set Gestapo men to watch Petiot. From this point on men in long overcoats and pulled-down hats stalked the doctor around Paris.

At rue Lauriston, Estébétéguy's brother Louis was becoming anxious at not hearing any news from his escaped sibling and approached

Pierre Bonny for advice on how to make contact with Argentina. 'Your brother is a fool,' snapped the former inspector. 'He did not appreciate Henri's generosity. He has already been forgotten.'[5]

Bonny was losing his nerve a little more every day as the war turned against the Germans. He'd slapped his own son when Jacques wanted to attend a surprise party for Joseph Joinovici that was being thrown by the cream of the Paris collaboration. Bonny didn't want his son dragged into that world. The former inspector spent his nights lying awake staring at the bedroom ceiling trying to convince himself that the Germans might still win the war.

Outside his window and across Paris, Communist activists chalked '1918' and 'Stalingrad' on the walls of the city, while the supporters of de Gaulle drew the Cross of Lorraine. The German patrols would wash off the graffiti and replace it with '1763' for the Treaty of Paris that ended the Seven Years' War, but few Parisians got the historical reference.

Joseph Joinovici was not the kind of man to lie awake worrying about his future. He had been smart enough to support the efforts of both sides. Despite the official closing of the black market, a few specialised buying bureaus were allowed to continue. The German-run business Primetex bought munitions and other supplies in the occupied territories, the SS created their own offices and Joinovici set up the L'Union Économique in avenue George V to sell to the Wehrmacht and other German military units. Chamberlin supplied the stake money and his protection allowed the firm to employ Jewish workers and keep the Nazis away.

Joinovici also funded a resistance group within the Paris police called Honneur de la Police, a senior member of which was Inspector Louis Métra. He kept a close eye on rue Lauriston.

Chamberlin knew nothing about his business partner's resistance activities and remained convinced that the Germans were on the road to ultimate victory. In March 1943, the Wehrmacht had recaptured the strategic Ukrainian city of Kharkov, German U-boats had been sinking huge amounts of Allied ships every day, and many in Europe still believed that it was impossible for the Allies to invade the continent.

Monsieur Henri had one more year before his life would fall apart.

PART III

FROM THE GESTAPO TO THE SS

13

IN THE CELLARS OF RUE LAURISTON

AS THE SPRING OF 1943 turned into summer, reality became harder to bear in Paris. Countess Mara Tchernichev-Bezobrazov quit the capital and bought a château called Bel Air. She moved in with an old friend called Renée de Mallet who was in the process of divorcing her husband and the pair lived gauzy warm days with butterflies dogfighting through the meadow grass and the lawns long and level for miles.

Collaborators, Russian émigrés and German officers came to stay. It was cocktails and casual affairs, while the gramophone played and old American films flickered black and white and grainy on the wall. The two friends visited golf tournaments and went on trips to Paris. The countess smoked opium supplied by a journalist friend and floated away on euphoric clouds of peace, soft as a dove breast. The war seemed a lifetime away.

A lovesick Hans Leimer tried to requisition the château just to get close to his former girlfriend, but Tchernichev-Bezobrazov was too drugged up to even notice when her Wehrmacht friends shut him down.

Back in Paris, those who were unwilling to numb the reality of life with narcotics had to make hard decisions about the future. The

Bulgarian mystic Ivanov dropped out of the rue Lauriston scene to be with his disciples in the Paris suburb of Sèvres. The Universal White Brotherhood had contacts with local resistance groups and also hid Jewish children in the villa. Former Mouvement Social Révolutionnaire leader Eugène Deloncle started talking with Allied agents on behalf of high-placed Abwehr officers who opposed Hitler. Some regular guests at the rue Lauriston parties made excuses to stop attending.

Others dived deeper into collaboration. Violette Morris drove Captain Giraud of the Légion des Volontaires Français around Normandy and passed back any useful information about the locals she came across to the Gestapo. Jean Luchaire wrote pro-Nazi editorials in *Les Nouveaux Temps*. The informant Émile Marongin continued to burrow into resistance groups.

In April 1943 Marongin joined the Défense de la France, an organisation that had sprouted from a literary newspaper that had once supported Pétain but changed its allegiance to de Gaulle. A blind eighteen-year-old student named Jacques Lusseyran who was involved in the group complained that he distrusted Marongin's voice and clammy handshake, but his comrades ignored his suspicions. Marongin passed information about the organisation back to Bonny but exaggerated his own importance and confused the newspaper with the resistance network. Enough of the information was accurate for Bonny to draw up a neat diagram of cells, leaders and couriers.

Défense de la France used a number of locations across Paris for meetings, including a bookshop called Au Vœu de Louis XIII on rue de la Bonaparte. Chamberlin told Bonny to prepare for a swoop on the resistance group.

While Bonny typed up an action plan, rue Lauriston loaned out men to the Gestapo for other operations. In June 1943, a Frenchman called Henri Déricourt, supposedly working for the British, gave up information regarding a resistance group called the Physician network. It was not clear whether Déricourt was a traitor or playing a more complex game for British intelligence, but the information he provided was accurate. Lucien Prévost led a group of gangsters posing as resistance fighters to the house of network leader George Darling. Prévost had charm to go with his acting skills and was sipping a friendly aperitif when German troops raided the property and the gangsters produced their guns. The Physician network crumbled in days.

A month later, Bonny organised a citywide swoop on the Défense de la France network. Maillebuau and others rolled up to locations around Paris tense and alert in their Citroën Traction Avants, all glossy black curves and rumbling horsepower. Bonny spearheaded the raid on the Au Vœu de Louis XIII bookshop. A resistance meeting was in progress when Louis Haré knocked at the shop's door pretending to be a customer.

'What would you like?' asked a young woman through a crack in the door.

'A Bible,' replied Louis.

'Please wait. The bookshop is occupied. You'll be served shortly.'[1]

Bonny's men then kicked in the door and the group stormed inside. One of the resistance members managed to get off a few shots before the shop was locked down and the group arrested.

The first prisoners began arriving at *3bis* Place de la États-Unis. They spent hours stewing in prison cells before the doors opened and big men in good suits who smelled of cigarette smoke marched them out of the building and into cars for the journey to 93 rue Lauriston. Then it was hours of questioning down in the cellars. A young man called Edmond Bidaud somehow managed to convince

Chamberlin that he was innocent. He walked out of rue Lauriston, but thirty-six other resistance members were marked for deportation to the concentration camps. The young woman who was in the bookshop, Geneviève Garnier, broke down and confessed to being the niece of General de Gaulle.

'When Bonny heard my name,' she later explained, 'it seemed to me that he did not have an air of triumph but, instead, for a few seconds, one of boredom.'[2]

When everyone had been processed and returned to the cells, Bonny went home for dinner and as usual made an effort to pretend that he worked a normal office job, but the mask slipped that evening. 'If I am still alive, it is because there is a merciful God,' he told his wife and son. 'I was shot at while stopping a resistance fighter. I had the instinct to kneel when he fired. I think he was wounded by the others.'[3]

He talked about the war, his doubts, then tried to convince himself that collaboration was the only option, that the Germans were too strong and that Britain wouldn't have lasted a week if an invasion had succeeded. His wife patted him on the arm and poured him another glass of wine. The next morning Pagnon was parked outside as Bonny put on his suit jacket and checked his Walther P38 pistol before heading downstairs for the regular ride to work.

It was the same routine every day. If the former police inspector was running late, Pagnon would enter the apartment and sit quietly in a corner. 'He is a brave man, who never asks questions,' said Bonny about his driver.[4]

Bonny liked not being asked questions as there were many things that he did not want to discuss. The gang used torture to extract information from members of the resistance. Paul Clavié called it 'administering a correction'. The first line of abuse involved beatings by fist, truncheon or any other blunt object that could break bones.

The slapping sound of fist hitting flesh was accompanied by blood spraying everywhere, then the first torturer would step away to soak his hands in cold water and another took over.

Haré once emerged from the cellars after beating a suspect with his shirtsleeves rolled up. He bumped into Chamberlin and one of his aristocratic girlfriends by the stairs.

'How do you feel today, Madam la Marquise?' asked Haré politely.

'Very well, very well. And you, *mon ami*?' responded the woman, ignoring Haré's right arm blood-spattered up to the elbow.[5]

On another occasion Bonny beat up a man who had testified against him during the Stavisky affair. The prisoner agreed to sign a retraction after Bonny beat him so severely he broke a ring on his face. After a different interrogation, Bonny had to have the bones in his hand set by a doctor after he punched a prisoner too hard.

Anyone who refused to talk during the beatings faced the '*baignoire*' (the 'bathtub'), a torture borrowed from the Gestapo professionals at 84 avenue Foch. A prisoner would have their head forcefully submerged in a bath filled with filthy ice-cold water. They would struggle for air until Chamberlin would pull them out by the hair and the questioning continued.

For the more resistant prisoners Chamberlin and Bonny experimented with a portable battery and crocodile clips that they would attach to testicles, nipples and other soft flesh. Everyone cracked eventually. Soon rumours were circulating in the collaborationist world about charred bodies being buried in the walled garden behind rue Lauriston.

As Ernst Jünger wrote in his diary: 'In the last war, when we saw each other again we used to talk about those who had been wounded and killed in action. In this war, we add to those names the ones who have been abducted and murdered.'[6]

Alongside the torture, political raids and infiltrations, the gang continued with its criminal activities. In occupied Paris there was always money to be made.

• • •

Dr Eugène Lapiné was an otolaryngologist in his late thirties who had a side business as a trafficker and black marketeer. He found himself in Cherche-Midi prison after scamming the DSK out of 1 million francs. The DSK shook down Lapiné's wife for repayment but refused to accept the 200,000 francs that she managed to scrape together. Luchaire's crony George Prade suggested she make a visit to rue Lauriston.

Andrée Lapiné put on her best dress and a pair of black market stockings and went to see Henri Chamberlin. He looked her up and down and suggested a deal. She had sex with Chamberlin until her husband was released.

Dr Lapiné eventually met the man who had slept with his wife, discovered he was too powerful to hold a grudge against and decided to let it go. The doctor began to orbit the fringes of the gang. He made good money selling tins of black market sardines and peas to Joseph Joinovici, but preferred easier ways of getting rich. Everyone knew that Chamberlin could spring people from prison with a telephone call to avenue Foch; Lapiné suggested monetising on this ability. Soon, his friends in the Jewish community and then all of Paris found out that loved ones did not have to stay behind bars if their families had enough cash.

In the remaining months of 1943, many men and women were set free from prison in exchange for money split between the gang and useful officials at avenue Foch. One rich businessman paid 6 million

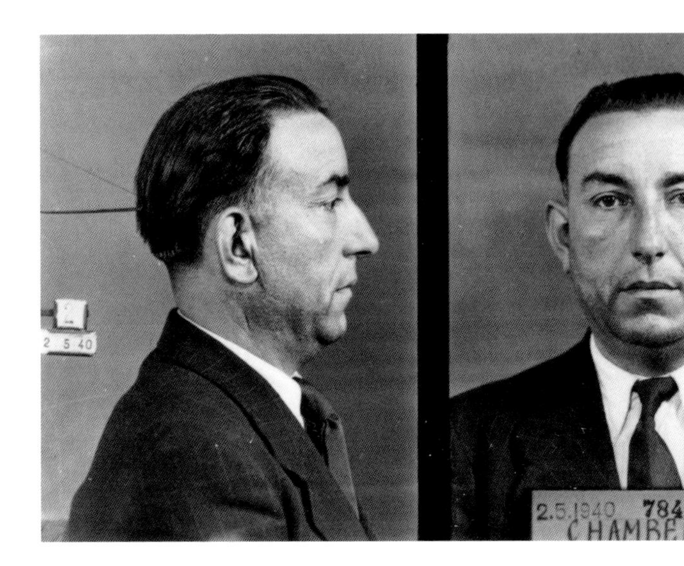

Petty crook and recidivist Henri Chamberlin, also known as Henri Lafont, under arrest in May 1940 and looking at deportation to French Guiana. Courtesy of Archives Nationale (France)

Marshal Philippe Pétain meets Adolf Hitler after the defeat of France in 1940, hoping for a place in the Nazi new order.
© Bundesarchiv, Bild 183-H25217/CC-BY-SA 3.0/CC BY-SA 3.0 DE

Occupying German soldiers watch the world go by outside a Paris café. © Bundesarchiv, Bild 101I-247-0775-38

FAR LEFT A pre-war photograph of Paul Clavié that gives little indication that its subject was the borderline psychotic nephew of Henri Chamberlin.

LEFT German war hero and author Ernst Jünger photographed in the interwar years before he entered the moral jungle of wartime Paris. © Ernst Jünger/Public domain

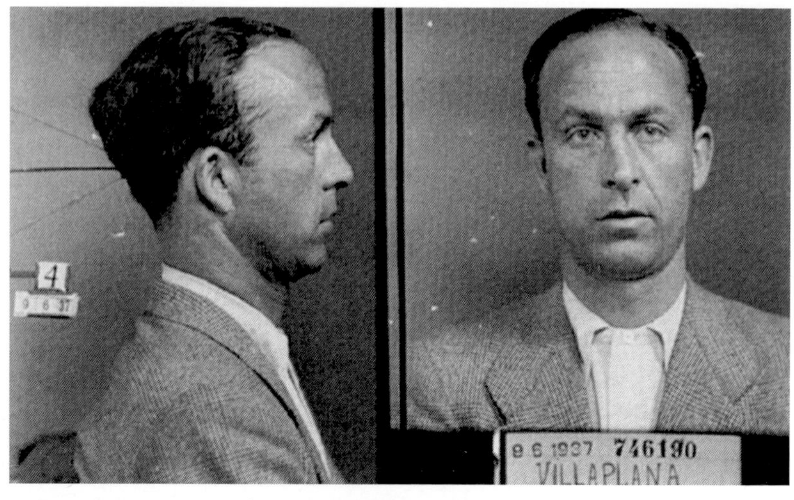

ABOVE Alexandre Villaplana, the former footballer who captained France at the 1930 World Cup, caught in a pre-war mugshot.
Courtesy of Archives Nationale (France)

LEFT France's best-known policeman Pierre Bonny (*centre, with moustache*) pictured during the 1934 Stavisky scandal that ended his law enforcement career.

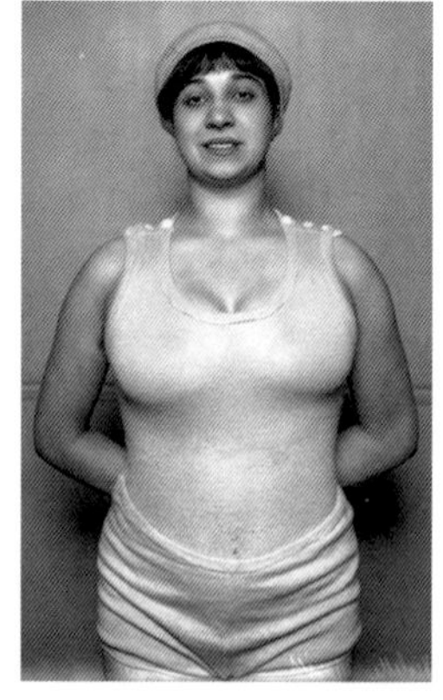

FAR LEFT The occupier meets the occupied as a French policeman salutes a German officer in Paris.
© Bundesarchiv, Bild 146-1978-053-30

LEFT Black marketeer and Nazi collaborator Violette Morris pictured in her pre-war sporting days.
© Agence Rol/Public domain

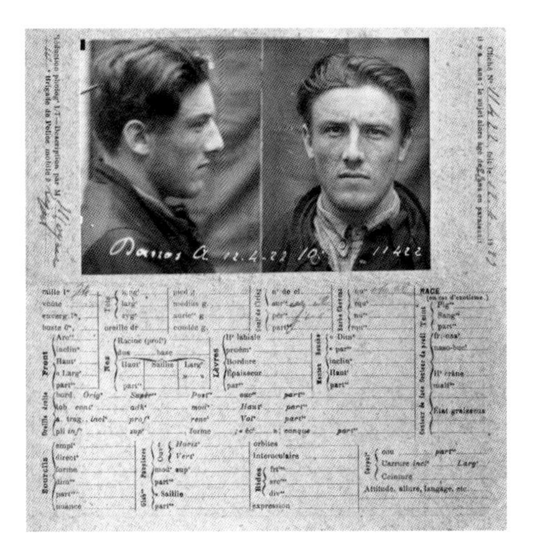

Armed robber and thug Abel 'Le Mammouth' Danos, photographed in 1922 for his first police file.
Courtesy of Archives Nationale (France)

The usually crazed alcoholic Pierre Loutrel, also known as 'Pierrot le Fou' (Mad Pete), manages to look amiable while being photographed after a 1935 arrest.
Courtesy of Archives Nationale (France)

Carlingue member and secret resistance supporter Jo Attia in a 1936 mugshot. Courtesy of Archives Nationale (France)

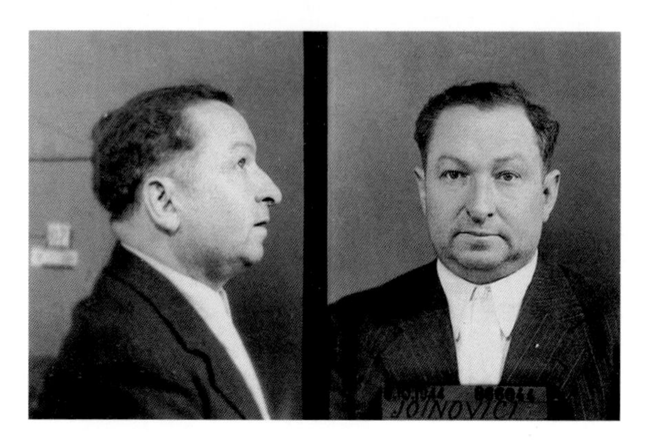

Jewish scrap metal dealer and rue Lauriston associate Joseph Joinovici tried to play for both sides during the occupation and paid the price. Courtesy of Archives Nationale (France)

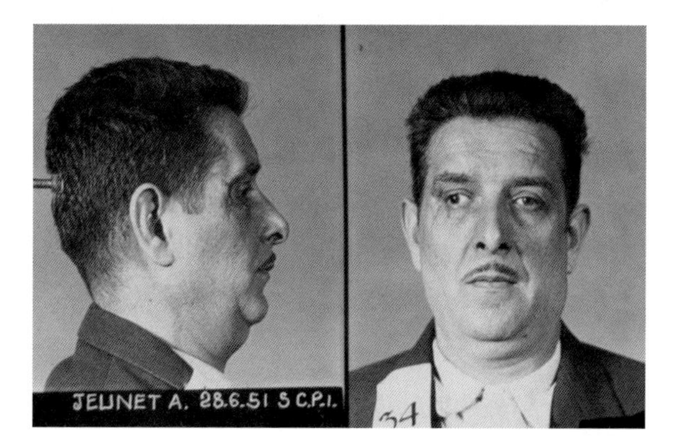

Pimp and Carlingue member Auguste 'Cajac' Jeunet is finally captured by the authorities in 1951. Courtesy of Archives Nationale (France)

A mugshot of career gangster Jean Sartore taken less than a year before he joined the gang in 1941. Courtesy of Archives Nationale (France)

FAR LEFT A German soldier chats to a French woman in the shadow of the Eiffel Tower. © News Dog Media

LEFT White Russian Countess Mara Tchernichev-Bezobrazov, black marketeer and girlfriend of Chamberlin, poses for a pre-war glamour shot.

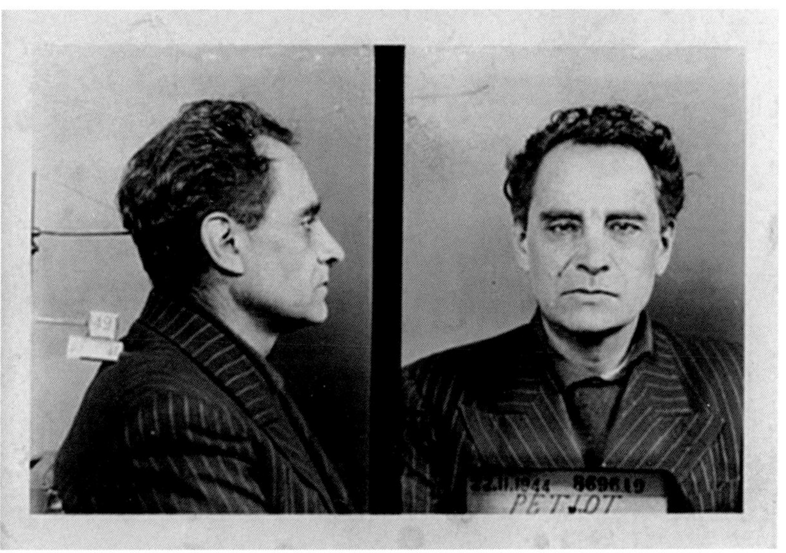

ABOVE Doctor and serial killer Marcel Petiot glowers out of his 1944 mugshot as he faces charges for multiple murders. Courtesy of Archives Nationale (France)

LEFT Algerian soldier and politician Mohamed El-Maadi in a Latin Quarter restaurant with fellow North African collaborators, 1943. Courtesy of Archives Nationale (France)

Members of the Brigade Nord-Africain pose for the camera at 93 rue Lauriston with a female friend and what appears to be a smirking Henri Chamberlin (*far left*).
Courtesy of Archives Nationale (France)

The medieval town of Sigmaringen in Germany, which became home to many French collaborators at the end of the war.
© Detroit Publishing Company/Public domain

Chamberlin's nephew Paul Clavié in Allied hands following the 1944 liberation of France.
Courtesy of Archives Nationale (France)

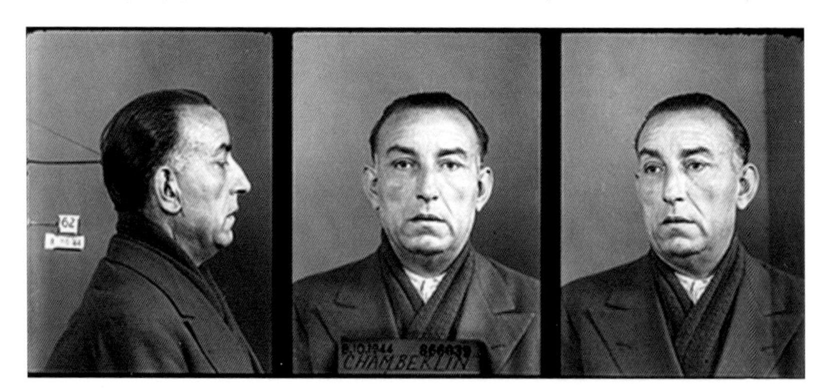

Henri Chamberlin reaches the end of the road with this mugshot taken after his 1944 arrest.
Courtesy of Archives Nationale (France)

A newspaper photographer captures a broken Henri Chamberlin in prison, 1944.

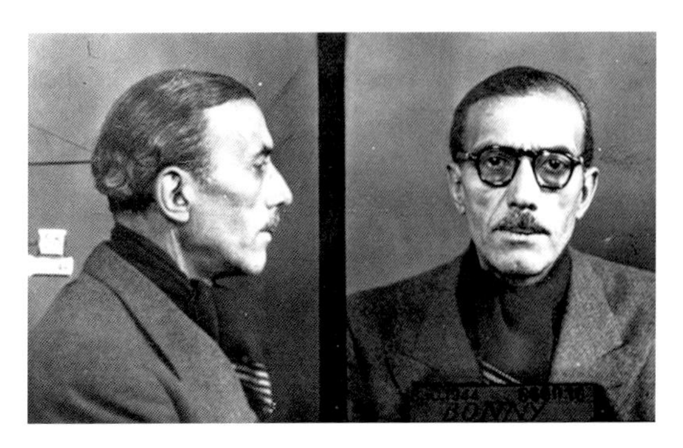

Pierre Bonny discovers what life is like on the other side of the law in this mugshot from autumn 1944. Courtesy of Archives Nationale (France)

The trial of the Bonny-Lafont gang leadership in December 1944: in the front row of the dock (*left to right*) are Chamberlin, Bonny, Clavié, Engel, Haré, Villaplana, Pagnon and Delehaye; sitting behind them (*left to right*) are Labussière, Lascaux, Delval and Tate.

Carlingue veteran Georges Boucheseich would go on to join the Gang des Tractions Avant and became one of France's most-wanted criminals in the post-war period.
Courtesy of Archives Nationale (France)

Today a memorial plaque outside 93 rue Lauriston commemorates the resistance members who died at the hands of the Bonny-Lafont gang.

francs to get out of prison. Georges Prade made twenty requests to free prisoners. Even the Vichy Chief of the Government Pierre Laval asked for a few favours after discovering that Chamberlin had more influence with the Germans than he did.

Laval and Chamberlin eventually met at a Paris dinner party. Luchaire made the introduction as thanks for Chamberlin lending him 1.5 million francs to settle de Wiet when his Théâtre de L'Avenue business went bankrupt; the situation had been getting nasty with accusations and threats. Laval and the gangster got on well. 'Personally, I was astonished,' said Chamberlin. 'I had a very different idea of a head of government and never imagined I could chat, drink and discuss important matters with a president.'[7]

Chamberlin did not charge for freeing Laval's friends, but could be equally generous for less powerful people. A florist based in the sixteenth arrondissement asked him to spring some friends and offered up an envelope full of cash. He waved it away and said: 'Send me flowers.'[8]

Chamberlin could also be generous in other ways. When a raid on a resistance flat uncovered only an abandoned wife and three hungry children, he gave the woman 20,000 francs and ushered his men out of the property.

By the middle of 1943, the Carlingue was over 100-men strong and operated in three unequal divisions. Bonny ran the anti-resistance operation, a second section under Alexandre Villaplana concentrated on crime, and a third, smaller faction run by André Lemoine had been set up on Gestapo orders to pass on the denunciations of Jews. Lemoine was enthusiastic but Chamberlin kept him on a short leash. The boss had little interest in anti-Semitism, which became apparent in September 1943 when Joseph Joinovici's enemies finally came for him.

The Jewish affairs IV–B4 office of the Gestapo had finally got permission to arrest the scrap metal dealer; its agents were watching the businessman's Clichy apartment. Radecke of the Abwehr suggested contacting rue Lauriston, clearly aware that his own agency's power was dribbling away a little more every day.

Chamberlin charged Joinovici 5 million francs to commission him as an official member of the gang. Monsieur Joseph received an identity card with his black and white photograph stamped with a Nazi eagle. Bonny wrote up a report which claimed that Joinovici had helped with various anti-resistance activities as far back as the arrest of Kellner in 1941 and had assisted the Nazis before the war. The IV–B4 was unconvinced and kept pushing for an arrest. Chamberlin had Bömelburg force his subordinates to drop the issue.

The second section of the Carlingue under Villaplana focused on the usual criminal schemes. Gold stings still brought in money, protection rackets continued to be profitable and the gang sold black market food to restaurants across Paris. Anyone who was able to supply good-quality produce could make a lot of money. In 1943, 23 per cent of French meat production was transported to Germany, which was up from 15 per cent in the previous year. Cereal production designated for Germany increased from 12 per cent to 17 per cent during the same period.[9] The French were slowly starving.

'There are whole families who have nothing but their daily bread ration each day,' wrote novelist and Nobel Prize winner Roger Martin du Gard. 'There is great unrest. You can see mothers of families weeping in the streets.'[10]

Villaplana's section of the Carlingue used its Gestapo affiliation as a shield. When the Paris police stopped a man named Bouillard unloading four tonnes of black market sugar from a truck he flashed a German police card in their faces and the police walked away.

However, the card didn't always help. On 14 July 1943, Sartore, Danos's old friend André Jolivot and an accomplice called Louis Largeron broke into a store of rationing tickets at Auxerre town hall. The police had been tipped off and a gunfight put Largeron in the hospital, Jolivot in the morgue and Sartore in a prison cell. Chamberlin set off in a two-car convoy with Bonny, Danos and a posse of armed gangsters. The local German police were surprised to get a visit from a man calling himself head of the 'Gestapo Parisienne' and Sartore was freed.

Loyal gang members could always rely on Chamberlin for help. Jean Sartore was allowed to spring a long-time crook friend named Pallatier, who belonged to the Marco Polo resistance network. Danos got help when his girlfriend Hélène Maltat was arrested early one morning trying to exchange a wad of Reichsmarks on the black market. She rang his apartment from the Hôtel Majestic, woke his other girlfriend and asked her to pass the phone to their mutual boyfriend. Even Bonny requested assistance after German soldiers arrested his son for chalking a '*V pour Victoire*' and de Gaulle's Cross of Lorraine on a bus stop. He gave his son a warning:

> You know, we live in times where the slightest gesture can have repercussions that we do not suspect, for you as well as for others, including your mother and me. If you think for example that the steps I had to make to release you have been fun for me ... These kinds of childish gestures can be very expensive, you see.[11]

It was a grim experience for the family, but Chamberlin found it amusing. 'When I told Lafont that our son had been arrested for Gaullist propaganda,' Bonny said to his wife, 'I thought that he was going to choke with laughter.'

Chamberlin always looked out for his own men. He sprang Villaplana from a camp in Compiègne after the former footballer was picked up by German police for stealing some precious stones. A mob of policemen who arrested Danos after a bar fight with a Corsican gangster found themselves dragged along to rue Lauriston where they were met by Chamberlin's gang waving MP40 submachine guns in their faces. 'France is rotten,' Chamberlin told them. 'You are sabotaging the work of the Germans.'[12]

By July 1943, Hamburg had been firebombed, Mussolini had been deposed and Allied troops had landed in Sicily. But Henri Chamberlin still thought that he was on the winning side and intended to prove it on the battlefield.

14

A NORTH AFRICAN CONNECTION

IN THE SUMMER OF 1943, an Algerian man in his thirties, with a face like a fox and thick black hair that started low on his forehead, visited rue Lauriston to ask for help. Chamberlin and Bonny invited him into the office for a talk.

'Why don't you ask the Germans?' asked Bonny.

'No,' said Mohamed El-Maadi. 'I only ask those from France.'[1]

El-Maadi had been born near Constantine, an ancient Roman city of dry hills and valleys strung together by a web of bridges. He was brought up as a loyal citizen of the French empire by his lawyer father, a Muslim with French citizenship. El-Maadi joined the army as a young man but quit in 1936 to form an organisation called L'Algérie Française in Paris. He campaigned for reform, equality between colonist and colonised and more opportunities for Algerians. As a man of the right, El-Maadi had no interest in independence. He blamed any unrest on Jews and Freemasons.

Right-wing North Africans were not uncommon. By the 1930s, around 100,000 Algerians and Moroccans lived in France, a third of them in Paris. The left liked to believe that all these citizens were angry anti-imperialists desperate for freedom, but plenty sympathised with the reactionary and anti-Semitic views of the far-right.

Solidarité Française militants in blue shirts and jackboots gave fascist salutes at the Grand Mosque when they buried an Algerian comrade who had been killed in the 1934 Stavisky riots. In the same year thirty-four Jews died during an anti-Semitic pogrom in El-Maadi's hometown of Constantine. El-Maadi had been on duty in the city as a 32-year-old adjutant in the French army and some thought he took part in the violence.

El-Maadi became more militant as the 1930s ticked on. He joined the far-right Cagoule terror group in a ceremony at a Paris café by holding a box full of red, white and blue matches and swearing allegiance to France. In 1937, the Paris police arrested him for membership of the group, and he received nine months inside. He was just out of prison when the Second World War came and the army called him up as a lieutenant. He was awarded medals for bravery during the fighting. Then came defeat and occupation.

A demobilised El-Maadi met Cagoule veterans who invited him to join Deloncle's new Mouvement Social Révolutionnaire. He rode the RNP merger into membership of the party's Comité Nord-Africain, which had been formed to strengthen North African support for collaboration. El-Maadi recruited for the Légion des Volontaires Français and wore the uniform, but he never left Paris. Deloncle's people peeled away from the RNP after the Paul Collette shooting and encouraged El-Maadi to join them; however, he preferred to go solo with his own newspaper project.

Er Rachid was a biweekly French-language newspaper aimed at Algerians and Moroccans who were sympathetic to the new order in France. The Abwehr helped with funding but had limited access to newsprint, so someone suggested that El-Maadi contact a man called Henri Lafont in the sixteenth arrondissement.

Chamberlin liked to do favours for people, and especially for men who had political influence. His meeting with Pierre Laval had planted seeds that were now sprouting into an ambition to become police prefect of Paris. Guests at rue Lauriston parties had to sit through long monologues about Chamberlin's miserable childhood in the thirteenth arrondissement and how things must change in the city. 'He thought a lot about the poor, the unfortunate who had nowhere to live and no job,' recalled one partygoer. 'He cared deeply about the condition of the little people in Paris.'[2]

Monsieur Henri talked about plans to empty the prisons in exchange for an underworld truce that would lead to rehabilitation for everyone and a city that was free of crime. More sophisticated party guests rolled their eyes at his utopian pipedreams, but everyone shook Chamberlin's hand and promised their support in his campaign. A gangster becoming the prefect of police seemed possible in the kind of city with a moral core so rotted out that even formerly loyal collaborationist newspapers complained about the corruption. Nobody could tell the police from the thieves any more. In October 1943, *La Gerbe* wrote:

> Every day, we read of a policeman engaging in blackmail, a gendarme taking up burglary in the evening. How can these men respect magistrates, under whose orders they function, when they see them go out of their way to acquit a high-ranking civil servant who has gained three or four million on the black market using trucks owned by the state, then hand down the maximum sentence to a mother who has fraudulently acquired a kilo of flour?[3]

Chamberlin secured El-Maadi's support for his future candidacy by leaning on Jean Luchaire to print *Er Rachid* on his own presses. As a result, the print run jumped from 30,000 to 70,000 a week.

Chamberlin also financed a canteen to feed hungry North Africans out of the former black market storage space in 40 rue Lauriston. A grateful El-Maadi sent over two bodyguards in exchange for his generosity.

'Thanks to you, I have peace in my heart,' he wrote in an accompanying letter. 'You have given me riches. Here are two faithful servants worth any two of yours. They will obey you like dogs. Treat them as you treat your other men, otherwise they will go soft.'[4]

Chamberlin was grateful for the extra manpower. A new front had opened up in the battle between occupier and resistance.

Maquis groups were waging guerrilla warfare in the countryside of France with raids, executions and ambushes launched on remote country lanes. Members of the group lived in forest camps, wore berets and hobnailed boots and hid their campfire smoke from German spotter planes. The Maquis were generally younger than their counterparts in the urban resistance, and less experienced. They gave each other boyish nicknames, pledged their lives to charismatic leaders and promised to withstand twenty-four hours of torture before they broke.

The British had sent in 400 agents to help the fight, parachuting them down by night onto fields lit by torchlight. Most belonged to the Special Operations Executive (SOE), which was a secret outfit based out of a few shabby hotels in central London. The SOE used every kind of dirty trick to undermine Nazi rule in Europe. It blew up railways in Greece, killed collaborators in Belgium and plotted to assassinate senior Nazis.

In its early days, the SOE attracted eccentrics and adventurers. Peter Kemp, a cheerful blond Cambridge man whose experience fighting for the Nationalists in the Spanish Civil War was valuable on commando raids, remembered dealing with a major from the Sussex Yeomanry who seemed at least half-deranged:

> On one occasion he visited an SOE camouflage station and returned with a papier-mâché cow's head, which he proposed to take with him to France, put on his head and push through some hedgerow beside a major road; thus disguised, he assured us, he would count German vehicles and troops passing by.[5]

By 1943, the eccentrics had been sidelined and SOE operatives were hard-hitting patriots with morals put on hold for the duration. In France, they ran intelligence-gathering outfits and escape lines and parachuted in to train Maquis sabotage teams. The Gestapo went after them like hunting dogs.

Anti-parachute operations were directed out of Paris by the pig-faced Sturmbannführer Josef Kieffer of the SD with assistance from Sturmführer Dr Kuhn. Kieffer had captured a transmitter, a code book and British SOE operative John Renshaw Starr, who had apparently converted to the Nazi cause. Holed up in a room at avenue Foch, Starr sent fake messages to London that requested supply drops and more agents. No one knew why Starr had decided to collaborate. When a curious Bonny met him, he discovered only that the man was calm, enjoyed his food and had an apparent eidetic memory that allowed Starr to remember the face of every person he had ever met.

Dr Kuhn supplied a turncoat Gaullist agent named Christian who posed as a member of the resistance for the SOE parachutists responding to Starr's messages. Once they had landed on French soil, he would escort them to Paris, asking leading questions on the way, and then leave the Carlingue to shadow the new arrivals around the city and sniff out their contacts. Back in rue Lauriston, Bonny made intricate diagrams of the resistance networks and their agents. The net would draw ever tighter around the prey until Kieffer gave the order for rue Lauriston and other French auxiliary groups to swoop in and make the arrests.

The Carlingue was involved in a dozen of Kieffer's operations, capturing eight Allied parachutists, a fistful of Maquis members and a Lieutenant-Colonel Émile Bonotaux, who was carrying 4 million francs when he was picked up. The missions spread outside Paris and stretched as far as Angers, Amboise, Dordogne, Limoges and elsewhere.

One member of the resistance remembered how the Gestapo crackdown made things increasingly difficult for the networks: 'The year 1943 had been a catastrophic year, a terrible year. Teams and organisations, French and Allied, were being broken, one after another, with depressing speed.'[6]

The French police estimated that the Germans arrested 8,000 people that year. An average of 129 arrests occurred every month from spring to autumn purely for acts of sabotage on the railways.[7] A German military court in Paris accounted for a third of all death sentences that were handed down in the entire country. Things were made even easier for the Gestapo when squabbling Gaullists and Communists settled political disputes by informing on each other.

Members of the resistance soon realised that Chamberlin had become the most powerful Frenchman in the capital. On 17 August 1943, a resistance chief reached out to the gangster through their mutual friend Jeannot Rossi, who ran the bar Le Chapiteau. Rossi arranged a meeting in a dark corner of the club. Chamberlin smoked and drank champagne while the resistance leader tried to persuade him to change sides. The chief's attempts to appeal to Chamberlin's patriotism and offer pardons for crimes committed took them through two bottles. Monsieur Henri smoked on his cigarette and then responded in his high-pitched voice.

'You can give me nothing I want,' he said, 'not women, not money, not power. And you want me to give that all up and launch myself into an adventure from which I might not return, a life of wandering, hiding and danger? No.'[8]

They drank a final glass of champagne and parted company with a handshake.

• • •

One evening during the viciously cold winter of 1943, Bonny took his wife and son on a trip to the cinema. When they returned home, their apartment door was swinging open. Bonny took out his pistol and entered to find the lights switched on, but nothing taken. 'They've found me,' he said. 'They must have used the service entrance.'[9]

Soon after the break-in, one of El-Maadi's men became Bonny's bodyguard. Every evening he would turn up with a Sten sub-machine gun tucked under his arm and a pistol on his hip. He quietly ate a meal in the kitchen and then sat silently facing the front door when the family went to bed. One evening he disappeared. Bonny later told his son that the man had walked into the street and shot dead a German officer before being killed. The former policeman seemed baffled by the event.

Chamberlin appointed Jean-Michel Chaves as a new bodyguard and gifted the family a large villa in Neuilly-sur-Seine, just west of Paris. However, they preferred to remain in their apartment in the city. Bonny was no longer sure that the resistance had been behind the break-in. The Carlingue had made a lot of enemies recently, from Corsican crooks to Gestapo impersonators to patriotic policemen.

In September 1943, rue Lauriston had been part of a large German operation against Maquis fighters based in Montbard, a small town on the river Brenne known for snails, wine and an eighteenth-century park. Bömelburg teamed them with the Bande des Corses, a group of Corsican gangsters run by Étienne Léandri who operated for the SS out of 11 rue Flandrin.

Early one humid morning, thirty men divided into five sections and set off for Montbard with Chamberlin's white Bentley leading the convoy. The procession of black Citröens behind the Bentley emptied out in the centre of town and the gangsters spread throughout the town to target anyone suspected of supplying the Maquis. One bakery was smashed up and a number of shops looted. Local men and women were dragged out of their beds and held at the Parc Buffon for the interrogations to begin. 'I want everything to go well,' Prévost told them, 'but I need information on the Maquis. These terrorists represent a serious danger to you and the Germans.'[10]

The gang arrested fifteen people that were suspected of helping the Maquis and took them back to Paris and avenue Foch. The operation was regarded as a success by the Gestapo, but during a house search in Montbard some jewellery went missing from a house belonging to a local family called the Plaits. Madame Plait went to the Germans and made an official complaint. Chamberlin never usually cared about theft, but the loss of the jewellery reflected badly on him as a leader. He assembled everyone who had taken part in the mission at his office at rue Lauriston.

'I received a telegram from the Feldgendarmerie of Montbard, a theft was committed. I want to know the thief. Nobody leaves until we know the thief,' he said.[11]

A long silence followed until a man called Ferrando, who was attached to the Corsican gang, raised his hand. Chamberlin ordered him to return the jewels and Bonny typed out a letter of apology to

Madame Plait. She made the trip to Paris to collect her jewellery, where Chamberlin kissed her hand and the two chatted politely over coffee. Monsieur Henri refused to work with the Corsicans again.

Reflecting on how his boss imposed discipline, Bonny explained that 'each time there was a theft, and unfortunately there were a few, Lafont never hesitated to punish the guilty person severely. Only, obviously, in this environment, it was a little bit difficult.'[12]

Chamberlin had a bigger problem than Corsican crooks in the form of Rudy de Mérode, the leader of a criminally minded Gestapo group in the Parisian suburb of Neuilly-sur-Seine. Born Frédéric Martin to a Luxembourg family in the disputed Lorraine region squeezed between France and Germany, he trained as an engineer in Germany before being recruited by the Abwehr. When back in France, Martin worked for the government until his spying was uncovered in the mid-1930s. He was still behind bars when the war began.

Martin escaped in the confusion of the German invasion. He returned to Paris and tracked down his former employers at the Hôtel Lutetia. He changed his name to Rudy de Mérode – sometimes Rudi von Mérode when Germans were around – and assembled a group that was involved in Amt Otto black marketeering. Hermann Brandl trusted him to deliver cash to the buying offices every week. Martin built up a gang of twenty or so men, which included disgraced policemen and famous faces from the underworld such as pre-war jewel thief Serge de Lenz.

The Neuilly gang graduated to the Gestapo and took part in the arrests of at least 300 members of the resistance. One woman who was interrogated by the gang tearfully asked how Martin could work for the enemy of France. 'Madame,' he replied, 'my parents raised me to drink chocolate in the morning, smoke a pack of cigarettes a day and travel by car. The Germans have furnished me with all these things.'[13]

Martin appeared on Chamberlin's radar when a Frenchman and his son visited rue Lauriston at the start of 1943 with a complaint. They had been robbed of 300 Louis D'Ors coins during a gold sale and then forced to donate a large sum of money to a supposed charity run by faux policiers. The men claimed that they had come from rue Lauriston.

Chamberlin identified Neuilly Gestapo gangsters as the fake police and confronted his rival. Martin promised to punish those of his group who were responsible but continued to allow his men to use rue Lauriston as a cover for their extortion. He found it hard to take Chamberlin seriously, remembering him as just another Amt Otto front man who had to wait for the money to arrive every week. It was a serious underestimation of Chamberlin's power.

In late 1943, Carlingue gangsters kicked in doors across Paris brandishing MP40 sub-machine guns and arrested most of Martin's gang. Serge de Lenz and his fellow faux policiers ended up in a German concentration camp. To explain away the arrests, Bonny typed up a report which claimed Martin had spied for the Allies.

Bonny's dossier wasn't quite believable enough and Martin was released. He attempted to re-establish his gang with help from the Wehrmacht. The Carlingue were having none of it and chased him out of Paris and warned him not to come back. Martin spent the rest of the war smuggling Spanish goods into Biarritz.

Rue Lauriston had also made more dangerous enemies on the other side of the law. In November 1943, six members of the Honneur de la Police resistance group were arrested by the Germans at a brasserie while planning the final stages of an attack on 93 rue

Lauriston. The group had access to detailed information about Carlingue security. Chamberlin and Bonny suspected they had an inside source and pulled in everyone who orbited the gang for an interrogation. Joseph Joinovici spent an afternoon in rue Lauriston praying no one realised that he had helped the resistance group. Joinovici's nervousness did not go unnoticed by Bonny:

> I have never seen a man so terrified. He sweated heavily and trembled in all his limbs. He knew Lafont's reputation and knew that a man's life was of little importance to him. Lafont let him stew in his juice for over two hours. 'Joano' must have lost at least five kilos that day. Finally, Lafont let him go and said, 'Be careful, Joano. If it goes wrong and I learn that you tried to screw me over, I wouldn't give a rabbit skin for your life!'[14]

Suspicion and paranoia were everywhere in Paris. The Germans arrested the resistance infiltrator Marongin at the end of the year. The 80,000-franc bounty that he had been collecting for each arrest had enabled the medical student to move from a room on rue de la Sorbonne to a more exclusive address in the sixteenth arrondissement. Sometimes he visited rue Lauriston for lunch, wearing a good suit that had been cut by a Jewish tailor that Chamberlin saved from deportation and bragging about the pleasures of sleeping with resistance girls. Behind the scenes Gestapo agents convinced themselves that Marongin had turned double agent. He was sent to a concentration camp.

Collaborationist fish were thrashing for room in a pool that no one wanted to admit was shrinking, but Chamberlin seemed to be more confident than ever. Knochen had left Paris in August 1943 after losing an internal power struggle and Bömelburg moved to

Vichy shortly afterwards to take up a post watching the decision makers of Pétain's government. Chamberlin now reported directly to Höherer SS-und Polizeiführer Carl Oberg, who put even fewer limits on the gang's powers.

As Paris welcomed in the new year of 1944 through snow and ice, Chamberlin began planning to dive even deeper into collaboration with the Nazis. He couldn't hear the hurricane howling in the distance. The Allied armies were six months from landing in France.

15

SS MOHAMMED

ONE EVENING, BONNY CAME home, slammed the door behind him and threw a brown paper parcel on the dining table. His wife watched him unwrap a feldgrau obersturmführer SS uniform with black collar tabs.

'Look at what that utter bastard Lafont gave to me,' he exclaimed. 'It's my size.'[1]

The fuse had been lit on Chamberlin's military dream by a Vichy defeat in 1943. Three hundred Frenchmen and a hundred Arabs of the Phalange Africaine unit had fought the invading Allies across Tunisia wearing Vichy's double-headed axe symbol on their breast pockets. The collaborationist press predicted that North Africa would remain secure, until the Phalange disintegrated in battle and de Gaulle's men shot any survivors.

Chamberlin followed the unit's rise and fall and thought that he could do better. He knew a little about the French colonies from his military service and liked to talk about launching his own '*petite expedition en Tunisie*'. French North Africa was in Allied hands before Chamberlin could do anything, but a seed had been planted, to be encouraged by Bömelburg a few months later when he casually suggested that North Africans could be recruited to guard Gestapo facilities.

In January 1944, Chamberlin grafted Bömelburg's idea onto his own fantasies of battlefield glory. He approached Carl Oberg with a plan to enlist 50,000 North African prisoners of war from German camps into a private army under a provisional Tunisian government in Paris. Chamberlin would be puppet master.

The plan came at the right time. Oberg was on the lookout for more manpower to combat the burgeoning zones controlled by the Maquis in the French countryside. The daily transfer of soldiers to the Eastern Front had forced the Germans to rely on collaborators and foreigners for internal security. Breton nationalists under Célestin Lané patrolled eastern France. Hindus and Sikhs of the Legion Freies Indien dug in at the Bay of Biscay. The Milice was expanding across France while Russians, Ukrainians, Georgians and Cossacks chased the Maquis through forests and fields. Chamberlin's North Africans would be a useful addition to the defence of mainland France.

Oberg handed over 1.2 million francs for a scaled-down version of Chamberlin's original proposal. The gangster's private army would start with a few hundred men to be recruited out of the North African community in Paris and his provisional government ambitions were vetoed. Oberg made Chamberlin an SS hauptsturmführer as compensation.

Chamberlin called a meeting of the Carlingue inner circle. He arrived wearing his hauptsturmführer uniform and ordered them to address him as 'Capitaine Henri'. 'I don't think the Krauts want you to command an armoured division,' said Danos in response.[2] Chamberlin slapped him hard across the face for the insubordination and announced that the Carlingue was joining the German war effort. Danos, Cazauba, Villaplana, Prévost and the rest of the gang had just been conscripted. After the meeting concluded, the gangsters dispersed in silence to sit around cafés smoking, drinking and thinking about the future. Chamberlin remained at rue Lauriston to quiz Emile Hess and Willy Kharlof – who were still serving their secondment from the Gestapo – about the inner workings of the German armed forces.

On 28 January 1944, the Brigade Nord-Africaine officially came into existence. Recruitment began through El-Maadi's *Er Rachid* and his contacts at the Grand Mosque in the fifth arrondissement. The pay was generous, with private soldiers getting 5,000 francs a month. The name was a deliberate echo of the Brigade Nord-Africaine de la Préfecture de Police, a corrupt department of the Paris police force based in rue Lecomte that kept an eye on the city's North African population. It had some murky links with El-Maadi, and no straight policeman in Paris would be seen near the place.

Chamberlin received 500 applicants and shortlisted 300, before stripping out another 100 individuals as being unsuitable. Around 15 per cent of the remainder had a criminal record, and one man joined up to escape a murder charge. Chamberlin saw such backgrounds as offering useful experience for his paramilitary adventure.

The first recruits were housed at 74 rue Lauriston, a hotel which had once been a Belle Époque mansion frequented by Marcel Proust. During the occupation it was used as storage space by Belgian black marketeer Oliver Allard. He owed Chamberlin a favour. Chamberlin's Moroccans and Algerians took over the building, sleeping in the conference rooms on cots. A nervy Tunisian military veteran called Abdelaziz Belhassine agreed to sign on as the unit's military leader under the pseudonym 'Ali Ouali' for 20,000 francs a month and his own room.

Joinovici supplied the uniforms for the unit: dark-blue tunic and trousers over a khaki shirt, a black beret and an overcoat in brown for the Moroccans and in blue for the Algerians. The soldiers wore daggers on their hips, brandished SS identity cards and had permits to carry weapons. Avenue Foch supplied Sten guns and bolt-action rifles that had been captured from Allied parachute drops. Chamberlin engaged in some aggressive verbal sparring with Joinovici as he bargained down the price of the uniforms from what had been originally agreed.

'After all, Joseph,' said Chamberlin, 'you're nothing but a dirty Jew!'

'And how much would it cost me to no longer be one, Hauptsturmführer?'[3]

As more recruits arrived, Chamberlin moved the brigade out of central Paris to a large property in the wealthy suburb of Neuilly-sur-Seine. In February 1944, the unit was divided into five units of thirty men, led by Cazauba, Maillebuau, Clavié, Villaplana and Prévost wearing SS untersturmführer feldgrau uniforms with black diamond collar patches. Each had four non-commissioned officers serving under him, which included men such as Danos, Chaves, Sartore, Fels, Haré, Bowing, Slovenski and others from the various teams that were run out of rue Lauriston. Pagnon became an untersturmführer in the reserve and El-Maadi was made hauptsturmführer but remained outside the brigade as a recruiter. Bonny was appointed obersturmführer, although his wife forbade him to wear the German uniform. 'Don't worry,' he said. 'I have no intention of disguising myself.'[4]

One day when the Carlingue were standing in a Neuilly park someone snapped a photograph of ten men standing together in uniform. Danos was crouched fat at the front, while Clavié smoked intensely in his untersturmführer uniform. The others in the group looked in turn sloppy, cheerful, apprehensive and bored.

Some of Chamberlin's gangsters refused to wear the German uniform. Labussière fell out with the boss and joined the Milice. Others like Ricord preferred to stay in Paris as part of a Carlingue skeleton crew. Chamberlin bullied twenty minor gang members, including a pair of brothers named Irwinsky and a man called Riffard, into joining up in civilian clothes. Four joined each section.

Chamberlin still found time to do favours for his friends in Vichy. The hardline collaborationist newspaper *Je Suis Partout* had been waging a press campaign against a Vichy official that it regarded as being unenthusiastic about Germany. The official telephoned Jean Luchaire who sent an intermediary to escort editor Pierre-Antoine Cousteau along to rue Lauriston. A shaken Cousteau later told his reporters what had happened:

> [The intermediary] picked me up in a huge American car, probably the only one driving in Paris. The driver was a horrible thug, hard on the eye. [The intermediary] spoke to him in a very friendly way. We stop on a street near avenue Kléber, rue Lauriston. A big bourgeois building. From the door, we dive right into a gangster movie. Everywhere guys with frightening mouths, real extras for *Scarface*, guarding the corridors, feet on the tables in rows of rooms, several in shirtsleeves, long guns like that on the hip. Others, no prettier, in German uniforms. [The intermediary] brings me to the chief: an SS officer almost two metres tall. He introduced himself: 'Captain Lafont'. With that accent, no doubt, he's a Frenchman. Very cordial, smiling, but completely categorical: 'You are attacking [the official]. He's one of my best friends. I won't let people say bad things about him. Your attacks must stop immediately. Otherwise, I would have to get you into trouble, and that would be a shame.'[5]

The reporters talked the matter over and quickly came to a decision. The attacks on the Vichy official stopped the same day.

In mid-February 1944, Chamberlin reached out to Marcel Déat of the RNP for extra manpower. Chamberlin's offer to equip thirty-seven paramilitaries if they agreed to support the Brigade Nord-Africaine came as welcome news to the collaborationist group. Déat's followers had become prime targets for attacks by the resistance, but the Germans didn't trust them enough to supply weapons; they were forced to buy guns and coshes on the black market. A few RNP men transitioned directly into Chamberlin's brigade at the end of February and others formed a separate support team. After meeting Chamberlin, Déat described the gangster in his diary as 'a strange figure for a policeman'.[6]

The gang secretary Delehaye turned 93 rue Lauriston into a logistics base, with the help of an unenthusiastic German non-commissioned officer who referred to the brigade as the 'SS Mohammed'. The pair's main business consisted of paperwork, organising the payroll and making preparations for injured soldiers. In March 1944, the Brigade Nord-Africaine received orders to leave Paris. To mark the occasion, Chamberlin put on a farewell dinner at the One-Two-Two brothel. Germans, gangsters and naked girls drank champagne as Monsieur Henri made a speech about his future ambitions.

'My friends,' he said, 'I will be either general or prefect, it doesn't matter. Personally, I like both uniforms.'[7]

• • •

Tulle was a manufacturing town in the southern part of France known for its lace, accordions and guns. The buildings of the medieval quarter were crammed like crooked teeth around a twelfth-century church. Chamberlin and three sections of the Brigade Nord-Africaine travelled to the town and set up headquarters in a requisitioned hotel and the neighbouring municipal theatre.

Bonny had arranged the billets a few days earlier but had gone on a personal mission to Brive and Bordeaux before the troops arrived. He gave Chamberlin a cover story about looking up family members but then drove off in search of some of his old friends who were now part of the resistance; Bonny was thinking about changing sides.

He failed to locate his friends and barely escaped a resistance ambush on a steep road just outside Mallemort, accelerating through a hail of sub-machine gun bullets. Seeing the corpses of German soldiers tortured to death by the road verge on the return journey hardened his resolve. 'It has become abominable on both sides,' he said. 'We do unforgivable things and so do they.'[8]

Back in Tulle, Bonny put on his obersturmführer uniform and joined Chamberlin in the hotel. The Brigade Nord-Africaine had orders to set up checkpoints and patrol the area together with a smaller German unit. In the first few days they uncovered a resistance group with a radio transmitter. The leader of the resistance group, Lieutenant Faro, was beaten half to death before he was sent off to meet his fate with the Gestapo. Shortly after, the arrest of a man stealing petrol uncovered another resistance group and some Jewish civilians hiding in the area.

On 1 March 1944, an ambush by a Maquis band wounded several North Africans. Morale began to drop and Chamberlin struggled to maintain discipline. Three gangsters were dismissed after stealing 10,000 francs in Tulle. A fat crook with gold teeth called Victor Paul then beat a local out of 19,000 francs; Chamberlin dealt with him and returned 15,000 francs. A woman complained that two North

Africans had stolen items from her grocery store, so Chamberlin slapped the men around in front of her and gave them six months in prison. Events began to escalate when the brigade looted some nearby houses and killed a local. Chamberlin was able to ignore a German order to burn down a village, but this was a small glimmer of mercy in an increasingly dark cave.

In early March, two sections under Maillebuau and Cazauba were sent to Franche-Comté in eastern France to guard a Peugeot factory in the town of Sochaux that manufactured tanks and V1 rocket parts. British aeroplanes had been targeting it over the previous year but the closest the bombers had got was a July 1943 raid that missed the factory and killed 125 locals. SOE agents then took over the mission and got the factory owners to plant explosives around their own grounds. A team of workers was creeping in one November night to detonate everything when a group of German guards who were playing football stopped them. After a few tense minutes the guards made it understood that they just wanted more players and the sabotage mission was delayed in favour of an international game of football. The factory was blown up two nights later. It was barely operational when Maillebuau and Cazauba arrived to prevent further sabotage.

The pair built a temporary prison in the Peugeot grounds for workers suspected of having Communist sympathies. The morale of their soldiers was wobbly from the start and Cazauba lost his authority after an attempt to ban North Africans from drinking in local cafés almost caused a mutiny. Men from the brigade climbed over the prison wire at night to rape female detainees. The Germans had enough and arrested the rapists and expelled the rest of the North Africans from the area, leaving only skeletal units under Maillebuau and Cazauba. Newly arrived RNP men reinforced them.

Two further sections detached from Tulle: Prévost's men headed for Objat and Juillac to do little except gather together the locals at odd times of the day so that their commander could lecture them about the inevitable German victory. Villaplana marched to Périgueux, the site of the German military command for Dordogne, and joined toad-faced fifty-something General-Major Walter Brehmer's 8,000-strong division of Wehrmacht troops and Georgian collaborators in a sweep for Maquis camps. The death of two SS officers in an ambush led to Villaplana's men participating in the reprisal execution of sixty hostages.

Chamberlin was called back to Paris later that March, leaving Bonny in command, after the mystery of Adrien Estébétéguy's disappearance was finally solved. On 11 March, black smoke began pouring from a town house chimney in rue le Sueur, not far from rue Lauriston. Firemen broke into the property and discovered an out of control blaze in the basement furnace. Body parts from ten people were scattered around the building. The house belonged to Dr Marcel Petiot.

The doctor was a serial killer. He promised escape routes to desperate people, many of whom were Jewish, and then injected his victims with poison that was disguised as vaccinations. One of the suitcases found hidden in the property belonged to Yvan Dreyfus and another contained silk Sulka shirts with the monogram 'AE' that had been handmade for Estébétéguy. He and Paulette had spent their last moments alive in a triangular room with a false door, while Petiot watched them die through a peephole.

Chamberlin arrived at police headquarters wearing his SS hauptsturmführer uniform, accompanied by a Moroccan bodyguard. He identified Estébétéguy's belongings and asked a lot of questions about the case. He seemed to believe that other members of his gang who had disappeared, including Tissier, might have been killed by Petiot. The police promised to inform him when the doctor was located.

When Chamberlin returned to Tulle he was subdued and thoughtful. Bonny handed back command of the troops and received permission to join the administration team at rue Lauriston. His wife was scared by the death threats and tiny wooden coffins that had been arriving at the apartment; personal details about Bonny's involvement in the brigade had been made public in a resistance bulletin:

> A special police section has just been formed to 'direct' all 'law and order services' in case of an Allied landing. It is headed by Bonny, Malbiaut [Maillebuau] and Henri Lafont. They expect to recruit 5,000 natives from North Africa at a tremendous price ... Men of good will who have nothing to do are reminded that Bonny still lives at boulevard Gouvion-Saint-Cyr, Paris, XVII.[9]

Abel Danos also decided that it was time to leave the battlefield. His girlfriend Hélène Maltat had come to join him in a billet at a small hotel in Tulle, arriving after a long train ride delayed by Allied bombing raids. At night they cuddled close and Danos insisted that he was not a traitor and that the feldgrau was only a uniform. He gave Hélène a copy of the Neuilly photograph of the gang in uniform but muttered that it had been a mistake. An infected dog bite gave him the excuse to leave Cazauba's section and return to Paris for medical treatment.

Once the wound was stitched up, Bonny refused Danos any more time away from the brigade and sent him back to Tulle. Chamberlin was more sympathetic and gave him a few days off, during which Le

Mammouth immediately deserted back to Paris with Hélène. The journey took twice as long on tracks that had been torn up by sabotage and aerial bombing. Policemen could barely keep the contempt off their faces when Danos flashed his Gestapo card to get through a railway station checkpoint.

Cazauba returned to Tulle with his mutinous section in the opening days of April and was immediately dismissed by Chamberlin. Charlot le Fébrile stripped off his uniform and returned to Paris, glad to be done with the military life. Maillebuau's section remained in Sochaux. The former policeman spent his time discussing the war with his wife Marinette and making secret contacts with the local resistance. In Périgueux, Villaplana's men went through provincial towns like a swarm of locusts and were a barely controllable mob as the Brehmer division tortured prisoners and executed hostages. All the while the Maquis watched and waited in the forests.

Even Eddy Pagnon the chauffeur was making his own plans to escape involvement in the gang. He had to make a choice between Henri Chamberlin and a beautiful red-haired aristocrat who had diamonds sparkling at her throat and a secret past as a prostitute. It wasn't a hard decision.

16

THE COMEDY IS OVER

HENRI CHAMBERLIN TREATED HIS loyal chauffeur like a dog. Pagnon was last in line when cash was being handed out and the first to be insulted. He spent his nights half asleep at the wheel of Chamberlin's white Bentley, ferrying his boss from nightclub to nightclub, listening to drunken insults and tirades about being an informer and a traitor as he drove through the streets of Paris.

As the clock ticked towards morning, Monsieur Henri would become sentimental and contrite and give the chauffeur a pay rise. The abuse would come creeping back the next day.

Pagnon had been forced into service with the Brigade Nord-Africaine. In Tulle, he wore SS feldgrau and watched the trees for Maquis snipers. He wrote a miserable letter to his lover Sylviane Quimfe, Marquise d'Abrantès, complaining about life in the brigade.

Quimfe took the train down from Paris to comfort her lover. A sleek-haired Irish playboy friend named Michael Farmer – who had become famous before the war as husband to Hollywood star Gloria Swanson – lived locally and offered her a room. Pagnon would slip away from his duties and lie in the marquise's arms and forget about the fighting, the brigade and rue Lauriston. They enjoyed a few sweet days before Chamberlin uncovered the love nest and sent

Quimfe back to Paris on the next train. He didn't want Pagnon to be happy.

The Marquise d'Abrantès had entered rue Lauriston in the first half of 1942 as black marketer de Wiet's escort at a Saturday night party. The plump businessman wore his usual pink silk shirt and light-grey suit. His companion accessorised her red hair with a low-cut dress that Chamberlin could not resist. Quimfe told worldly stories of her aristocratic beau monde with its money and glamour, and winters spent in Saint-Moritz, spring in Cannes and summer in Deauville. After a few glasses of champagne, Quimfe dropped hints about how she worked as a spy before the war and knew something about a resistance circle that helped soldiers to escape from France. Chamberlin liked what he heard and invited her to return for a private dinner the next day.

Pagnon saw Quimfe entering rue Lauriston one Sunday. He recognised her as somebody that he used to know. She hadn't been an aristocrat back then.

Quimfe was born in September 1912 to a family transplanted from Alsace to Paris. There wasn't much money growing up, but Sylviane was pretty and looked good in an evening gown. She worked as a shop girl, then a model and finally a working girl in an upmarket *maison de rendez-vous*. Influential men who liked to pay for sex found her entertaining company. A pin-up photograph of Quimfe in modelling disguise appeared in the August 1935 edition of girlie monthly *Paris-Magazine*.

The future marquise met Pagnon at the Moderne Garage on avenue de la Grande-Armée. At the time he was working as a salesman with a sideline in illegal gambling dens and lottery fraud and she needed her car fixed. Pagnon's wife had recently run off with a Moroccan and things were looking shaky with his new girlfriend

Suzanne Daniel. Quimfe flirted and Pagnon flirted back but it went nowhere. Quimfe had higher ambitions than dating a car salesman who had underworld connections. The pair became friends and eventually drifted apart.

Soon after, contacts from the brothel introduced Quimfe to the Marquis Maurice LeRoy d'Abrantès. They entered into a marriage of convenience that would require neither party to change their lifestyle to any degree. Quimfe continued to see wealthy men who gave her presents and the marquis took a percentage.

She was in Nice when the defeat arrived and a fog of desperation settled on the bars and restaurants as the wealthy tried to keep the pre-war party going. An Austrian baron gave Quimfe expensive jewellery but stepped aside for Lionel de Wiet. The profiteer was in Nice negotiating a complicated and unsuccessful attempt to buy local film companies on behalf of the Italians. He found time for a brief affair with Quimfe. Lust burned itself out, but they remained friends and returned to Paris together. De Wiet took her to a party at rue Lauriston and explained that the building belonged to an important friend who had sprung him from prison.

Chamberlin treated the marquise to a private dinner at rue Lauriston, but lost interest when Pagnon whispered Quimfe's backstory into his ear. He aborted the seduction but remembered to pass on the stories about an escape network to the Abwehr. The agents checked scrupulously, found nothing and soon Quimfe was no longer welcome at rue Lauriston. She made an attempt at seducing Bonny, but the policeman remained faithful to his wife and his bourgeois life. Her next target was Pagnon, who reciprocated. The couple moved into a requisitioned apartment at *48bis* rue des belles-Feuilles, just a few doors along from Joinovici's abandoned wife and children.

Around this time the chauffeur began doing faux policier robberies with Clavié, Maillebuau and Terrail, which they kept quiet from Monsieur Henri and split the takings among themselves. Pagnon wanted to buy nice things for Quimfe. The marquise continued to sleep with rich men in the afternoons for money; the couple seemed happy.

By spring 1944, Pagnon was with the Brigade Nord-Africaine in Tulle. After Chamberlin broke up the scene at Michael Farmer's house, a humiliated Quimfe sent a flurry of angry letters from Paris offering an ultimatum: Pagnon had to choose between her and the Carlingue. 'My decision is made,' he wrote back on 1 April 1944. 'I am leaving Henri.'[1]

Pagnon deserted to Paris a few weeks later for a passionate reunion. Lying in bed, they discussed plans for the future and the need for money. The owner of a bar in the rue Darcet called Guy Lavigne was planning a faux policier scam on a Jewish man looking to sell some bolts of cloth and Pagnon agreed to take part. The plan was straightforward: the group would pretend to be buyers and then pull out the chauffeur's Gestapo card and walk off with the cloth. Faux policier scams had been part of the occupation since the earliest days of the war and showed no signs of drying up. The French police recorded 820 incidents between October 1941 and March 1944, with many more going unreported.[2]

Pagnon supplied a car for the scheme and he and Lavigne drove off to the rendezvous, with Quimfe excited and chattering in the back seat. It turned out to be a trap and the three were arrested by members of Friedrich Berger's rue de la Pompe operation; a gang of Gestapo auxiliaries who tortured their victims at an elegant house just a short walk from rue Lauriston.

The German Berger was a thuggish, half-deaf brute, unrefined as crude oil. He had joined the Abwehr in 1933 and gone undercover into the French Foreign Legion. Berger spent three years reporting back to Berlin before quitting the Legion with a disability pension for an inflammatory ear condition called chronic suppurative otitis media. At the start of the occupation he was based at the Hôtel Lutetia in Paris. A mission to infiltrate the Vichy Deuxième Bureau in 1940 went wrong and Berger ended up in an Algerian prison with a death sentence. It took the Abwehr two years to free him.

Back in Paris, he opened an Amt Otto office and did some black marketeering before transitioning to the Gestapo at rue des Saussaies. He had a side business in faux policier scams, refined by the addition of torture for anyone reluctant to give up the rest of their stock. In April 1944, Berger moved into 180 rue de la Pompe and expanded his operations into chasing down members of the resistance.

He was the leader of a multi-national gang. Members included the Guicciardinis, who were an Italian man and his two sons; the former taxi driver Rachid Zulgadar who claimed to be Iranian or Georgian depending on his mood; the amateur pianist Zimmer from Luxembourg; Manuel Stcherbina from Georgia; and Favriot the Frenchman who liked hurting women. The group infiltrated resistance groups and took prisoners back to the rue de la Pompe to be stripped naked and drowned half to death in a bath, while Zimmer played classical pieces on the piano. Berger's red-haired lover Denise Delfau perched herself on a chair and watched everything while recording confessions in a notebook.

'They are shits and human sewage,' said Henri Chamberlin, morally outraged for once.[3]

Eddy Pagnon's Gestapo card meant nothing at the rue de la Pompe. Berger locked the trio up. A Gestapo source contacted

Chamberlin in Tulle and advised him to come and collect his chauffeur before Berger lost control.

• • •

The resistance opened hunting season on collaborators in the spring. On 26 April, members machine-gunned Violette Morris to death as she stepped out of her Citroën Traction Avant on a Normandy country road between Épaignes and Lieurey. Morris was acting as chauffeur for a local butcher named Bailleul, his wife and their two young children. As they rounded a corner, they came across a carriage blocking the road. The Citroën stopped and Morris got out with a pistol in her hand. The sub-machine guns opened fire from the trees and Violette Morris and her passengers were all killed.

The murder was an act of revenge for her activities as an informant. Morris had moved from the Abwehr's Service Léopold to the Gestapo. A few months before her death, Morris had told the Gestapo about a network that was involved in sabotage and parachute groups.[4] Frenchmen working for the Gestapo arrested six people, including a colonel and his wife. All of them were executed. Later, she passed on information about a resistance arms cache near Montlhéry. The German troops moved in and seven resistance fighters were killed and another ten dragged off to Paris prisons.

No one from rue Lauriston noticed the death of the woman who wore men's clothes and had attended their parties for a number of years. They were too busy fighting and looting their way through the French countryside.

Alexandre Villaplana and his men had spent the last month trailing the German army around Dordogne. They robbed and blackmailed every village, leaving a trail of destruction. Villaplana assuaged his guilt about the rural crime wave by occasionally helping out locals. In the south-western town of Eymet, a man called Raynaud had been accused of making contact with British parachutists, but denied everything. A German officer threatened to burn down the neighbourhood and gave Raynaud five minutes to confess. Villaplana intervened, had the execution pushed back a few hours, and did some detective work. The man had been denounced by a family named Lormand, so he decided to pull them in for questioning, along with a family friend called Morganti. Villaplana soon uncovered the truth:

> I resumed the interrogation of the entire Lormand family. It was a real family drama that was happening in this village, in which everybody is very small-minded. At six o'clock, Monsieur Morganti gave me an indication and caused me to understand that this could [have] come from Monsieur Lormand's beautiful daughter-in-law. I asked him why. He said, 'Because she is in the process of divorcing Monsieur Lormand's son; she has already sent a first letter and I saw her take 50,000 francs from her father-in-law's safe. She must have done this for revenge.'[5]

The daughter was tracked down and confessed to framing her father-in-law over delays in her divorce. Raynaud was released. Villaplana congratulated himself and went back to squeezing the Dordogne dry. In a nearby village, a married couple with a small child were accused of hiding six boxes of explosives. Villaplana's men burst into their home in the early morning as Monsieur Maceron was just getting out of bed.

'I asked whether they would let him eat a little bit and get dressed,' said Madame Maceron. 'They agreed immediately. My husband then ate breakfast. These men, accompanied by the Germans, asked if they could eat breakfast with him, telling me they would pay. I said: If you want to eat, eat with my husband, just help yourselves.'[6]

The air of strained cordiality continued until Villaplana's men began searching the property and found 50,000 francs in a strongbox. Villaplana switched to threatening charm. 'I am French,' he said, 'and I have already saved fifty-five Frenchmen. I want to make your husband the fifty-sixth. Give me this money. I will leave you 25,000 francs to raise your son.'[7]

The Macerons agreed to the deal and Villaplana and his men left, no longer interested in the explosives. Other families bribed their way out of real or imagined trouble in the same way. Some captured resistance commanders were released with instructions to remember Villaplana's mercy. His faith in a German victory was fading away.

In early May 1944, Villaplana was ordered to leave his unit and return to Tulle as temporary commander of the brigade headquarters. Chamberlin had been called to Paris for a tactical meeting with Pierre Laval and Joseph Darnand. The Vichy pair were in the capital as part of a delegation to watch Marshal Pétain speak to 10,000 people from a balcony of the Hôtel de Ville and attend mass at Notre-Dame. 'La Marseillaise' was sung publicly in the capital for the first time, while suspicious German soldiers stroked their rifles and watched the crowds.

Chamberlin agreed to free some prisoners being held by the Germans, in exchange for Milice manpower to support the Brigade Nord-Africaine. The three men parted with a handshake, assuring each other the Nazis would win the war; any alternative was unthinkable. Afterwards, Chamberlin had one last task before heading back to Tulle. He visited 180 rue de la Pompe in his hauptsturmführer uniform and ordered Berger to release Pagnon, Quimfe and Lavigne. The German was disappointed about missing out on a 'beautiful nudism session', as he referred to his interrogations, but he obeyed Chamberlin. Outside on the street, Chamberlin tore up Pagnon's Gestapo card and threw the pieces in his face. The chauffeur was expelled from the Carlingue.

Chamberlin returned to his headquarters in Tulle and operations continued throughout May. However, the additional Milice paramilitaries made no difference in the fight against the Maquis and by the end of the month Chamberlin's fantasies of military glory had crumbled like an old sea wall. He could not win against an enemy that lived behind every tree and hedge and blank-faced stare in the neighbourhood.

He dictated a report to his boss Carl Oberg stating that the Maquis remained strong, that German troops were overwhelmed and that occupation policies were making things worse. He took credit for protecting the Peugeot factory and blamed any setbacks on his unruly North African troops. Shortly after this report was sent, Chamberlin lost all interest in military life. On the night of 25 May 1944, the Brigade Nord-Africaine pulled out of Tulle and returned to Paris, leaving behind only Maillebuau's RNP group in Sochaux and Villaplana's old section, now under the command of Raymond Monange, busy committing atrocities in Périgueux.

Monange was a 31-year-old house painter with a vicious streak. He'd served a stint in the Foreign Legion before settling down into the family business of paint-stained overalls and turpentine.

When the war came, Monange joined the regular army and won the Croix de Guerre. He returned to occupied Paris and discovered that no one needed their houses painted in the middle of a war. He moved into the pimping business with the help of some underworld friends but was arrested. A collaborator colleague freed him and brought Monange into a Gestapo network. Later, some men from rue Lauriston mentioned that their boss Henri Lafont was recruiting a paramilitary outfit of North Africans; Monange decided to sign up. 'The more fights there are, the happier I am,' he said.[8]

He visited his family home wearing a German non-commissioned officer's uniform. His mother rushed up and hugged him, but his father turned away from him in disgust. In Tulle, Monange was promoted to untersturmführer in Villaplana's absence and became leader of the section at Périgueux. He was assisted by fellow crook Jean Delchiappo and a legendarily mean faux policier called Mathieu Fioravanti whose girlfriend was always complaining that he never passed on the spoils of his crimes. 'Only once, for Christmas Eve last year,' she said, 'he brought back a diamond necklace that he allowed me to put on the same evening and took back the next day.'[9]

Monange was drunk and violent and was convinced that every local belonged to the Maquis. A family attending a funeral were beaten and robbed; a young man stopped and searched was shot in the leg; and anyone who was suspected of knowing something about the Maquis was tortured. Sometimes Monange lost control and his own men had to hold him back. 'Ah, you do not know what the Gestapo is,' Monange screamed at one prisoner. 'Well, I'll show you.'[10]

Everything suddenly changed on 6 June 1944 when Allied forces launched the largest seaborne invasion in history at the beaches of Normandy. In one day, 160,000 Allied troops crossed the channel to France. They brought with them tanks, assault craft, fighter planes, artillery and gliders. The soldiers slogged their way up the beaches and dunes of Normandy into an onslaught of German machine-gun fire. Within a week the Allies had carved out territory sixty miles long and fifteen miles deep in the north of France. A worried Chamberlin telephoned Luchaire and Prade and his other underworld contacts. 'If you still have any friends you want freed, let me know quick,' he said. 'I can still do a lot of things, but probably not for long.'

From their foothold in Normandy, the Allies were able to force through the German defences and into open country. Fierce fighting commenced: villages were blown to rubble; houses cleared with flamethrowers; snipers shot out of hedgerows; bridges dynamited into rivers. Within a month, a million Allied troops were on French soil. Chamberlin finally seemed to understand that Germany would lose the war. On the evening of 23 June, he was in a bar on boulevard Rochechouart in Paris, drunk, depressed and rambling to friends:

> I have eyes to see and ears to hear, and what I see, what I hear, old friends, is not good at all, not good at all. It's over for the Krauts, finished, kaput! They still want to shout, march, shoot! But they know that their beans are cooked. The comedy's over, guys, over! Give me a drink.[11]

The barman tried to cheer him up, but Chamberlin waved him away. 'I don't care. I lived like a prince, like a crazy guy, like I wanted! But I'm a good sportsman. The time of holding four aces in my hand is over.' By the time he got up to leave, he was staggering drunk. He ignored all the advice and slaps on the back: 'I bet on a bad horse. I lost.'[12]

As he stumbled out of the bar someone else tried to console him by calling him 'Henri' in a familiar tone. He spun around and shouted that it was '*Monsieur Henri, Capitaine Henri*', and smashed a glass on the floor. A long silence followed, then he gave a nervous laugh and tottered out of the door and into the blacked-out street. The next day, a hungover Chamberlin instructed Bonny to find a small property hidden away somewhere outside Paris where the two could retreat if the Allies got close. Bonny borrowed a Jaguar from the rue Lauriston garage and loaded it up with his son and a corpulent former police colleague who had stayed loyal to him down the years. They drove off to check some farmhouses.

The trio got as far as a country road about sixty miles south-west of the capital. A resistance group had blocked the road to check the identity papers of anyone travelling south. As Bonny brought the car to a stop, the roadside was suddenly full of unshaven men in berets brandishing machine guns. For the trip, Bonny was posing as a butcher from Avranches and had adopted the pseudonym of Debouche. He handed over a fake identity card and some cigarettes and told the men with guns that he was simply looking to buy a place for his family away from the fighting.

The men studied the card, looked at Bonny's face, looked back at the card and then offered up some useful information about real estate prices in the area. Bonny drove on through the checkpoint, but his hands shook so badly that he turned the Jaguar around and drove back to Paris. A few days later a letter arrived from his former police colleague, who had continued the property search alone. He had located a farm for sale near Bazoches-sur-le-Betz. Bonny told his family to pack their bags and be prepared to leave at a moment's notice.

17

LA TOUR DE BABEL

THEY SHOT PHILIPPE HENRIOT dead in a corridor outside his apartment. The propagandist looked like a silent film comedian, but beneath his smirk and black moustache was a devout Roman Catholic who gave up poetry to dedicate his life to hard-right nationalism. Before the war, Henriot shouted down leftists in the French Parliament and was one of those journalists who roasted Pierre Bonny in newspaper columns during the Stavisky scandal. Vichy gave him the post of Secretary of State for Information and Propaganda.

After his assassination huge posters went up on street corners across France with Henriot's face looming over painted waves of blue, white and red. 'He spoke the truth,' read the text. 'They killed him!'

Henriot made daily lunchtime broadcasts from Paris that savaged the regime's enemies with a corrosive commentary. The whole country would stop work to tune in and listen, but on Friday 28 June 1944, Pierre Laval took the microphone instead. 'You have tuned in, as you do every day, to hear the voice of Philippe Henriot,' he said. 'You will not hear him. Philippe Henriot was murdered this morning at the Ministry of Information.'[1]

A resistance group disguised as Milice paramilitaries had marched into the Ministry of Information office on rue de Solférino, where Henriot kept a secure apartment. The group planned to kidnap the politician and transport him to London for a trial. Henriot and his wife were persuaded to leave their apartment with talk about an emergency, but the plan went wrong almost immediately. A suspicious Henriot started asking questions for which his abductors had no good answers and the sub-machine guns opened up. The 55-year-old broadcaster died and his wife was wounded.

Vichy held a public funeral that was full of flowers and tricolore ribbons at Notre-Dame Cathedral. Parisian bureaucrats named a boulevard in the city after him and in the newspapers Jean Luchaire mourned the country's loss and urged a more hardline collaboration with Germany. The Milice put up a reward of 20 million francs for information on the assassination. There wasn't much left to spend it on in Paris. As the war ground on, some locals had resorted to eating millet and hemp seeds from the bird stalls on the banks of the Seine. Ernst Jünger noted that French women spent their last clothing coupons on tall hats. 'This is the couture of the Tower of Babel,' he wrote in his journal.[2]

The Place des Invalides was cordoned off around a camp of anti-aircraft guns and nervy-looking German troops. The Commander of Greater Paris, General Dietrich von Choltitz, had orders to destroy the capital before the Allies could take it and dynamite was packed under every monument across the city. The general wasn't sure he would be able to take that decision when the time came.

Others in the Wehrmacht felt even less loyalty to the government in Berlin. Men at the Hôtel Majestic talked obliquely about removing the Führer in vague conversations filled with historical allusions and talk about honour and oaths. Small groups in feldgrau strolled the hotel corridors muttering about the Eastern Front and camps in occupied Poland and what would happen when the war was over. 'One day,' said one officer called Ravenstein, 'my daughter will pay for all this in a brothel for n*****s.'[3]

They tried to involve Ernst Jünger in their complaints, but the writer cared only about his son who had been arrested for criticising the Führer. During the last days of occupation in Paris, he spent the time calling anyone in Berlin who could help.

Resistance attacks and Gestapo counterstrikes continued in the streets of the French capital and people disappeared every day. It became a common sight for the concierge to force open the door to an empty apartment and find two chairs close together in the hallway with German cigarette butts left on the tiled floor by the interrogators.[4] Family and friends queued daily at avenue Foch to beg for information about their loved ones.

The queues got longer after a group of Wehrmacht officers finally took action against Hitler. On 20 July, a badly wounded aristocratic Wehrmacht veteran with one eye and only a few fingers remaining on both hands slid a briefcase under the table of a hut in East Prussia before quietly walking away. Adolf Hitler and his generals were still discussing the war situation when the bomb went off. Oberstleutnant Claus von Stauffenberg headed for Berlin to start a coup, convinced that everyone in the room had been killed.

The bomb plot failed. Hitler survived the bomb blast and the Wehrmacht officers who had taken control of Berlin and Paris and other cities across Europe were arrested that evening. In France, Höherer SS-und Polizeiführer Carl Oberg rounded up the families of those involved in the bomb plot, their friends and anyone remotely suspicious. Countess Mara Tchernichev-Bezobrazov and former lover Hans Leimer were two of the many who found themselves in prison.

Tchernichev-Bezobrazov had quit her opium addiction and returned to Paris earlier in the year to work for Joseph Joinovici. She was arranging raw material sales to the Germans when the men in leather overcoats marched her away for questioning. They wanted to know about her earlier Spanish trip. At the same time, Leimer was scooped up from his post outside Paris for interrogation before being sent to fight in the hell storm of the Eastern Front. Tchernichev-Bezobrazov found herself in the women's wing of Fresnes prison desperately looking for a way to contact her former lover Henri Chamberlin.

Knowing someone with political influence was the only way to get out of prison. Those who didn't have the right connections sat despairingly in their cells while relatives queued at avenue Foch to plead their case. A woman with green eyes, high cheekbones and a bun of dark hair spent a lot of time standing in line that summer. Marguerite Donnadieu was a baby-faced thirty-year-old who had been born to French teachers working near Saigon in French Indochina. In early June 1944, she spent her days working as a Vichy civil servant and her evenings plotting with a Communist resistance group led by fellow bureaucrat François Mitterrand. Any spare time that she had went towards writing novels under the name Marguerite Duras.

One day, the Germans raided her Saint-Germain des Près apartment and dragged her husband away. Donnadieu visited avenue Foch every day with all the other desperate wives and mothers.

A tall 43-year-old man with sleek dark-blond hair and blue eyes behind tortoiseshell glasses said he could help. Charles Delval was a Frenchman working for the Gestapo. The self-employed art appraiser had been arrested for running a private pawnshop and then denounced as a Gaullist. Delval convinced the Germans that he had been falsely accused. 'There always comes a moment when you must choose and decide,' he said. 'I opt for Germany, from love of order and discipline, and also for idealism. I don't want to stand there with folded arms, neutral and passive, doing nothing, not taking part.'[5]

Delval took Donnadieu aside and offered to treat her to a meal at a restaurant that was reserved for Germans and collaborators. She agreed and more meetings followed. Donnadieu convinced herself that she was befriending a German agent in order to help her husband, while Delval's wife thought that he was simply buying meals for a hungry young intellectual. Donnadieu's resistance group friends suspected she was having an affair and Mitterrand decided to have the pair watched.

Fate would entangle Delval with the rue Lauriston gang. There were already rumours that he had worked with them in late 1943 advising on the value of artwork they came across in their looting sprees. Crooks claimed to have seen him wandering rue Lauriston like a lamb among gangster lions, carrying a copy of Paul Valéry's *Monsieur Teste* under his arm, a challenging novel about a superhuman intellectual who abandons conventional society to dive into the mysteries of the human mind. Delval denied ever visiting the Carlingue headquarters but proudly admitted to working for the Germans at avenue Foch.

It was a bad time to be boasting about collaboration. On Bastille Day in 1944, Parisians celebrated by draping blue, white and red clothes on their balconies. Women wore the colours of the tricolore in the streets and workmen placed blue, white and red pencils together in their shirt pockets. The Germans pretended not to notice.

As Nazi Paris crumbled around them, Delval tried to persuade Donnadieu to sleep with him in exchange for her husband's freedom. She gave him letters and presents to pass on to her husband, but he kept them for himself. Delval never asked for money, although he did take 400,000 francs from another woman in exchange for releasing her husband from prison. Instead, he asked Donnadieu to give up Mitterrand in exchange for her husband's freedom. She refused.

They saw each other for the last time at a black market restaurant in the hot middle days of August 1944. Outside in the street, he suggested spending the afternoon together at a friend's empty studio. Donnadieu refused and walked away.

'I almost crossed the Rubicon that day,' she said later.[6]

As Donnadieu fought off the arms of the Gestapo, Tchernichev-Bezobrazov finally managed to get a message through to her friend Henri Chamberlin. On 13 August 1944, she was allowed out of prison with a German escort to collect some of her belongings before being transported to Berlin for trial. At the château, she managed to tell her chauffeur to contact Chamberlin.

The chauffeur drove down to 93 rue Lauriston. It was empty.

• • •

The last time anyone saw Henri Chamberlin in public had been two months earlier in June 1944. He spent most of the month after his military failure at Tulle slumped at nightclub tables, drinking and complaining about the people who had once flocked to him but now wouldn't answer his calls. 'I'm tired,' Chamberlin muttered in Le Chapiteau. 'Tired and sickened by the cowardice of people, their ingratitude, their pettiness.'[7]

Jeannot Rossi nodded sympathetically and tried not to show his nervousness. Rossi had recently arranged the execution of Cizeron Étienne, known to all as 'Cheucheu le Stéphanois' and a close friend of Jean-Michel Chaves. Étienne and Chaves had come up with a drunken plan to shoot performer Yves Montand for singing some of his act in English. Rossi organised the murder of Étienne to save his star singer but had lived in fear that Monsieur Henri might find out ever since.

Chamberlin either didn't know or he didn't care. He had aged decades in a matter of months; his well-groomed and suave appearance had crumbled. He muttered drunkenly about having lived three lives: as an orphan, as a criminal and as a power player in occupied Paris. He was forty-two years old and could see the end coming.

A few weeks earlier, Chamberlin had received orders to send men from the Brigade Nord-Africaine to Limoges for a fresh operation. Clavié's section got the job, walked into the buzzsaw of a resistance ambush and returned a week later carrying their dead. When the Germans requested another forty men, Chamberlin dispatched a group of North Africans but refused to send any of his gang members; a German officer had to take command.

Chamberlin took to wandering around Paris, drinking heavily and melancholic. He dropped into the gang's old haunts and constantly talked about the end. He didn't share the delusions of men such as Robert Brasillach, Joseph Darnand or Pierre Drieu la Rochelle, who were expecting the arrival of German miracle weapons and ultimate victory. Chamberlin was not surprised when the Allied tanks broke through Germans lines in July 1944 and headed for Paris.

Nervous-looking Wehrmacht soldiers began searching people coming out of Paris Métro stations, patting down the men for weapons and checking women's identity cards. The phone stopped ringing in the rue Lauriston office and the orchids wilted in their vases.

Chamberlin ordered the discreet dismantling of the Carlingue. Bonny wanted to hold on to the intelligence files, seeing potential bargaining power in all those typed and cross-referenced pages. But Chamberlin had no interest in post-war leverage. 'You're not going to start your machinations and rubbish all over again,' he said.[8]

Bonny burned the files in the garden of rue Lauriston. A few documents were kept, weeded of anything incriminating and added to an archive that avenue Foch was shipping out to Stuttgart. Then Bonny called in the rue Lauriston regulars. North Africans from the Brigade Nord-Africaine received a substantial advance on their wages and were immediately released from service. The gang members received larger payoffs. Bonny destroyed their documentation and handed over blank identity cards and envelopes full of cash. The Carlingue was finished.

Longstanding member Auguste Ricord suggested they all leave Paris. He had already reserved a place in a Wehrmacht convoy. 'The Yanks will arrive and the terrorists will hold the whip hand,' he said. 'Then, fuck that, we will be shot. It's fucking obvious! Guys, I do not see this as good for us. We must get away quickly before it's too late.'[9]

Abel Danos listened to the advice. He hid his mistress Hélène in Paris then left for Montreuil in northern France with his girlfriend Simone. The gold traffickers Jean Sartore and Robert Gourari preferred to con their way into the Marco Polo resistance network along with Charles Cazauba, whose hands now quivered worse than ever. The trio proved their loyalty by murdering a married couple in a murky affair that was organised and then immediately denied by the Marco Polo leadership. Cazauba disappeared somewhere in Clichy soon after and it was assumed that resistance colleagues had recognised and shot him. Brigade Nord-Africaine leader Paul Maillebuau met a similar fate in Franche-Comté; lured out to a wood with three of his RNP men and executed by the resistance. He thought that he was changing sides.

The rest of the gang chose to burrow beneath the skin of the city and trust to underworld friends, fake identity cards and attic rooms with bad wallpaper. Raymond Monange and the last remains of the Brigade Nord-Africaine joined them. In Périgueux, Monange had written to the local German commander claiming that his group was demoralised and couldn't be trusted in action any longer. The commander believed him and sent the unit to join the defence of Paris. Once back in the capital, Monange and the others threw away their uniforms and disappeared underground.

A few Carlingue veterans went for one last score. Paul Clavié had met Anne-Marguerite Garnier in a bar near rue Lauriston. She was a prostitute with an apartment on the Champs-Élysées and a morphine addiction. It was getting harder to make money on the streets. Legions of amateurs were driving down prices.

'Ah! Sluts,' said a disgusted professional. 'You have no idea.'

'But don't you do the same thing?' asked someone.

'Excuse me, greenhorn. That's my career. They're just sluts.'[10]

Garnier knew an elderly retired actress named Madame Deryeux who lived with her nurse in a nearby apartment. The place had a wall safe. Garnier suggested Clavié rob the place and give her a percentage.

In the early evening of 3 August, a car rolled up to the apartment with Clavié, Haré, Engel and a crook called Bernard at the wheel. Garnier introduced Clavié as a friend and then left. His oily smile quickly disappeared as the rest of the team came in through the unlocked door. They tortured the old woman and her nurse for the safe combination with hot coals and a knife until the evening of the next day. The two women died before the safe could be opened;

Clavié and the others scattered their dismembered body parts around a forest outside Paris. As they returned to the city, they saw that German troops had taken up defensive positions around the Hôtel Majestic.

Meanwhile, Alexandre Villaplana was busy running faux policier scams out of a bar on rue Coquillère with his former theatre director friend Alex Bowing. The pair squeezed $900 and a gold ring out of an Armenian teacher and promised to return for the rest of the man's valuables. 'What we're up to isn't good,' said Bowing, 'but we'll be fucking done by next week. I'm going to Germany.'[11] He didn't get the chance. On Tuesday 15 August 1944, the Paris police went on strike and the next day collaborationist journalists and newsmen left the city early in the morning. Resistance supporters took over their offices. Vichy radio propaganda shut down and German snipers took to the roofs of Paris.

A man outside a Métro station sold tricolore rosettes from an upside-down umbrella as Allied artillery pounded in the distance. The *drapeau tricolore* was hoisted aloft outside the Jardin de Plantes, while convoys of Wehrmacht men left the city. French crowds rushed every building abandoned by the Germans to strip it for food and coal. Communist posters were plastered on walls across the city.

The insurrection began on Saturday 19 August when the resistance came out of the shadows to attack columns of retreating Germans. Bodies lay piled thick in some districts, while the atmosphere was quietly normal in others. People sunbathed on the banks of the Seine as German tanks fired shells into buildings just a few streets away. Radio bulletins faded in and out with the failing electricity supply. By the time a French armoured division led by General Philippe Leclerc fought its way into the city at the end of the week, fake identity cards for the resistance group Forces Françaises de L'Intérieur could be bought for 10,000 francs. 'Heroes have multiplied,' wrote the journalist Jean Galtier-Boissière. 'The number of last-minute resisters, armed head to foot, wearing ammunition belts in the style of Mexicans, is considerable. Some heroines too, revolvers in their belts.'[12]

The next day, General Dietrich von Choltitz disobeyed orders to burn Paris and surrendered the city to the Allies. An SS garrison at the Palais du Luxembourg held out to the last before finally surrendering. Paris was in French hands again; at least 1,500 people had died in the fighting.

Shortly after, on 25 August, Charles de Gaulle arrived to unify his homeland and shut out the Communists who hoped to claim power. He gave a speech from the Hôtel de Ville as diehard collaborators took pot-shots from the rooftops: 'Paris! Paris outraged! Paris broken! Paris martyred! But Paris liberated! Liberated by itself, liberated by its people with the help of the French armies, with the support and the help of all France, of the France that fights, of only France, of the real France, of the eternal France!'[13]

Leclerc's soldiers kicked down the doors of 93 rue Lauriston to find an empty building, with the ashy remains of a bonfire in the walled garden out back and the graffiti of names and dates scratched into the cellar walls. Chamberlin and Bonny had vanished, along with every other collaborator who feared for their life.

PART IV

FROM THE SS TO THE FIRING SQUAD

18

DAS SCHLOSS

THE MAN ARRIVED AT the town beneath the castle with a false name, a young wife and a tiger-striped cat. The identity card from the Paris police described him as being a sales representative named Louis François Deletang, with brown hair, blue eyes, 1.79 metres tall. It was a good fake identity card with a stamp from a real policeman at the prefecture, but the photograph fixed to the yellow card was familiar to anyone who followed the French literary scene. That fox-thin face, widow's peak of hair, a scrub of beard on the chin and sour expression. The man in the photograph was Louis-Ferdinand Céline and he was on the run.

Everyone in France knew Céline. Before the war he'd been the famous author of *Voyage au Bout de la Nuit* (*Journey to the End of the Night*) and *Mort à Credit* (*Death on Credit*), avalanches of cynical filth about desperate lives and their messy physicality. Back then, most novelists stopped at the doors of the bedroom and the outhouse, but Céline barged in and took notes.

Away from the typewriter Louis-Ferdinand Céline had a third identity under his real name of Louis Ferdinand Auguste Destouches, a veteran of the First World War and a doctor who worked in a dispensary for the Paris poor. All those years treating weeping sores and pus-packed abscesses had filled Destouches with contempt for anyone who claimed that life could be beautiful.

Many on the left loved Destouches until he started writing racist tirades that blamed Jews, Africans and Freemasons for everything that was rotten about France. Then the right started buying his books.

> Our French Republic is no more than a great gullet swallowing the negroising of the French at the command of the Jews. Our governors are a clique of sadistic yids and yellow-bellied masons sworn to swallow us up, to bastardise us further, to boil us down by all the grotesque, primitive means of inter-mixture, part negro, part yellow, part white, part red, part monkey, part Jewish, part everything.[1]

When the German war machine punched through French lines in the summer of 1940, Destouches was running an ambulance with his third wife Lucette Almanzor, a dancer half his age. They fled towards the coast in grinding columns of traffic, bandaging up wounded soldiers and dodging air strikes on the way. In June, the Germans entered Paris and the war was over for France; Destouches returned to his dispensary in the north-western suburb of the city.

He kept writing during the German occupation. He published novels such as *Guignol's Band*, political pamphlets like *Les Beaux Draps* (*A Nice Mess*) and letters to newspaper editors calling for the extermination of the Jewish people. In his journal, Ernst Jünger described Destouches as giving 'the impression of a maniac who cannot really be made responsible for his declarations'.[2]

Destouches thought he was the only sane man in Paris. Few

agreed with this diagnosis, not even the diehard fascist collaborators in the capital or the self-professed patriots of the government at Vichy. They preferred to put their faith in the scientific anti-Semites from Berlin who seemed to be winning the war.

Jünger and the German forces had a few years of triumphant victory before their empire fell apart. To the east, the invasion of the Soviet Union ultimately failed in ice storms and waist-high snow. When Jünger got to his office at the Hôtel Majestic on the morning that Allied troops landed on the French coast, he found panic and ringing telephones. General Erwin Rommel, overseer of Western defences, was back in Germany for his wife's birthday and no one knew what orders to give as chaotic fighting raged on the beaches of Normandy. Jünger felt defeat like a stone in his stomach and hoped that Paris would survive the battle of liberation: 'What a marvel it would be', he wrote, 'if she, like an ark laden to the brim with a rich old cargo, were to reach the port of peace after this deluge, and were to remain to us for future centuries.'[3]

French men and women who had been too friendly with the Nazis cared more about saving themselves than the city around them. Everybody seemed to know a collaborator who'd been murdered by the resistance. Dr Destouches received three tiny wooden coffins at his Montmartre apartment high above the grey roofs of Paris. Later he heard someone sentence him to death on a radio station broadcasting out of London.

The German authorities provided Destouches with a pistol and a firearm permit, but within days of the Allied landing he procured a fake pair of husband and wife identity cards from a policeman friend. He and his wife started packing.

When the fighting pushed inland, they walked to the Gare de l'Est with a retinue of suitcases and their cat Bébert curled up in a basket. Their train rolled out towards Germany. Destouches was aiming to reach Denmark where he'd stashed pre-war royalties from *Voyage au Bout de la Nuit*. He got as far as a small German town in the state of Baden-Württemberg, which had become home to an exile French community full of desperation and backstabbing.

A torrent of French citizens with suitcases and knapsacks had gone rushing for their lives into the Reich when the Allies approached. The remains of France's Vichy government washed up in the medieval town of Sigmaringen on the Danube, joined by every collaborator, fascist and vocal anti-Semite who'd cheered them on during the Nazi occupation. They packed out hostels, rented every spare room and filled the sports halls with sleeping cots. Part of the local monastery was turned into a maternity ward for women who had become pregnant by German soldiers.

• • •

The schloss dominated the town, a castle of white stone and red roofs overlooking the river from its perch on a green-veined cliff. The 88-year-old Marshal Philippe Pétain lived on the castle's upper floor and claimed to be a prisoner of war. The old soldier had kept his position through four years of collaboration and changing fortunes until the former Gestapo chief Karl Bömelburg evacuated Vichy at gunpoint in August 1944 as the Allies approached. In Sigmaringen, the marshal finally abandoned collaboration and spent his days talking to his wife and staring out of the window.

Pétain's dishevelled former Chief of Government Pierre Laval was on another floor of the castle, also refusing to serve the Germans for reasons of his own. Former ministers who were less scrupulous formed a government in exile on the castle's lower levels. Another

2,000 Vichyites and collaborators lived in the surrounding town as they fought among themselves and tried to believe that the Third Reich might still win the war.

Fascist leader Jacques Doriot had already split to form a rival exile centre forty miles away at Mainau island. Doriot had been an ardent Communist until he fell out with Moscow back in the mid-1930s and then formed the far-right Parti Populaire Français. Now he was at the heart of last-ditch collaborationist plans to parachute fascist guerrillas behind Allied lines.

The Germans needed all the manpower they could get. In Sigmaringen, paramilitaries with flopping black berets from Vichy's Milice were sent away to join the French Charlemagne division of the Waffen-SS in an apocalyptic battle to save the Reich. Those who enlisted understood that they were marching to their deaths.

Even among the chaos and plotting, Destouches's arrival in the town in late October 1944 caused excitement. He was still one of France's best-known authors, with a reputation for scabrous invective and crazed anger. Everyone was disappointed to find a quiet, depressed man who cared only about his wife and cat. Destouches found a billet and went to work as a doctor for the French colony in the town; he refused to get involved in politics beyond predicting Germany would lose the war.

Many in his host nation secretly agreed, including Ernst Jünger, who'd escaped the fall of Paris and now led a Volkssturm home guard unit in the small town of Kirchhorst. His eldest son had been killed in Italy, but Jünger would not receive the news until the following year. He spent his time reading books about shipwrecks while waiting for the Reich's inevitable defeat.

Not everyone thought that the war was lost. In Sigmaringen, Jean Luchaire had been promoted to the exile government's Minister of

Information. As part of his propaganda campaign, Luchaire tried to talk Destouches into picking up a pen for the German cause. The pair knew each other from the days when the doctor used to write angry letters complaining that Luchaire's papers weren't anti-Semitic enough. Later Destouches applauded Luchaire's turn towards '*résolutions racistes*' but called for more extreme measures. He sent furious rants to the French press:

> Count on me to put Jews, Jesuits, Freemasons, synarchists, parish priests, the English, Protestants, the lukewarm, soft, vague anti-Semites in the same boat and sink it in the waters of Nantes! All these people, for me, cling to this rotten civilization – and must disappear. We need racism for a few centuries at least.[4]

Luchaire wanted Destouches to write for his four-franc daily newspaper, *La France*. The paper paid well but the doctor wasn't interested. Soviet troops in eastern Poland had liberated the first concentration camps and their newsreels were showing the rest of the world what racist resolutions could look like. Destouches remained depressed and awaited the coming apocalypse.

As Christmas 1944 approached, the doctor's pessimism seemed to be premature when German tank columns punched through Allied lines in the Ardennes forests and pushed on towards the coast. Adolf Hitler's generals had plans to encircle the Americans and British, cut off the essential ports and force a peace treaty in the West.

Luchaire splashed the news about the winter offensive through *La France* and the radio station Ici la France, the dregs of his once huge propaganda machine. The German offensive through the Ardennes seemed to be a gift from God. The exiled government made excited broadcasts and held endless meetings about possible futures. Some believed that they might get back to Vichy, maybe even Paris.

During the day, the exiles read triumphant German news reports about Panzer tanks and dead Americans. At night, they huddled around the wireless to listen to the forbidden Allied stations broadcasting out of liberated France. The announcers talked about the trials and executions of collaborators: Frenchmen who joined the Gestapo to torture and murder members of the resistance; criminals who got rich during the occupation doing dirty work for the enemy; Milice members who shot hostages in town squares. Journalist and collaborator Georges Suarez was the first to be executed. It took an incompetent firing squad three volleys to kill the journalist at Fort de Montrouge in Paris one November morning.

The trials of collaborators were part of a push by de Gaulle's new government to establish authority and to put an end to the vigilante justice that had killed approximately 10,000 people. Resistance groups, outraged patriots and anyone with a grudge came knocking at doors in the middle of the night to get their revenge. Across the country bodies lay in ditches by the roadside or were left to rot in obscure fields, executed to even the score for the 90,000 French who had died in the resistance or in front of the German firing squads.

French women who had slept with Germans were paraded in public, stripped naked and had their heads shaved. A prostitute in the eighteenth arrondissement was kicked to death in the street. Girls from the One-Two-Two were dragged out of the brothel and marched through Paris to be spat on by crowds. Similar acts of public shaming happened everywhere across France.

The film director Louis Malle remembered events in his own town: 'I also have a very keen memory of the liberation of Montceau-les-Mines, the marches, the red flags, the settling of scores, the girls accused of having slept with the Germans, walked around naked, with shaven heads and notices on their stomachs – "I am a bitch of the SS."'[5]

The women in the monastery maternity ward in Sigmaringen heard about these events and shivered. They prayed for the success of the German offensive through the Ardennes.

Luchaire also prayed. Through the first half of December 1944, he had heard some familiar names on the radio. Twelve men from the rue Lauriston gang were in a Paris courtroom and were facing the death penalty. Lawyers for the prosecution talked about murder, money, collaboration, torture, gambling dens, bribery, beautiful women, Jews freed from prison for money, suitcases of gold coins, protection rackets, theft and extravagant dinners in rue Lauriston with celebrities like the singer Maurice Chevalier. The newspapers in France called it the trial of the century.

The Vichyites who were listening on the radio in Sigmaringen could pretend they didn't know the people from rue Lauriston. Black marketeering and gangland shootings hadn't been a part of their war. Pétain's ministers had sat around an elegant spa town talking about the rebirth of conservative France and the necessary compromises to be made with Germany. Their motto was '*Travail, famille, patrie*' ('Work, family, fatherland'); the depravity of occupied Paris had seemed very far away.

But not for everyone in Sigmaringen. Laval and Luchaire knew the gang well, as did Karl Bömelburg of the Gestapo, who was running security in the town but thinking of his chicken farm near Giverny. Ernst Jünger had often visited his novelist friend Banine in rue Lauriston, where the gang stored stolen goods on the ground floor of her apartment block. Even Destouches had been accused of contact with the Carlingue, through his dancer wife Lucette. Chamberlin's tentacles had slithered in through every open window across Paris.

The French in Sigmaringen wondered if the rue Lauriston gang would escape the firing squad. Perhaps a last-minute deal, a sudden confession or the German assault through the Ardennes would change things. If not, their fate would be the same as every other collaborator. After what had been done during the occupation, how could they expect mercy?

19

PICKING MUSHROOMS

ON 30 AUGUST 1944, the police moved in and surrounded the farm at Bazoches-sur-le-Betz. An officer disguised as a tramp had scouted out the property earlier in the day and reported that it consisted of a farmhouse and a retinue of crumbling outbuildings among the overgrown fields. It was populated by two men, two women, a teenager and two children.

The farm had been purchased a few months previously. One of the new owners was a man who drank in the village café and claimed to be a refugee from the fighting up north. He was tall and spoke with a high voice. When the police charged through the farmhouse door, they found him in shirtsleeves repairing a chair.

'Lafont, I'm arresting you!' shouted an inspector.

The other man in the building had a black moustache and slicked-back hair. He calmly held out his hand. 'Do you have a search warrant?' he asked. The inspector jabbed at him with a sub-machine gun: 'Here's my warrant,' he sneered.[1]

The police search of the property uncovered 3 million francs, handfuls of jewellery, firearm certificates, some resistance documents and German passports in the names of Pierre Bonny and Henri Chamberlin. It was all over for the leaders of the Carlingue.

The village of Bazoches-sur-le-Betz was a settlement of chirping trees, squirrels, country lanes and church spires piercing the sky in the distance, all of it just south-east of Paris. Chamberlin and Bonny arrived at their newly purchased farm towards the end of July 1944. Bonny's Jaguar contained his wife, teenage son and their dog named Jules Patrick II. Chamberlin drove his two children and their governess Anne-Marie Jeanne Douflos in his white Bentley. The group planned to head down to the Spanish border if the Nazis lost France.

After arriving, they hid their cars and employed a woman from the village to cook and clean. For a month all was tranquil.

Early one morning in the opening days of the Paris insurrection, an unshaven gang of resistance fighters appeared at the door of the farmhouse. Someone had told them about the vehicles hidden away in the outbuildings. Chamberlin turned on his smile and invited the group inside. Glasses of wine were filled and refilled as he charmed his guests into believing that the cars had only dropped them off at the farm before driving on elsewhere. Everyone shook hands as the men filed out. When they had left, Bonny buried some money and gold coins at the base of a tree.

At 5 p.m. on the same day, another group from the resistance appeared at the door. The chief member climbed the creaking stairs to a first-floor room where Chamberlin sat smiling in a chair with his hand under a cushion holding a pistol. 'You hid your cars well,' stated the chief, 'but we are obliged to requisition them.'

Chamberlin attempted to bargain the man down to taking one car, but he got nowhere and their last resort of escaping over the Spanish border disappeared. 'You're still bastards,' said Chamberlin with a laugh. 'You take everything from us, like the others! Oh well, since it is for France, I give it to you willingly.'

'You know,' replied the chief, 'you are entitled to a receipt and they will be returned or you will be compensated after the war.'

'I should hope so,' said Chamberlin, still laughing.[2]

When the mob had left, Chamberlin and Bonny spent the night discussing other options. The next day Bonny's son set off on his bicycle to Paris with instructions to contact Joinovici and request two fresh cars. Chamberlin knew the risks of giving away his location to Monsieur Joseph, but he could see no other option. 'Difficult to do anything else,' he said. 'But I'm confident. He's smart; he's always been straight with me.'[3]

Jacques Bonny cycled all day and survived being shot at from the air by an Allied fighter plane and then being stopped by suspicious German soldiers and a resistance roadblock. Night had fallen by the time he reached the capital and he could hear gunfire in the streets. A good friend provided the teenager with a bed and the next morning he headed off to Joinovici's seventeenth-arrondissement apartment in rue du Dobropol.

When he arrived, he found the flat had become an open house for resistance fighters. Everybody was wearing armbands and carrying pistols and Sten guns. Jacques Bonny wandered through the rooms until a shocked Joinovici pulled him aside. 'What are you doing here? What do you want?' he demanded.

Jacques explained about the cars. Joinovici took down the farm address and told him not to worry. When the boy returned to Bazoches-sur-le-Betz, Chamberlin and Bonny were disturbed to hear about the scene at Joinovici's apartment and decided to move fast. Jacques was sent off to the nearby town of Sens to contact a car thief that his father had known back in the police days.

The man provided two vehicles and he and Jacques drove one each towards the farm. The cars pulled up on the outskirts of Bazoches-sur-le-Betz and Jacques rode a rutted track on his bicycle the rest of the way.

As he rounded a corner near the farm a man jumped out of nowhere and asked him what he was doing. 'Mushroom picking,' responded Jacques.[4] The man punched the teenager to the ground and dragged him into the farmhouse by his hair. Inside the dog was lying dead in a pool of blood. Jacques was beaten by members of the resistance, who told him that his parents were dead and then began arguing among themselves over where to execute him. The police returned to the farm as Jacques was being pushed up against an outside wall and took custody of the boy.

'You came very close,' shouted the resistance leader as Bonny's son was led away to a police car.[5]

In a Paris prison, he was beaten and interrogated again, but could divulge little new information. At one point he saw his mother framed in the window of her cell like the queen of hearts on a playing card.

His father was also being questioned nearby. The inspector's former colleagues pretended that they didn't recognise the once-famous Pierre Bonny as guards led him down a corridor to the office of Inspector Georges Clot, who headed the anti-Gestapo section and was building a case against rue Lauriston. When the door to the office closed, Bonny told him everything. The note-taker could barely keep up with the avalanche of words that cascaded from the Carlingue second in command. Bonny talked about the Abwehr spying, the mission to Algiers, black marketeering, the Kellner arrests, the Tissier murder, the Duke of Ayen affair, the theft of the American embassy silverware, the Gestapo arrests and the Brigade Nord-Africaine. The Bonny-Lafont gang story was threaded together like pearls on a necklace.

Chamberlin said nothing and endured three days of beatings, but then started to talk. He took responsibility for the crimes that had been described by Bonny, but denied murdering his ex-con friend Tissier, whose body had never been found. When questions about Joinovici came up, Chamberlin pretended that the scrap metal magnate had always worked for the Allies in an attempt to protect the man that he could not believe had turned traitor.[6]

During a break in the interrogations, Chamberlin tried to commit suicide by hanging himself in his cell, but the guards cut him down just in time. Across Paris, the other members of the Carlingue were being rounded up.

• • •

The drug addicts of Paris knew Inspector Louis Métra as 'Loulou'. He had worked the vice beat for twenty years and arrested every junkie and back alley dealer in the city. Before the war, Métra's biggest score was taking down a major smuggling operation that imported opium from Turkey into France on the Orient Express and somehow involved the Chief Rabbi of Brooklyn.

Short, fat-bellied and mild-mannered, Métra spent the Second World War juggling police work with his secret life as a member of the resistance. When the capital rose up against the Germans in the summer of 1944, he stalked the streets hunting down Carlingue members. On 24 August he picked up Alexandre Villaplana and Alex Bowing, who were carrying guns and fake police identity cards. The pair refused to talk, but Métra got a break when he discovered Sylviane Quimfe at her hairdresser's the next day.

Pagnon and Quimfe had reached out to Lionel de Wiet for help in the aftermath of their escape from Berger and his rue de la Pompe gang. The fake baron offered them a house in Barbizon, a small town near the Fontainebleau forest, and the couple hid out before returning to Paris and staying with some aristocratic friends. One day Quimfe ventured out to get her hair done and was arrested.

As Quimfe was sitting in a prison cell, someone with a posh voice who claimed to be a friend telephoned the police and offered to give up Pagnon if she could go free. Métra took the deal. Pagnon soon cracked and spent eight hours taking the police around every gang hangout, apartment and front business in the city. Paris was still smoke-stained from the fighting and the streets were full of Allied soldiers, journalists, counterintelligence officers and the munitions specialists who were carefully defusing German boobytraps hidden in piles of horse dung. American war correspondents took over the Hôtel Scribe; Ernest Hemingway had come to town and was staying at the Ritz. Edith Piaf sang for French officers at Ciro's, a sixteenth-arrondissement restaurant, while British and American soldiers ate for free at the Tour d'Argent.

Some crooks took advantage of the chaos. The faux policier scams returned as former collaborators flashed Allied identity cards and accused the innocent of working for Nazi Germany. The black market proliferated. 'Chocolate? Tobacco? Gauloises? English cigarettes?' called men from the shadows of the Strasbourg – Saint-Denis Métro station.[7]

Inspector Métra used Pagnon's information to cast his net across the city. Twenty-two people were arrested inside a fortnight. Paul Clavié was picked up organising a plan to free Chamberlin; he showed no remorse for his actions. 'My uncle and Bonny,' he said, 'are the kind who deserve freedom.'[8]

Jacques Labussière was picked up on 4 September and the police found André Engel six days later. Edmond Delehaye was arrested on 9 September, released in error and then picked up again three days later. Louis Haré was arrested a week afterwards as he lay wounded in a hospital bed after helping liberate the city from the Germans. Police arrested Jean-Michel Chaves the same day. Small-time gang members were dragged out of bars and apartments, their pockets full of cash and fake identity cards and scraps of paper with incriminating phone numbers.

The police raided Tchernichev-Bezobrazov's château and found a Brazilian passport in the name of Mary Garat, a collection of opium pipes and a cigarette lighter in yellow metal engraved with an inscription that read '*Pour ma petite femme chérie – Henri*'.[9]

The would-be intellectual Charles Delval landed in a cell on 14 September 1944 after resistance fighters raided his apartment on a tip from a neighbour. He fell into the hands of Marguerite Donnadieu and her resistance colleagues. Donnadieu took special pleasure in treating Delval's wife badly. 'You don't have the right to a bed,' Donnadieu told her. 'You sleep on the ground.'[10]

Lionel de Wiet was arrested in early September. Police found him in an expensive Paris apartment with a gang of men standing around a table piled with sub-machine guns and fake resistance identity cards. 'The robber-baron Lionel de Wiet, administrator of the *Les Nouveaux Temps*, friend of Lafont–Luchaire–Prade, is behind bars,' said *Ce Soir*.[11]

By the middle of September 1944, forty-three people connected to the gang had been arrested, most of them given up by Pagnon. Inspectors threw the chauffeur in prison and reneged on whatever deal they'd done with Sylviane Quimfe. She was re-arrested and charged with espionage and theft.

Quimfe initially insisted that she was a spy for the Deuxième Bureau, but soon broke down and confessed that it was all lies. She eventually found peace in religion. The prison chaplain agreed to help her communicate with Pagnon and she wrote heartfelt notes every day: 'I would like you to see the chaplain for confession and communion, which would bring me great joy, and put you right before God, which we both need … Try to behave as though you were free. Again, a thousand caresses. I will communicate tomorrow.'[12]

Other members of the gang were less enthusiastic about seeing Pagnon again. Chamberlin's long-standing suspicions about his chauffeur being an informer had come true and the boss blamed Pagnon for everything when they met in prison. 'I'll take you with me to the stake,' Chamberlin spat.[13]

Jean Sartore and Robert Gourari were arrested outside Paris in mid-November 1944 when a local reported them to the police. They claimed that they had been members of the Marco Polo resistance network since 1942 but couldn't account for the 683,000 francs that they had stashed in their rooms. The police missed Abel Danos by a few weeks; he had ditched girlfriend Simone following the liberation and returned to Paris for his other lover Hélène then holed up in a café-hotel in the Yonne, south of Paris, owned by Sartore.

'One evening we went by motorbike to Sartore's place,' Hélène remembered. 'A nice man, with a certain charm, I have to say. I remember his wife, a very sophisticated blonde, and also, who knows why, the ceiling of their bedroom was decorated with stars.'[14]

The couple returned to the capital in October 1944 when Hélène fell pregnant. Danos partnered up with a former Brigade Nord-Africaine member Victor Paul, and the pair went on a crime spree that lasted a few weeks before Danos got himself arrested on 18 November after a shootout with the police. He claimed to be a resistance fighter named Paul Richard.

Police were already preparing a case against the Carlingue. Gang members lied, pleaded and bargained in an attempt to save themselves while Chamberlin sat depressed in his cell, muttering about the illegality of the charges against him. He had a visit from some of de Gaulle's intelligence agents looking for information about Gestapo operations, but didn't know enough about the inner workings of the organisation to give them anything very useful.

The prison guards feared that the former gang leader might try to kill himself again; they confiscated his tie and offered up some false hope. British MI6 officer Malcolm Muggeridge was invited to meet with Chamberlin and discuss his case with clear instructions to humour the gangster and nothing more.

Muggeridge was a Cambridge graduate in his early forties whose hard-left convictions had crumbled away after seeing the 1930s Ukraine famine up close. The Second World War pushed him from journalism into intelligence work and he spent time in Mozambique and Algeria before his Francophile world view and admiration for de Gaulle led to a posting in liberated Paris.

The police offered up an interrogation room full of walnut finish and black leather at the Sûreté Nationale on rue de Saussaies. Chamberlin entered looking pale and battered. He quietly explained his hope that the Allied military authorities would take over his case. Muggeridge read through the gangster's file and listened to Chamberlin complain about the unfairness of being prosecuted by a police force that had worked alongside the Germans during the occupation and his belief that de Gaulle had no authority to prosecute him, as the general had been in exile when the crimes had taken place. Chamberlin seemed to believe that General Eisenhower would take an interest his case.

Some of Chamberlin's old charisma and confidence returned as he talked. He flattered Muggeridge and claimed to have helped downed British pilots escape to Spain and to have sent Red Cross food parcels to a girl in Hull throughout the war, who was his one true love. Muggeridge believed none of it but promised to take the matter to his superiors. The guards came back into the interrogation room and Chamberlin visibly wilted as the handcuffs clicked back on his wrists. Muggeridge later reflected on his encounter with the man who once controlled most of Paris:

> It was a relief to get away and out onto the street but the memory of my macabre encounter with him continued to haunt me. The thought of that ego of his, lifting its head and darting out its cobra tongue; that vanity, emerging, inviolate, fresh and new as a Pharaoh's treasure after centuries in a dark tomb, from the beatings and thumpings at the Sûreté, the questionings and shoutings, the bright lights shining and the dead hours passing.[15]

Muggeridge's bosses had no interest in Chamberlin's case. The Allied forces were rolling through France and Belgium as the Third Reich collapsed into chaos. Mayors of small German towns gave speeches about fighting to the last and then went home to pack their bags, while teenagers waited in ditches with rifles for the American tanks to arrive.

The trial of the members of the gang from 93 rue Lauriston was set for the start of December 1944.

20

THE TRIAL

IN THE WINTER OF 1944, the Seine froze thick and solid around the Île de la Cité, an island shaped like a diving whale harpooned by nine bridges. Twelve men sat shivering in an antechamber somewhere deep in the bowels of the Palais de Justice's labyrinthine corridors. For months, the courts had been feeding the firing squads a steady stream of collaborators, including the journalist Georges Suarez, the broadcaster Lucien Felgines, and the Milice men who shot hostages in revenge for the death of Philippe Henriot. The turn of the Carlingue came on 1 December 1944.

The prosecutors were taking no chances. They had an avalanche of evidence to bury Henri Chamberlin, Pierre Bonny, Paul Clavié, Louis Haré, André Engel, Alexandre Villaplana, Louis Pagnon, Edmond Delehaye, Jacques Labussière, Jean-Damien Lascaux, Charles Delval and Maurice Tate, the last being an unconnected Frenchman who had informed for the Gestapo against his resistance colleagues. Anne-Marguerite Garnier had been due to appear alongside Clavié for her part in the attempted robbery of the elderly lady and her nurse, but the government had postponed her case at the last minute.

The accused sat waiting for their trial to start on the other side of the door in a cavernous barn of a room called the Salle des Assises. Chamberlin no longer seemed to care about his fate:

> The games are over. Those who queued yesterday for me to receive them, pretend not to recognise me any more. Who wouldn't want to dislike me? But now, all that tires me. I had everything I wanted. I lived like a king. Now nothing matters any more. I look forward to keeping company with my contemporaries.[1]

The guards opened the door to the Salle des Assises and the prisoners shuffled through into a long wooden dock in the huge, cold cavern of a courtroom. Those present included the defence team, the prosecutor Marcel Reboul, a four-man jury and a crowd of angry spectators who were wrapped in overcoats and scarves. Above the dock was a fresco depicting the moment that King Louis XIII took his vows in 1610. The artwork had been commissioned under the Vichy government and the paint still smelled fresh.

After the preliminaries, Judge Ledoux addressed the defendants and stated: 'You are accused of intelligence with the enemy.'[2] He then read out the accusations, detailing crimes, names and places. Chamberlin looked bored and put his head in his hands as the judge spoke. He had already told his lawyer that he would commit suicide if he got a prison sentence rather than the firing squad, but only once he had killed Bonny for having talked so much to the police.

The trial lasted for eleven days. Judge Ledoux directed the questioning but it was prosecutor Marcel Reboul who had the job of hammering a stake through the heart of rue Lauriston. He was a tall, dark and big-chinned 39-year-old from Provençal who had been a judge under Vichy but had successfully kept his hands clean enough to survive the post-liberation purges. His oratory was as flowery as a botanical garden. 'You believed that your leather seat cushion would be your life preserver,' he told Lauriston's office manager Delehaye. 'It will be your shackles!'[3]

The collaborationist author and journalist Robert Brasillach, who was in custody and awaiting his own trial with Reboul, laughed himself sick when he read that in the newspapers. The prosecutor toned down his language to discuss the gang's contacts with Otto Abetz, Pierre Laval and Jean Luchaire. Witnesses were called, including the sister of Jacques Paul Kellner who had been shot for his involvement in the resistance, a selection of police officers and a resistance man who had been beaten half to death at rue Lauriston.

Marguerite Donnadieu testified for the prosecution and described how Delval had betrayed resistance groups, while the prosecution emphasised how her husband was still suffering in a concentration camp somewhere in Germany. Delval responded by annoying both the judge and prosecutor with calm speeches about his admiration for Nazi ideology.

Bonny was accused of torturing prisoners. He denied everything until he was baited into admitting that he assaulted one man who had lied about him during the Stavisky affair. 'There you are, Monsieur le Président,' Bonny said. 'It was only once and I think he deserved it.'[4]

Proceedings then moved on to accusations about the Brigade Nord-Africaine. Reboul painted a picture of foreign mercenaries murdering their way across France under the command of amoral gangsters. Chamberlin claimed that he had not been present when any atrocities occurred and insisted that he had ensured that any prisoners were given coffee, butter and meat, every morning and every evening. A sick-looking Delehaye admitted that Maillebuau had discussed rapes committed by North African soldiers under his command. Villaplana admitted commanding a section and stealing two bottles of aperitif from a farmhouse but blamed everything else on a German officer. 'I'm not a murderer. I've never killed anyone,' he pleaded.[5]

Clavié, Engel and Haré looked emotionless as the murder and torture of the elderly actress Madame Deryeux and her nurse was described. Chamberlin wiped tears from his eyes as he listened. Pagnon talked at length about the Carlingue's work for the Gestapo and arrest of resistance members.

Chamberlin and Clavié were defended by René Floriot, a talented and forensic advocate known as the most expensive lawyer in Paris. He specialised in quick divorces for the wealthy, but he had a sharp mind and a more straightforward manner than Reboul. The other defendants had their own, cheaper advocates.

Under defence questioning, Haré and Engel claimed that they had protected people from the Germans. Bonny blamed the other defendants for everything, while Chamberlin accused his former subordinate of lying to escape the death sentence and admitted only to looting supply drops from Allied planes. He claimed that the gang members not yet on trial had committed the worst crimes. 'The ones really responsible,' he began, 'Cazauba, Sartore, Jeunet, and a dozen others, are not here at my side.'[6]

Delval's lawyer described him as a naive idealist who had no direct connection to the Bonny-Lafont gang and whose joining the Gestapo in 1944, as the German hopes of victory were waning, proved his detachment from reality. Delval undermined his own defence by talking about his political opinions: 'I was not a Gaullist then, and I am not one now.'[7]

Floriot brought in the witnesses for the defence, which included Lionel de Wiet, Georges Prade, Dr Eugène Lapiné and Guy de Voisins, who all testified about the people that Chamberlin had been able to free from prison. His treatment of the Duke of Ayen was discussed and Inspector Clot, who had interrogated Bonny, was persuaded to say some positive things. 'I owe it to the truth to say that, since Lafont, who had betrayed his country, released a great many Frenchmen, he did good to individual people, without doubt.'[8]

The trial ended on 11 December with a condemnatory final speech delivered by Reboul that was full of fire and damnation. The defence countered by portraying Delehaye, Bonny and Villaplana as being victims of Chamberlin, while Lascaux and Labussière were described as victims and little more than office boys. Clavié's advocate pleaded for the guillotine rather than a firing squad.

During the closing speeches Delehaye fainted and was carried out. His diabetes had been untreated since he was arrested. The other defendants then stood to hear Ledoux direct the jury and ask them for any last excuses. Engel claimed that he had only acted as a chauffeur, Bonny described himself as merely a functionary, Delval talked briefly about his exemplary war record. The other members of the gang simply shrugged. Chamberlin stepped forward and stated: 'Rue Lauriston is no more than a legend.'[9]

The judge instructed the jury to retire and decide whether Chamberlin and his gang were guilty of twenty-two counts of intelligence with the enemy. The prisoners shuffled back through the door into the Palais de Justice and began the long walk back to their cells. In the morning they heard that Delehaye had died in the hospital.

At midday on 12 December 1944, the four men of the jury returned and gave their verdict: all the defendants were guilty. Lascaux and Labussière received life imprisonment with hard labour due to the extenuating circumstances of their youth and relationship to Bonny. All of the other members of the Carlingue were sentenced to death and the executions were set for two weeks' time.

Villaplana closed his eyes when the verdict was read, Chamberlin and Delval smiled, Bonny coughed and turned grey. The others remained unmoved.

• • •

The walls on Bonny's cell dripped with damp and his only furniture was a horsehair pallet on the floor. The former policeman's health had deteriorated and he had started coughing blood. On the cell wall he wrote out a calendar with a pencil and crossed through the days leading up to his execution. He added in the extra months of January and February 1945, in the hope of a pardon. His wife prayed and philosophised and wrote to him regularly.

> Life, you know, is a very short passage. I lost my mother while she was still young; and you, you lost your father. We are all destined to pass. No matter what time. We know that life is not finished, that it begins for eternity and that the family will end up there. I have vowed to go to Lourdes with you to thank the Virgin, if we are reunited again.[10]

An appeal for clemency was submitted to de Gaulle by Bonny's lawyers, but it was denied. Bonny wrote a last letter to his wife on 22 December 1944 full of religious pleadings, expressions of love and worry for his son. Jacques received a separate letter in which his father talked of all of the good that he had done as a policeman and made bitter remarks about the Stavisky affair as the moment everything went wrong for him.

Bonny spent his remaining days writing a short memoir, which were part meditation on his trial and part examination of his actions. He couldn't understand why the jury had found him guilty.

> Nothing villainous has been blamed on me, neither for robbery, concealment, faux policiers, scams, nor trafficking in gold, nor torture, nor abuse, nor kidnapping. At rue Lauriston, I served as secretary and steward, cashier, accountant, responsible for directing domestic staff. The maids confirmed it overall. There is not and there has never been any question of espionage or counter-intelligence. Am I a traitor? Have I done acts of treason? And against whom? I worked for Lafont. It is a fact. Working for him, I worked for the Germans. That was collaboration. But were we at war? I never touched a centime of theirs.[11]

Meanwhile, Chamberlin sent one final letter to his son Pierre. It was written in a semi-literate hand and each letter had been formed with effort. Attached was a long list of individuals that Chamberlin had helped under the occupation.

> Dear son, I think that you will receive my letter again in time and that I will be able to see you one last time. I made the request. But in case I do not see you any more, know that I have always loved you. Do not listen to what you will hear others say about me. You will judge for yourself later. And when I'm gone, I charge you, the man of the family, to watch your sister. Try not to allow any mistakes that she would later regret. As for yourself, try to learn a good job, as a mechanic for example: it will serve you everywhere in life. Finally, in you, I have confidence: we have about the same character.[12]

On 23 December 1944, Chamberlin received a final visit from counterintelligence agents sent by de Gaulle's Cabinet. They wanted information about war criminals who were still on the run.

Chamberlin claimed that he knew nothing but offered to personally track down Hermann Brandl and others who had fled France; he offered to leave his children behind as collateral. The representatives ignored the offer and Chamberlin didn't seem surprised. Later, he wrote a letter in which he admitted responsibility for everything.

> De Wiet wasn't part of the service, he worked the black market. His wife is innocent. Lapiné was involved in the money side. His wife is innocent. Countess Tchernichev is a lunatic who had more to do with the Allies than the Germans. Villaplana and [another gang member] Keller are innocent. Estébétéguy, Louis had nothing to do with the service. Engels, André also didn't do anything.[13]

The authorities clipped this admission into a file with the rest of the paperwork on Chamberlin. The other gang members wrote last words to their lovers, mothers, wives and children. An old priest did the rounds of the cells. Some listened, some did not.

'Well, granddad,' said Chamberlin, 'have you come to give me a passport to paradise? I'm not going. All my friends will be somewhere else and I don't like solitude.'[14]

He laughed as the old man hurried away; Monsieur Henri could already hear the dirt hitting the coffin lid.

The German counterattack through the Ardennes in the middle of December 1944 smashed Allied complacency. Civilians fled Paris in cars that were piled high with suitcases and furniture. Some collaborators even taunted the guards from their cells, but Bonny, Chamberlin and the rest did not share their optimism. They smoked cigarettes and looked through the bars of their cells up at the dark winter sky.

21

LONG LIVE FRANCE, ANYWAY

FORT DE MONTROUGE WAS a hulking block of stone just outside Paris. The place had been an artillery depot and police barracks since its construction in 1843 as a link in the city's defensive chain. After the liberation it had a new career as an execution ground.

Early in the morning of Tuesday 26 December 1944, the condemned cell in the Fort de Montrouge was thick with cigarette smoke. The prisoners drank champagne. Some had got a haircut from the prison barber at Fresnes before the transfer in a last act of human vanity. They talked with their lawyers or to each other or remained silent. Bonny appeared disgusted by the griminess of the cell. Chamberlin was detached and spoke ironically. 'I lived the equivalent of ten lives,' he said to a lawyer. 'The least I can do is give you one of them.'[1]

The number of prisoners awaiting execution had been reduced to eight. The Gestapo informer Maurice Tate escaped the firing squad when his death sentence was commuted for bravery shown fighting against the Germans. He joined Lascaux and Labussière breaking rocks for life.

The guards came for the first batch of prisoners a little after 9 a.m. Charles Delval, Louis Haré and Pierre Bonny stood up as their names were called. Delval handed his lawyer a letter for his wife Paulette promising his eternal love. He didn't know she was already pregnant by another man. Bonny was wearing his old police cloak and as he left the cell he slid his glasses into a suit pocket.

'Courage, guys,' said Chamberlin as the three departed. 'Let nobody fail.'[2]

Outside in the yard, the three men braced themselves against their wooden stakes like sailors facing a storm. Their faces showed regret, determination and resignation. The officer who was in charge raised his sword and swept it down. The rifles cracked and a smoke cloud rose into the air and then the prisoners lay on the ground, each body twisted around a stake. Delval's glasses had been thrown from his face when the bullets hit. The bodies were lifted into cheap wooden coffins by the prison guards.

Down in the cell, the remaining five prisoners waited their turn. Chamberlin steadied Villaplana. 'This one penalty you can't save, my friend,' he said. 'No need to dive.'

The guards came for Chamberlin, Pagnon and Villaplana next. The former footballer joked with the officer about what he should do with his coat, before they smoked their last cigarettes and uttered last words. Chamberlin refused to wear a blindfold, saying that he wanted to see the sun as he died. The guards finally roped him to the stake with a cigarette still smoking in his mouth. 'I didn't deserve this fate,' he said, 'but long live France, anyway.'[3] At 9.50 a.m. the firing squad raised their rifles and it was all over for the leader of the Carlingue.

Clavié and Engel were the last of the gang to be tied to the stakes. 'I deserve to die,' shouted Clavié, 'and I'm going to die.'[4]

The fodder kept coming for the firing squad. Robert Brasillach was found guilty on 19 January 1945 at the Palais de Justice.

Petitions for clemency from writers on both the left and the right were ignored and he was executed at Montrouge on 6 February. By this time, the Ardennes offensive had failed in the deep snow of Belgium and the Americans were launching a counter-offensive. The hope finally died among the Vichy exiles in Sigmaringen. Jean Luchaire attempted to keep up morale with games and quizzes on the back pages of *La France*. On 12 March 1945, a clue for the crossword puzzle read 'contemporary bandit'; the answer was 'resistant'.[5]

Nazi Germany collapsed within two months, with Hitler dead in his bunker and the Third Reich in flames. The victorious Allies and Soviets carved up Europe between them.

Brigade Nord-Africaine members Jean Delchiappo and Mathieu Fioravanti were tried and executed a few days after the end of the war. The press baron Jean Luchaire and resistance infiltrator Émile Marongin also paid the price for their collaboration. The Allies arrested Jean Luchaire in Italy; on the morning of 22 February 1946 a firing squad shot him at Fort de Châtillon, south of Paris. He walked to his death chain-smoking and accompanied by the Jesuit priest who had baptised and married him. Marongin survived the German camps but was identified on his return to France and tried in October 1946 for leading Gestapo agents into the heart of the resistance. The prosecutor read out accusation after accusation, while Marongin hopelessly tried to butt in. 'If I'm allowed to explain myself…' he stuttered before being found guilty.[6] A firing squad executed him in December 1946.

On the outer orbits of rue Lauriston's solar system, the 6th Duke of Ayen died on 14 April 1945 at Bergen-Belsen concentration camp. The camp was liberated by British troops one day later. Adrien Estébétéguy's murderer Dr Marcel Petiot went on trial the following year, charged with the deaths of twenty-seven people.

The black market exploiter Rudolphina Kahan was tracked down living under a false name in the sixteenth arrondissement and gave evidence against the man to whom she had introduced Jewish families. Petiot insisted that the dismembered bodies in rue le Sueur belonged to collaborators. The jury didn't believe him and on 25 May 1946 the insane doctor with the dead eyes was guillotined.

Other individuals associated with the gang escaped execution. Chamberlin's Abwehr contact Max Stöcklin was stopped at the Swiss border in the autumn of 1944 and sent to Fresnes, which was already crammed with fellow collaborators. He got a life sentence in 1946 and was lucky to escape more charges for the mysterious murder of an Amt Otto business partner who had been thinking of helping the authorities. The French government demanded 20 million francs' worth of compensation from Stöcklin, but he insisted that he was penniless. In 1950, the Swiss government exchanged high-level correspondence with Paris about swapping prisoners; both sides agreed not to include Stöcklin in any exchange.

Things changed two years later when a pardon for collaborators returned him to a low-profile life in Switzerland. Most of those who were still in prison for their wartime crimes were released in 1954 after another general pardon and the remainder were freed early in the next decade. By 1964, nobody who had been convicted of wartime treason remained behind bars in France.

Danos's friends Robert Gourari and Jean Sartore were among those who benefited from the early release programme. On 8 May 1948, they received ten years' hard labour but were back on the streets of Paris within a few years. Auguste Jeunet, who had dropped out of the gang after being knifed by Tanguy the pimp, was arrested in 1951 and spent two years waiting for a trial. He admitted his guilt with a shrug and received five years but served less. The

Corsican François Suzzoni was arrested on 15 November 1944 on treason charges, but his work for the resistance saw them dropped. It helped that he'd been kicked out of rue Lauriston before the Brigade Nord-Africaine days for his involvement in an unauthorised jewellery store robbery. The judge gave him five years for various other crimes. Anne-Marguerite Garnier, who had set up Clavié's final robbery and murder, received three years in prison in 1946 and a 3,000-franc fine.

In May 1945, American soldiers located Countess Mara Tchernichev-Bezobrazov living at Garmisch-Partenkirchen, a ski resort in the Bavarian Alps that had hosted the Winter Olympics in 1936. She refused to reveal what had happened after she was deported to Germany and the Americans sent her to Fresnes prison.

On 5 June 1947, Tchernichev-Bezobrazov was tried and received two years for intelligence with the enemy and a penalty of 26 million francs. However, more evidence emerged the following month that upgraded her sentence to five years. A blizzard of appeals and legal arguments meant she was released inside a year. The Russian aristocrat declared herself bankrupt but somehow managed to keep her château. She lived for a while with friend Renée de Mallet and a prison acquaintance who acted as her housekeeper and spied for the police. Tchernichev-Bezobrazov then became involved with a Swiss jewel thief, bounced between Paris and Mexico and finally settled with her brother in America to fade out of history.

Sylviane Quimfe mourned Pagnon and managed to avoid a trial until 1950. In court, she denied everything but received eighteen months in prison and a 30,000-franc fine. After her release, she found more rich lovers, suffered a number of business bankruptcies and disappeared into anonymity.

Lionel de Wiet continued to masquerade as a war veteran and

persuaded gullible doctors that he was too sick to attend a trial. The court let him live in Toulouse on bail and the 1952 amnesty set him free without having served any prison time. Luchaire's politician friend Georges Prade got seven years in 1947 but was released from prison the following year. He died in Spain sometime in the mid-1970s.

The Bulgarian mystic Mikhaël Ivanov avoided being accused of any collaboration charges but received four years in prison in 1948 for committing sexual offences against underage girls. His followers remained loyal to him throughout the case; legal manoeuvring reduced the charges and set him free after two years. After release, he refined his name to Aïvanhov and went on to build up his White Brotherhood operation. He died in 1986 and still has followers today.

• • •

Prominent Carlingue member Lucien Prévost was never found. Rumours circulated that he had escaped to Spain through Marseille and then sailed for South America, or that he had been murdered, or that he had got rich, or he joined the secret police in Cuba. A few French conspiracy theorists have even claimed that Prévost played important roles in the assassinations of the American mobster Bugsy Siegel and President John F. Kennedy.

It is most likely that Prévost lived and died in Spain. General Francisco Franco's dictatorship proved to be a haven to many fleeing fascists, including collaborationist gang leader Frédéric Martin, better remembered as Rudy de Mérode. The chief rival to rue Lauriston slipped across the border into Spain after the liberation and started a new life under the name of the Prince de Mérode. His death remains mysterious, but he probably died in 1970 somewhere near Madrid.

Other collaborators took alternate escape routes out of France.

Friedrich Berger of the rue de la Pompe gang escaped from custody in 1947, was sentenced to death in absentia and then died in his bed in Munich thirteen years later. Brigade Nord-Africaine organiser and *Er Rachid* proprietor Mohamed El-Maadi retreated to Germany in August 1944 and then made it to Tunisia at the end of the war. He settled in Egypt and died there in the 1950s. The renegade British SOE agent John Renshaw Starr also left France with the retreating Germans. He turned up in Switzerland among some recently released concentration camp inmates shortly before the war ended. Starr claimed to have only worked with the Nazis to gain information; British authorities investigated but couldn't find enough evidence for a prosecution. He eventually moved back to Paris, and then to Switzerland where he died in 1996.

On the German side, Abwehr chief Hermann Brandl was arrested in Munich at the end of the war. Allied soldiers locked him up in Stadelheim prison, but he hanged himself in his cell on 24 March 1947 awaiting trial. Gestapo chief Karl Bömelburg had died in Munich the previous year after slipping on ice and cracking his skull. He had been living under a false identity and helping wanted Nazis escape into Spain when the accident happened. Brandl's subordinate Wilhelm Radecke left France in the spring of 1944 after the Abwehr was disbanded by a suspicious Hitler. He spent the rest of the war in Berlin and later worked for the Soviets in the German Democratic Republic.

SS Standartenführer Helmut Knochen, who had been responsible for security in Paris, received a death sentence from the British in 1947 and another from the French in 1954, but both were commuted. At his trial in Paris he threw a handful of mud at the Carlingue's memory. 'I never had any confidence in Lafont,' he said, 'who was, in my eyes, a defective person without moral courage.'[7]

Knochen was released from a French prison in 1962, along with his superior Carl Oberg who had been convicted at the same trials. Oberg died in Flensburg in 1965 and Knochen in 2003 at Baden-Baden.

Marshal Philippe Pétain left Sigmaringen and crossed into Switzerland in early May 1945; he then voluntarily returned to France for trial. He was sentenced to death but spent the next six years in prison, becoming progressively more senile until he died at the age of ninety-five in 1951. His despised underling Pierre Laval was executed in October 1945 after a farcical trial that did no one any credit.

Those who had been on the winning side at the time of the liberation had their own legal problems after the war. Inspector Louis Métra took early retirement in 1948 and opened his own detective agency. However, former colleagues became suspicious about some of the company that he kept and in 1955 he was arrested on the landing outside a drug addict aristocrat's apartment in possession of a kilo of opium. He received two years in prison for drug smuggling.

Joseph Joinovici thought that he was safe. He had got the Resistance Medal for bankrolling the Honneur de la Police, then ordered 12,000 portraits of Charles de Gaulle to be put up in schools across France and made cash donations to every new political party that emerged after the war. It all came crumbling down in September 1944 when the military police discovered his safe conduct pass from the Gestapo and his business links to rue Lauriston. In his defence, Joinovici said: 'I was intent on passing in their eyes as a major trafficker of enormous means, all with the aim of camouflaging my actual activities as a resistant. My relations with rue Lauriston were a cover.'[8]

The police agreed and he was freed within two months. Shortly after, a fresh investigation turned up stronger evidence and Joinovici fled to the American-occupied zone in Germany. He returned to Paris and claimed to be a victim of Nazi anti-Semitism in the hope that the police would show him clemency. Around 70,000 foreign

Jews living in France had been deported to the camps during the war, together with 6,000 Jewish citizens. Only 2,800 returned.[9]

By the time that Joinovici's trial came round in 1949, the French public had got used to the idea of Jewish collaborators. The French businessman Michel Szkolnikoff made big news when his charred corpse turned up at the side of the Madrid to Burgos road in June 1945. His death was linked to a wartime fortune made selling uniforms, art and jewellery to the Germans. The jury gave Joinovici five years for economic collaboration; some newspapers could barely conceal their disgust. 'Prodigiously active and shrewd,' said *Le Monde*, 'without scruples, simultaneously greedy and generous, alert, amoral, this jovial, rotund, little Israelite is a character made for a latter-day Balzac, with his highly characteristic profile, his vivid, minuscule porcine eyes, his Balkan accent, fat lips rolled back into a capital U.'[10]

Joinovici claimed serious health problems and managed to swap a prison cell for house arrest in a room at a hotel in Mende, Lozère. He rebuilt his scrap metal empire over the telephone and made friends by funding the local football team. In August 1957, his guards got complacent and Joinovici fled to Israel on a fake Moroccan passport to join his sister in Haifa. A long legal row that lasted most of the rest of the decade ended with Israel deporting Joinovici back to France where he was imprisoned once again. He was let out in 1962 and settled in Clichy. Joinovici died on 7 February 1965 at the age of sixty, villain to some and hero to others. Representatives of the Honneur de la Police left a wreath at his grave.

The sound of the firing squad and the slamming prison door echoed across France for many years after the liberation. The Courts of Justice in France executed 1,500 people between October 1944 and January 1951, sentenced 29,927 to life terms in prison, 2,702 to forced labour for life, 10,637 to shorter sentences of forced labour and 3,578 to the loss of various other civil rights. Nearly 7,000 were acquitted of the crimes.[11] When the punishments finally ended, the Carlingue was dead and buried in an unmarked grave.

Some of its alumni went on to bigger things. Many of France's most notorious post-war public enemies got their start at rue Lauriston, and so did the heroin-smuggling masterminds of the scheme that became known as the French Connection.

22

AN OLD PHOTOGRAPH OF OUR YOUTH

AUGUSTE RICORD WAS A diminutive 61-year-old with a bald head and white sideburns thick as sheep wool. His bony arms stuck out of an orange sports shirt; thin ankles disappeared into polished loafers. 'Do I look like I deal in narcotics?' he asked the journalist.[1]

The walls of his three by four metre cell were covered in family photographs and tourist posters of France. A watercolour of a Paris street painted by Ricord during the long hours of boredom stood on an easel in the corner.

It was the summer of 1972 and the journalists crowding into the jail cell in the Paraguayan capital of Asunción had a lot of questions to ask. Two years earlier, a single-engine Cessna 210 light aircraft had touched down at Miami International airport. The American authorities found forty-two kilo bricks of heroin on board. The pilots of the plane cracked under questioning and named Auguste Ricord as head of an international drug smuggling ring that was based out of Paraguay. 'I do not understand the accusations against me,' said Ricord. 'They are a mystery.'

The flood of heroin across the Atlantic had proliferated after the Second World War. Corsican crime families got rich by refining Turkish opium and selling it on to Mafia dealers in New York. By

1960, gangs based in Marseille were smuggling twenty tonnes of heroin a year into the New World. Two years later, the operation took a hit when the New York police found fifty kilos of heroin in a Buick that was owned by the French television personality Jacques Angelvin, host of *Paris-Club*.

The transatlantic route closed down and the Corsicans moved their operations to the soft underbelly of Central America. The heroin was then sold directly to Cuban exiles fronting for Argentinian-Italian crime families. Argentina and Brazil became narcotic warehouses, and Paraguay served as the gateway to the north.

'A variety of methods are used to smuggle heroin in bulk,' noted a 1971 CIA report, 'including caching it in new European automobiles with false gas tanks, inside dead bodies being returned to South America for burial, and other methods equally bizarre.'[2]

From Paraguay, the heroin made the last stage of its journey into the USA as individual kilo packs that were carried by travellers, hidden behind partitions in planes by commercial aircrew or stacked in light aircraft. Paraguay had no narcotics laws and the dictatorial President Alfredo Stroessner turned a blind eye, provided that his cronies got a split of the drug money. The President's fierce anti-Communism protected him until the CIA lost patience and leaked the lists of Paraguayan officials involved in the heroin trade to an opposition newspaper. The embarrassed government reworked its drugs policy and Ricord found himself in prison shortly afterwards.

Auguste Ricord had grown up in Marseille and started his criminal career with a mob led by veteran villains Paul Carbone and François Spirito. The pair ran prostitution networks, protection rackets, arms sales and an opium empire. They had met in Egypt before the First World War when Carbone's success in trafficking

European prostitutes angered rivals into burying him up to his neck in the desert sand. Spirito dug him up and a criminal partnership was born.

The Marseille gang provided a criminal education for Ricord. He served time for extortion, theft, violence and carrying weapons. When the police pressure got too much, he shifted operations to Paris and moved in with a young art student called Jeanne. The two supported themselves running a brothel bought from another Corsican gangster. Jeanne had a talent for keeping the girls in line.

The couple were happily losing their money at the gaming tables of Monte Carlo when the Nazis invaded. Back in Paris, they were muscled out of the brothel business by a new breed of wartime pimp with links to the German occupiers. Ricord was rebuilding his finances through a gold scam act when the Carlingue recruited him. He returned to the rackets and got rich running a chain of gambling joints popular with the gang.

Chamberlin liked the little man from Marseille but had no time for the more established Corsican gangsters. Ricord was probably the only member of the rue Lauriston gang who mourned when his old mentor Carbone died in a train derailment in late 1943 engineered by a resistance group targeting collaborators and German soldiers. Carbone managed a laconic gangster's death, straight out of Hollywood, as he lay crushed in the wreck. He spent his last hours smoking, encouraging rescuers to help others who still had a chance, and muttering: '*C'est la vie.*'

Six months later, Allied tanks came rolling towards Paris. Ricord and Jeanne joined a retreating German convoy with friends from rue Flandrin's Bande des Corses. Ricord took with him millions in francs, pesetas, dollars, gold coins and diamonds. The group made it to Munich and feigned enthusiasm about a spy mission the Germans had planned for them in Italy. Once they were across the border they dropped out of sight, separated in Milan and went underground.

Ricord and Jeanne settled in an apartment overlooking the Piazzale Loreto in Milan, a flat expanse of concrete and apartment blocks. They held an open house for any rue Lauriston veterans on the run who passed through Italy.

And then the war was over. On 29 April 1945, Ricord watched as a mob strung up the corpses of Mussolini, his mistress and three other Fascist leaders from the grid-work on a garage in the Piazzale below. Hitler was dead a day later and the Third Reich fell with him.

Italy was suddenly full of American and British soldiers, hungry civilians, emaciated Jewish refugees, black marketeers selling cigarettes and tights, Italian Communists marching through the streets and women selling themselves to foreigners.

Swimming in this chaotic sea were Nazi war criminals looking for a way out of Europe. Many claimed to be Dutch or Swiss and lived in constant fear of discovery. SS Obersturmbannführer Adolf Eichmann – the logistical brain behind the Nazi extermination of the Jews – remembered his years hiding behind a fake identity:

> In the five years I spent underground living as a mole, it became second nature to me, whenever I saw a new face, to ask myself a few questions, like: Do you know this face? Does this person look like he has seen you before? Is he trying to recall when he might have met you?[3]

Networks of Nazi officials, SS men and collaborators sprouted up across post-war Europe. Underground forgery workshops turned out passports and identity documents. Some Nazis escaped through a northern route that ran into Sweden and a few with Celtic connections got to Ireland, but everyone else headed south to Italy or tried to enter Franco's Spain.

Jeanne and Ricord moved to Genoa hoping to secure passage on a boat to South America but were arrested by suspicious American troops. Jeanne didn't spend long behind bars, but Ricord served two months in prison under a fake name. In the autumn of 1946, he was released and managed to cross into Spain and onto a boat destined for Argentina using the name Lucien Dargelès. His new identity documents had been stolen from a French chef who thought that he was getting into the entertainment business when he handed them over to a music hall artist in a Paris bistro.

Jeanne joined him in South America, along with Ricord's sister and nephew. Ricord received a death sentence in absentia. He set up prostitution rings across Argentina, Brazil and Venezuela, with girls sourced from France. Nightclubs with names like Chez Danielle and Le Fetiche served as fronts for brothels and human trafficking enterprises.

Soon after, Jeanne decided that Buenos Aires did not suit her and returned to France, but Ricord stayed on, made money and got comfortable. As Ricord started a new life for himself in South America, other former Carlingue men were still on the run back home.

• • •

The Gang des Tractions Avant was born from a meeting in a Paris street between two wanted men. In the autumn of 1945, Pierre Loutrel was wandering through Montmartre when he encountered Abel Danos for the first time since the days of the Carlingue. Loutrel had spent the last months of the occupation working with the Nazi SD at avenue Foch, where one of his colleagues was the Dutchman Seelen whose girlfriend had doubled as Chamberlin's mistress. An attempt to integrate the erratic Loutrel into a team run by René Launay failed in a tussle of discipline. Loutrel started his own team to hunt down parachute drops and resistance networks.

Off duty he drank, got into bar fights and wandered Paris openly carrying his sub-machine gun. Loutrel took part in his last Gestapo mission on 7 July 1944 with a raid on nightclub Chez Bob that saw three men arrested. A few weeks later he earned the nickname 'Pierrot le Fou' (Mad Pete) by shooting Inspector Ricordeau. The two were arguing over something insignificant when Loutrel pulled a pistol and put two bullets in the policeman's chest and one in his neck. The inspector was lucky to survive.

The Gestapo refused to protect Loutrel. He fled to Toulouse using the name Pierre Déricourt and became a lieutenant in the Forces Françaises de L'Intérieur. His comrades thought him pleasant and calm.

Loutrel quit the resistance in the chaos of the Allied invasion and returned to Paris and a chance meeting with Abel Danos. Le Mammouth had escaped custody on 18 January by climbing out of a jimmied police station window. He reunited with Hélène and his son for a life of hotels, train journeys, stolen cars and false identities. Danos would occasionally leave his family to fend for themselves before returning with money. 'We were an ordinary couple,' said Hélène.[4]

Loutrel and Danos were drinking in La Roulotte nightclub when a withered figure with a suit hanging off him like a sail appeared in the doorway. It was their old Carlingue colleague Jo Attia, back from the concentration camp Chamberlin had sent him to after discovering his involvement in the resistance. Deportees were returning to Paris every day, stepping out of train carriages looking hunched and malnourished with black, decayed teeth. Old women would give up their seats on the Métro to them. Attia had just been awarded the Legion of Honour by Charles de Gaulle for his bravery. Loutrel and Danos bought their former partner food, drink, a girl and a new suit of clothes. They apologised for allowing him to be deported. 'What a bastard I've been,' said Danos. 'Poor Joe, blow after blow, it would have been better for him to have taken down rue Lauriston than suffer through all that pain.'[5]

The trio drank and talked and Loutrel sketched out a new approach to crime. The war years of sub-machine guns, fast cars and kicked-in doors had opened up his horizons. He had an idea for a new kind of gang that would speed to a target, hit hard and spray bullets, and then be gone before the police knew what was going on; the Gang des Tractions Avant was born.

Loutrel, Danos and Attia recruited Carlingue veterans Henri Fefeu and Georges Boucheseiche; former soldier Marcel Ruard; a young man named Julien le Ny; and resistance fighter turned crook Raymond Naudy, who looked like a 1920s gigolo with his pencil moustache and slicked-back hair. The gang divided and subdivided, hitting targets in Paris and the Côte d'Azur simultaneously, picking up and shedding members as they rampaged around the country.

The gang continued on their spree for months until a witness identified Loutrel after the robbery of a Nice post office in July 1946. Two months later, a 350-strong police task force with automatic weapons and armoured cars cornered some of the gang at a Champigny-sur-Marne inn. Loutrel drove through a storm of bullets at the police roadblocks to rescue Attia and Fefeu, while

Boucheseiche escaped by hiding at the bottom of a well and breathing through a straw.

Breathless newspaper stories romanticised the gang, but the real Loutrel was an alcoholic happy to kill anyone who got in his way. The gang stole 80 million francs from banks, jewellers and security vans until the police crackdown turned other members of the underworld against them. It was probably a rival underworld crook who supplied the information that got Ruard arrested after a robbery in Cassis and Fefeu apprehended while sitting at a Montmartre café.

During the drunken raid of a jewellery shop on 5 November 1946, Loutrel managed to shoot himself in the groin and bled to death during the long trip between hospitals and hideouts. The others buried him on the Île de Gillier, in the middle of the Seine.

Attia and Boucheseiche were arrested in July 1947 and Danos on 30 November 1948 after a police raid in which Naudy was killed. Le Mammouth found himself behind bars with the former Brigade Nord-Africaine commander Raymond Monange, who had been arrested for carrying a gun while pimping, and fellow Carlingue member Victor Paul.

Danos looked haggard and worn-out in court as he shuffled into the dock and put on his reading glasses. He was the father of two small children and his own father had hanged himself three years earlier; the newspapers claimed it was from shame.

Two years later, on 14 March 1952, Danos and Monange were executed by firing squad for their wartime activities. Fellow prisoners called out as they made their long walk.

'Courage, Abel.'

'*Adieu*, Mammouth.'[6]

Danos refused a blindfold, telling the officer in charge of the firing squad that 'death should be looked in the face'.[7]

Victor Paul received twenty years of forced labour but served less and returned to crime on his release. Georges Boucheseiche got eight years, while Jo Attia received only three thanks to testimonies from important men he had helped in the concentration camps, including the recent Minister of the Armed Forces, Edmond Michelet.

The police refused to believe that Loutrel was dead until his decomposing corpse was exhumed two and half years after its burial. Another crook called Pierre Carrot earned the nickname 'Pierrot le Fou numéro 2' for his tactic of robbing the same locations on multiple occasions. In July 1948 Carrot escaped a police station with a cardboard revolver and a safety pin to unlock his handcuffs. His fellow escapee was former Carlingue member René Mâle, better known as Riri l'Américain. Mâle was looking at life on a murder charge. They launched a series of robberies but soon ended back behind bars.

As the Gang des Tractions Avant fell apart, Auguste Ricord was enjoying the good life in Argentina. He had been granted citizenship, secured a passport and found himself a wife.

Ricord had got out of the brothel business in the 1960s after his Corsican partners were deported in connection with a murder committed back in France. The shifting of the French Connection heroin routes from across the Atlantic to South America opened up new opportunities. Ricord moved to Paraguay to head up the drug business for some of his friends in Marseille. It helped that his old gang boss François Spirito knew the heroin smuggling racket from before the war and still had a hand in the business from his new home in Canada.

Everyone made a lot of money until the American crackdown in the 1970s made Ricord a useful fall guy for Paraguayan President

Stroessner. The American public were already horrified by what they had seen in the 1971 Academy Award-winning film *The French Connection*, a fictionalised version of French actor Jacques Angelvin's arrest. However, the situation on the ground was far more complicated. Some saw Ricord as more of a figurehead for a smuggling operation rather than a drug kingpin, with the real power lying in the hands of younger bloodthirsty French expats, including Christian David and François Chiappe. Others thought that David and Chiappe ran a rival gang and were happy to see Ricord gone.

In his cell, Ricord claimed to be simply a restaurant and hotel owner who had been set up by rogue CIA informers who were unable to get at the politicians who really ran the drug trade. He said that he had never heard of Henri Chamberlin. The sceptical reporters wrote it all down and threw in some local colour to interest the readers back home, like the young woman who visited every day and claimed to be Ricord's niece.

Within a few months, Ricord was in a Nassau County jail near New York. The court found him guilty on a conspiracy charge and handed down a penalty of twenty-two years' imprisonment. Ricord served ten, received a pardon and in 1983 returned to Paraguay. He died two years later at the age of seventy-four from a combination of diabetes and heart problems.

His old Carlingue colleagues Jo Attia and Georges Boucheseiche were already dead. Attia spent the decades after being released from prison becoming a serious crime boss in the Paris underworld, while doing dirty work on the side for former fellow concentration camp inmates who had gone on to work as senior intelligence figures. He made newspaper headlines in 1956 when a mission to kill an important Moroccan nationalist in Tétouan went wrong and French intelligence had to extract him in front of the world media.

After that he had a daughter, established a network of bars in Pigalle, before once again serving more prison time. He died of cancer in 1972 at the age of fifty-six.

Boucheseiche went into the brothel business after leaving prison and had operations in France and Morocco. He was linked to some murky intelligence circles through Attia and was involved in the October 1965 kidnapping and murder of Moroccan nationalist Mehdi Ben Barka in Paris. Boucheseiche flew to Casablanca the day after Ben Barka's disappearance, while anyone involved in French intelligence or associated with the Moroccan royal family denied responsibility. Boucheseiche received a life sentence in absentia and died in Morocco in the early 1970s.

Boucheseiche and Attia had lived long enough to see the Gang des Tractions Avant enter French popular culture. Novels emerged that were based on their crimes, and Jean-Luc Godard even borrowed Loutrel's nickname for his classic 1965 film. Later developments included movies such as Jacques Deray's *Le Gang* and the black-and-white *Le Bon et les Méchants* (*The Good and the Bad*) by Claude Lelouch, both of which were filmed in 1976.

Other gang members continued to have low-profile criminal careers. Chamberlin's key ally Jean Sartore was still getting arrested in the 1960s as an elephant-eared pensioner with shaved head in dark glasses and a sheepskin jacket. When he died early in the 1970s, a friend called Jacques Chatillon asked the young writer Patrick Modiano to write a biography, but Modiano refused. Chatillon wrote a letter to the author:

> I sincerely regret that you couldn't write Jean Sartore's memoirs. But you're wrong to think he was an old friend of Lafont's. He used Lafont as a screen for his gold and currency smuggling,

> since the Germans were after him more than the French. That said, he knew plenty about the Lauriston bunch.[8]

Modiano wasn't sure that he believed anything that Chatillon said about Sartore. He preferred to use fictional representations of rue Lauriston as a ghostly theme in his novels about the occupation of Paris. It helped him cope with buried family secrets and guilt and led him to the Nobel Prize for literature in 2014. Through Modiano, Henri Chamberlin would become world-famous.

23

GHOSTS OF PARIS

TODAY, PARIS IS A beautiful city filled with so much history that the ghosts are coming out of the walls. Side streets offer glimpses of the Eiffel Tower looming like a metal monster, the avenues are dotted with four-storey Gilbert Joseph bookshops and the pavements are filled with imperious businesswomen in high heels marching to work with a fruit juice in one hand and croissant in the other.

The Museé d'Orsay is a glorious shell of an old railway terminal stuffed with a fine selection of nineteenth-century art. The parks are still full of the kinds of elegant faces that Picasso sought out for portraits. There are also regular riots, homeless camps, piss-stinking streets and the kind of casual corruption that undermines faith in humanity.

Paris is a literary city and books are everywhere. Strap-hanging passengers read on buses, while customers in cafés crack the spines on a new paperback as they stir the sugar into their coffee. The streets are named after writers; there is an avenue Marcel Proust near the Seine and a small and cramped rue Huysmans further inland. This love of literature has fooled many writers into thinking that their words mean something. It fooled Jean-Paul Sartre.

'Every writer of bourgeois origin,' wrote Sartre in the first editorial for *Les Temps Modernes* in 1945, 'has known the temptation of irresponsibility. I personally hold Flaubert responsible for the repression that followed the Commune because he did not write a line to stop it.'[1]

It was guilt guiding the pen. The gang at rue Lauriston would not have put down their weapons to discuss the curse of freedom or to read a poem. Sartre was attempting to claw back some self-respect after the passive waiting and watching and surviving of the war years. Within a few years he would be existential king of the black polo neck brigade, talking philosophy in smoky cellar jazz bars where no one asked difficult questions about what he did during the occupation.

The first book on the Carlingue appeared out of Brussels in early 1945 while the war was still raging. Someone using the name Rowland W. Black wrote *Histoire et Crimes de la Gestapo Parisienne* (*History and Crimes of the Parisian Gestapo*), a low-budget paperback that combined Paris gossip, newspaper reports and inside information. By the third edition of the book, a section on the trial by a French journalist – who may not have been paid for his efforts – had been inserted as a final chapter in a different font.

A few years later the Bonny-Lafont gang turned up in a more unexpected literary corner. The petty thief and male prostitute Jean Genet had spent twenty-one months behind bars during the Second World War. During one stretch in prison he wrote *Notre-Dame-des-Fleurs* (*Our Lady of the Flowers*) on sheets of brown paper supplied to prisoners to be made into bags. A limited edition of the book was published anonymously at the end of 1943 and sold to connoisseurs of gay erotica.

The book was republished after the liberation with the more pornographic parts removed and became a literary success. It saved Genet from a recidivist's life sentence a few years later when the judge accepted that the man in the dock had cultural significance. In 1949, he wrote *Journal du Voleur* (*The Thief's Journal*), a semi-fictionalised account of his experiences before and after the war. Among the muscles and cocks and thieves and rent boys, Genet included a section about the Bonny-Lafont gang. The author had a fetish for betrayal and treason, and his fascination with the gang was compounded after discovering that one of his lovers had been on its fringes during the war. Genet collected newspaper pictures of the gangsters during their trial and remembered seeing Labussière driving around Paris in the war with a girlfriend. In *Journal du Voleur*, Genet wrote: 'The French Gestapo contained the following two fascinating elements: Treason and theft. With homosexuality added it would be sparkling, unassailable. It would possess the three virtues which I had set up as theological [...] What could be said against it? It was outside the world.'[2]

As Genet's literary talent kept him out of jail, another writer looked set for a prison sentence. Louis-Ferdinand Céline's 1950 trial was the last major collaborationist court case. In the final days of the war he had fled Sigmaringen and gone to ground in Denmark. His trial began in Paris while Céline was still being held in a Danish cell. Shortly before the proceedings began, Georges Cahn, a radio journalist, wrote to the newspaper *Combat* and claimed that there was a link between rue Lauriston and Céline:

> In March 1942 I was detained for a few hours by Henri Laffont's [*sic*] gang at its seat on the rue Lauriston. During my detention, and without there being any possibility for doubt on this matter, I overheard a cordial telephonic conversation between one of the members of that gang and a correspondent who was none other than Céline's companion [Lucette Destouches].[3]

Céline denied that he owned a telephone, defended his wife and claimed Cahn could only have been at rue Lauriston to pick up a bribe. No one ever bothered to ask Lucette for her side of the story or if the dance school she ran had any connections to gang associates such as Chamberlin's showgirl friend Esméralda.

Cahn's story did not seem to affect the outcome of the trial. Céline received one year's imprisonment before being granted an amnesty. He returned to France in 1951 and continued his medical career before making a literary comeback with novels about Sigmaringen, which included *D'Un Château L'Autre* (*Castle to Castle*) and *Nord* (*North*). Céline and his wife became more reclusive as the years passed, although he was a hero to visiting writers from the Beat Movement, such as William Burroughs and Allen Ginsberg. He died in July 1961. His wife outlived him, dying in November 2019.

Authors from less high-brow circles also took an interest in rue Lauriston. José Giovanni used Abel Danos as a character in his 1958 crime novel *Classe Tous Risque* (*Consider All Risks*), although he later admitted to only meeting Danos for a few minutes while he was on death row. They had exchanged some inconsequential words after Giovanni gifted the condemned man some chocolate and stamps. Danos's attachment to his wife and child touched the future author.

Giovanni's real name was Joseph Damiani and he was a Parisian of Corsican descent. A decent education lost out to the appeal of collaboration and he joined Doriot's Parti Populaire Français in 1944 and then worked for the Germans in Marseille, where he hunted down and blackmailed those dodging work service in the Reich. After the liberation he formed a gang with his brother Paul and some former collaborators. They targeted businessmen with phoney accusations of collaboration and then tortured them until they gave up money. Three died.

The inevitable arrest meant that Damiani was put on death row, but his sentence was commuted to hard labour for life. In the end he served eleven years in prison. His lawyer encouraged him to write about his experiences once he was released. His first book *Le Trou* (*The Hole*), about a failed prison break, came out in 1957 under the name José Giovanni and was a success. Soon after, he developed the Danos character into a novel based on their brief meeting in prison and in 1960 it was made into a hit film. He went on to write many more novels and died in 2004.

Another writer wrestled with how much to reveal and conceal about what happened during the war years. After the war, author Marguerite Donnadieu's husband returned from his imprisonment at Buchenwald, but their marriage did not last long. She left her husband to be with her wartime lover Dionys Mascolo and in 1947 they had a baby. By this time, Mascolo had already fathered a child with Paulette Delval, the wife of executed Carlingue member Charles Delval. Their relationship had started while Delval was in prison awaiting trial.

Donnadieu's complicated love life did not get in the way of a long literary career under the name Marguerite Duras. She became best known for the screenplay of well-regarded 1959 avant-garde film *Hiroshima Mon Amour* and the 1984 global bestselling novel *L'Amant* (*The Lover*). A less popular but more personal work was *La Douleur* (*The War: A Memoir*), a collection of six texts about her experiences during the war. The story entitled 'Monsieur X. Here Called Pierre Rabier' concerned her dealings with Charles Delval. She claimed that Delval was actually a German using the French identity of his cousin but failed to mention the tangled relationships between its principal characters.

Paulette Delval dismissed Donnadieu as a liar and others blamed the story's inaccuracies on Donnadieu's alcoholism. She died in 1996 at the age of eighty-one.

• • •

One young writer was less squeamish about uncovering the secrets of rue Lauriston. Jean Patrick Modiano debuted with the 1968 novel *La Place de L'Étoile* and found immediate success. He went on to make a career out of revisiting a past that much of France wished to forget.

Modiano's mother was a Flemish actress named Louisa Colpeyn, who was born in Antwerp back in 1918 to a working-class family. After attending youth group drama classes, she began working in film and spent some time as a chorus girl in Brussels. When the Germans invaded, she did some radio work and performed for Flemish workers. In June 1942, she moved to Paris and a job writing subtitles for French films. She moved in a vaguely artistic milieu, was ambivalent about collaboration and drank like tomorrow would never come.

In October 1942, Colpeyn met Albert Rodolphe Modiano, who had been born in Paris to a Jewish family out of Tuscany by way of Thessaloniki. Albert's father had died young and his childhood had consisted of attending expensive boarding schools on family money. He soon discovered the attractions of the Parisian bars and making easy money. In the early 1930s he was involved in a petrol smuggling racket, various dubious companies, a Romanian petrol business and a stockings and perfume shop at 71 boulevard Malesherbes. He became friends with Chamberlin's chauffeur Eddy Pagnon.

Albert Modiano was in the army when the Germans arrived in Paris. He avoided registering as a Jew and returned to the kind of business that he'd done before the war. Soon he was selling metals to an Amt Otto purchasing office that was run by two Armenian brothers.

By the time Colpeyn entered Albert Modiano's life, the Germans were after him for escaping arrest after a raid on a black market restaurant. The pair fell in love and went underground until the liberation.

Patrick Modiano was born in July 1945. He had a brother who died young from leukaemia and the death affected Patrick's parents in ways that he didn't understand. Modiano grew up a resentful child, clever enough to get into the Lycée Henri-IV, the top secondary school in France, but rebellious enough to quit at the age of seventeen.

His parents refused to talk about the war, but echoes of the past were everywhere. People talked knowingly about the Carlingue over aperitifs at their parties. His father had an office at 1 rue Lord-Byron, the same building used by Max Stöcklin for his black market activities. In the early 1960s, Modiano sold some stolen suits and a music box to a second-hand dealer in the rue Jardins Saint-Paul. The man came from Clichy and boasted of being an old friend of Joseph Joinovici.

All of this was poured into the books that Modiano began writing in his early twenties. His first novel *La Place de L'Étoile* follows a delusional protagonist taking a hallucinatory stagger through the anti-Semitic obsessions of mid-century France. His next two books, *La Ronde de Nuit* (*Night Rounds*, 1969) and *Les Boulevards de Ceinture* (*Ring Roads*, 1972), took oblique looks at the rue Lauriston collaborators. Chamberlin and Bonny appear under their own names or in thin disguise, accompanied by Violette Morris and a cohort of decadent black marketeers.

The books won prizes and acclaim and awoke a new interest in the rue Lauriston gang. In 1970 Philippe Aziz wrote *Tu Trahiras sans Vergogne: Histoire de Deux Collabos Bonny et Lafont* (*Shameless Betrayal: The Story of Two Collaborators, Bonny and Lafont*), a serious look at the gang that is built on interviews with policemen, members of the resistance and former gang members. It remained the best study of the Carlingue until 2002 when Grégory Auda wrote the thematic history *Les Belles Années du 'Milieu' 1940–1944* (*The Golden Years of the 'Milieu' 1940–1944*) from Paris police records.

After his avant-garde trilogy, Modiano began producing literary deconstructions of the detective thriller in which the conventions of mysterious phone calls, femme fatales, notebooks with clues and intimidating desk clerks were subverted by passive narrators who wander through the dreamlike fog of Paris in search of vanished streets and lost memories. 'So, are you awake?' asks a character in 1992's *Un Cirque Passe*.

'I'm not sure,' replies the narrator. 'I'd rather keep it vague.'

Modiano churned out books like a highbrow Georges Simenon, transposing his angry adolescent relationship with his distant parents and a teenage flirtation with crime back through time into the war and its aftermath. Each book obsessively rewrites the same basic story from a slightly different angle.

By the mid-1970s, Louis Malle was working on a screenplay about a wartime collaborator. Modiano became the obvious choice to help him write it.

Malle was a young boy during the war and remembered seeing Jewish pupils at his school being rounded up by German soldiers. By the 1950s he was a successful film director and journalist who hung around with the rightist literary movement known as the Hussards, a gang of young writers who flaunted their love of fast cars and playboy living in the faces of the serious-minded disciples of Sartre. Malle thought they were 'happy, pessimistic dandies, mocking the Bourgeois-Stalinist intelligentsia of the period'.[4]

Malle made *Ascenseur pour L'Échafaud* (*Elevator to the Gallows*) with leading Hussard writer Roger Nimier, who would die at thirty-six by crushing his sports car into a tin can against the barriers of a motorway. In 1974, Malle turned to a very different kind of writer in the form of Patrick Modiano to collaborate on a film. *Lacombe Lucien* tells the wartime story of a teenager in a small French town who is denied membership of the resistance and ends up joining with the local Gestapo auxiliaries by chance.[5] The leader of the gang is obviously based on Chamberlin, a blond playboy stands in for Prévost, a black gang member is based on a real collaborator but also symbolises the Carlingue's North African brigade. The protagonist helps betray resistance groups but falls in love with a Jewish girl. The couple escape to an idyllic pastoral hideaway as the war comes to an end and the closing screen laconically states that Lacombe was executed by the resistance.

The title character was played by 22-year-old woodcutter Pierre Blaise, who had never acted before. He gave a convincingly naturalistic performance and looked to have a bright cinematic future but died the following year when his car hit a tree near Moissac in the pouring rain. The film was a controversial hit that jangled nerves in a France that was already deep into an unwelcome reassessment of its role in the Second World War. The narrative of heroic resistance members and snivelling collaborators long pushed by de Gaulle supporters now seemed too simplistic.

'I knew some Lucien Lacombes,' wrote Richard Marienstras in

the magazine *Le Nouvel Observateur*. 'They were not in the Gestapo but in the Maquis: and the weapons they brandished brought them the same compensation (the taste of power, the will to be important, easy women and money at hand).'[6]

After his work with Malle and cinema, Modiano went back to writing novels. For the next thirty years he mined away at the hard rock of collaboration, guilt and exile and in 2014 won the Nobel Prize for literature. The academy stated that he had been given the award 'for the art of memory, with which he has evoked the most ungraspable human destinies and uncovered the life-world of the occupation.'[7]

The prize led to a programme of international translations accompanied by introductory essays, magazine articles and book-length studies. All attempted to carefully explain Modiano's obsession with the man known as Henri Lafont and his cronies at rue Lauriston. The few survivors who remembered the Carlingue boss found it hard to believe that he had become an international literary character, studied by professors and students, parsed in footnotes.

Chamberlin's old headquarters at rue Lauriston still stands, tall and thin and the colour of weak tea. The address has become infamous. A low-budget and heavily fictionalised 2004 Canal Plus film called itself *93, rue Lauriston*, confident everyone understood the reference. On the wall today is a grey stone plaque:

> In homage to the resistants tortured on this site during the occupation of 1940–1944 by Frenchmen and auxiliary agents of the Gestapo from the group known as 'Bonny-Lafont'.

In 2009, the site was occupied by the Franco-Arab Chamber of Commerce, which pressurised local politicians to change the address to *91bis* but failed in its efforts and moved out. In 2014, the plaque was replaced during renovation work with a more general one that honoured the resistance. The original wording was reinstated after an outcry in the press.

Chamberlin, Bonny and the Carlingue haunt the streets of Paris. Once, they allowed the French to pretend that only lowlife crooks and professional failures worked with the enemy. Later, when the stain of collaboration had spread like damp and the traitors could be counted in the hundreds of thousands, the rue Lauriston gang became a Gothic horror story peopled by killer doctors and Gestapo torturers creeping the dark heart of an occupied city.

In reality, the Carlingue was a gang of poorly educated working-class men who were motivated only by self-interest, greed and contempt for conventional morality. They spent their lives in and out of prison, were violent and ruthless, and came together in the chaos of occupation under the leadership of a petty crook who got lucky. The luck didn't last. It never does.

Decades after the war, Henri Chamberlin's daughter encountered some former members of the Carlingue while she was in Paris. Although they were older and greyer, they remained unrepentant. 'Only the good die young,' said one. 'I was rotten so I'm still alive.'[8]

NOTES

INTRODUCTION: IN A STATION OF THE MÉTRO

1 Philippe Aziz, *Tu Trahiras sans Vergogne: Histoire de Deux 'Collabos', Bonny et Lafont* (Paris: Fayard, 1970), p. 44.
2 Henry Sergg, *Joinovici: L'Empire Souterrain d'un Chiffonnier Milliardaire* (Paris: Le Carrousel-FN, 1986), p. 116.
3 Alphonse Boudard, *L'Étrange Monsieur Joseph* (Paris: Pocket, 1998), p. 152.

1: THE MAN WHO LOVED ORCHIDS

1 Thomas Maeder, *The Unspeakable Crimes of Dr. Petiot* (New York: Open Road Media, 2016).
2 Rowland W. Black, *Histoire et Crimes de la Gestapo Parisienne* (Brussels: Exclusivités de Vente ASA, 1945), p. 32.
3 Philippe Aziz, *Tu Trahiras sans Vergogne*, p. 44.
4 Alice Yaeger Kaplan, *The Collaborator: The Trial and Execution of Robert Brasillach* (Chicago: University of Chicago Press, 2000), p. 81.
5 Philippe Aziz, *Tu Trahiras sans Vergogne*, p. 44.
6 Serge Jacquemard, *La Bande Bonny-Lafont* (Paris: French Pulp, 2016).
7 Nicholas Shakespeare, *Priscilla: The Hidden Life of an Englishwoman in Wartime France* (New York: Harper, 2014), p. 250.

2: ONE HOUR BEHIND GERMANY

1 Julia Lopez, 'Pétain and the French: Authority, Propaganda, and Collaboration in Vichy France', undergraduate thesis, Mount Holyoke College, 2014.
2 Nicholas Atkin, *Pétain* (London: Longman, 1998), p. 9.
3 Julien Hervier, *Drieu la Rochelle: Une Histoire de Désamours* (Paris: Gallimard, 2018), p. 36.
4 Julia Lopez, 'Pétain and the French'.
5 Eugen Weber, 'The Vanquished and Their Prey', *American Scholar* (Winter 1983), vol. 52, no. 1, pp. 107–19.
6 Philippe Aziz, *Tu Trahiras sans Vergogne*, p. 44.
7 David King, *Death in the City of Light: The Serial Killer of Nazi-Occupied Paris* (London: Sphere, 2012).
8 Philippe Aziz, *Tu Trahiras sans Vergogne*, p. 68.

3: PLAYING TO WIN

1 Bruce Chatwin, 'An Aesthete at War', *New York Review of Books* (5 March 1981).
2 Bertram M. Gordon, 'Review of *La France du Marché Noir (1940–1949)* by Fabrice Grenard', *Business History Review* (Autumn 2009), vol. 83, issue 3, pp. 669–72.

3 Grégory Auda, *Les Belles Années du 'Milieu' 1940–1944*, p. 85.

4 Kenneth Mouré, 'The Faux Policier in Occupied Paris', *Journal of Contemporary History* (2010), vol. 45, no. 1, pp. 95–112.

5 Grégory Auda, *Les Belles Années du 'Milieu' 1940–1944*, p. 86.

6 'Alexandre Villaplane, un Traître, un Vrai', Parlons Foot (30 August 2010), http://www.parlonsfoot.com/archives/2010/08/30/alexandre-Villaplane-un-traitre-un-vrai/ (accessed April 2020).

7 Morvan Lebesque, *Chroniques du Canard* (Paris: Éditions J-J Pauvert, 1960).

8 Bruce Chatwin, 'An Aesthete at War'.

9 It was rumoured that Carlingue member Terrail was a scapegrace member of the family that owned the Tour d'Argent restaurant.

10 Jacques Bonny, *Mon Père L'Inspecteur Bonny* (Paris: Éditions Robert Laffont, 1975).

4: THE GREAT MISTAKE

1 Robert Paxton, *Vichy France: Old Guard and New Order 1940–1944* (London: Knopf, 2015).

2 David Bellos, *Roman Gary: A Tall Story* (London: Vintage Digital, 2010).

3 Angelo Tasca, David Bidussa and Denis Peschanski, *La France de Vichy: Archives Inédits d'Angelo Tasca* (Milan: Feltrinelli, 1996), p. 297.

4 Kenneth W. Estes, *A European Anabasis: Western European Volunteers in the German Army and SS, 1940–45* (New York: Columbia University Press, 2003).

5 Bertram M. Gordon, 'The Condottieri of the Collaboration: Mouvement Social Revolutionnaire', *Journal of Contemporary History* (April 1975), vol. 10, no. 2, pp. 261–82.

6 Philippe Aziz, *Tu Trahiras sans Vergogne*, p. 78.

7 Grégory Auda, *Les Belles Années du 'Milieu' 1940–1944*, p. 89.

5: ROTTING FROM THE HEAD DOWNWARDS

1 Piers Brendon, *The Dark Valley: A Panorama of the 1930s* (London: Vintage Digital, 2016), p. 145.

2 Jacques Bonny, *Mon Père L'Inspecteur Bonny*.

3 J. G. Katz, 'The 1907 Mauchamp Affair and the French Civilising Mission in Morocco', *Journal of North African Studies* (2001), vol. 6, part 1, pp. 143–66.

4 Joel Colton, *Leon Blum: A Humanist in Politics* (USA: MIT Press, 1974), p. 144.

5 Alastair Hamilton, *The Appeal of Fascism: A Study of Intellectuals and Fascism, 1919–1945* (London: Blond, 1971), p. 194.

6 'Carbuccia et le Gérant de Gringoire Sont Acquittés', *L'Humanité*, 1 December 1934.

7 Alan Riding, *And the Show Went On: Cultural Life in Nazi-Occupied Paris* (New York: Knopf, 2010).

8 Rowland W. Black, *Histoire et Crimes de la Gestapo Parisienne*, p. 45.

9 Jacques Bonny, *Mon Père L'Inspecteur Bonny*.

6: GREEN FRUIT

1 George Bree and Germaine Bernauer (eds), *Defeat and Beyond: An Anthology of French Wartime Writing 1940–45* (New York: Pantheon, 1970), p. 154.

2 Kenneth Mouré, 'La Capitale de la Faim: Black Market Restaurants in Paris, 1940–1944', *French Historical Studies* (April 2015), vol. 38, no. 2, p. 312.

3 'Le Cabaret des Fleurs: Chez Loulou Presle', *Vedette*, 24 January 1942.

4 Rowland W. Black, *Histoire et Crimes de la Gestapo Parisienne*, p. 69.

5 Yasmine Youssi, 'Violette Morris, Amazone Chez les Nazis', Raymond Ruffin, 3 October 2010, http://raymond-ruffin.over-blog.com/pages/Violette_Morris-2253930.html (accessed April 2020).

6 'Violette Morris (Gouraud) (1893–1944) Part I: Sports Champion', A Gender Variance Who's Who, 25 May 2015, https://zagria.blogspot.com/2015/05/violette-morris-gouraud-1893-1944-part.html#.XqAga1NKj-Y (accessed April 2020).

7 Anne Sebba, *Les Parisiennes: How the Women of Paris Lived, Loved and Died in the 1940s* (London: Weidenfeld & Nicolson, 2016).

8 Louise-Marie Frenette, *The Life of a Master in the West: Omraam Mikhaël Aïvanhov* (Journey with Omraam, 2016), p. 381.
9 Philippe Aziz, *Tu Trahiras sans Vergogne*, p. 195.
10 Grégory Auda, *Les Belles Années du 'Milieu' 1940–1944*, p. 90.
11 Ibid., p. 91.
12 Philippe Aziz, *Tu Trahiras sans Vergogne*, p. 195.
13 Ibid., p. 138.
14 Grégory Auda, *Les Belles Années du 'Milieu' 1940–1944*, p. 58.

7: THE BIG SCORE

1 Philippe Aziz, *Tu Trahiras sans Vergogne*, p. 79.
2 Eric Guillon, *Abel Danos, Le Mammouth: Entre Résistance et Gestapo* (Paris: Fayard, 2006) p. 26.
3 Ibid., p. 100.
4 Ibid., p. 119.
5 Serge Jacquemard, *La Bande Bonny-Lafont*.
6 Eric Guillon, *Abel Danos, Le Mammouth*, p. 122.
7 Allan Mitchell, *Nazi Paris: The History of an Occupation, 1940–1944* (New York: Berghahn Books, 2008).
8 Philippe Aziz, *Tu Trahiras sans Vergogne*, p. 101.

8: REVERSE OF THE MAP

1 Alan Riding, *And the Show Went On*.
2 Graham Robb, *Parisians: An Adventure History of Paris* (London: Picador, 2010).
3 Grégory Auda, *Les Belles Années du 'Milieu' 1940–1944*, p. 75.
4 Henry Sergg, *Joinovici: L'Empire Souterrain d'un Chiffonnier Milliardaire*, p. 123.
5 Ibid., p. 125.
6 Philippe Aziz, *Tu Trahiras sans Vergogne*, p. 140.
7 Ibid., p. 141.
8 Ibid.
9 Henry Sergg, *Joinovici: L'Empire Souterrain d'un Chiffonnier Milliardaire*, p. 35.
10 Cédric Meletta, *Jean Luchaire, 1901–1945: L'Enfant Perdu des Années Sombre* (Paris: Perrin, 2013).
11 Ibid.
12 Ibid.
13 Serge Jacquemard, *La Bande Bonny-Lafont*.

9: NIGHT AND FOG

1 Karl Dietrich Bracher, *The German Dictatorship: The Origins, Structure, and Effects of National Socialism* (New York: Praeger, 1970), p. 418.
2 Rowland W. Black, *Histoire et Crimes de la Gestapo Parisienne*, p. 88.
3 Philippe Aziz, *Tu Trahiras sans Vergogne*, p. 234.
4 Grégory Auda, *Les Belles Années du 'Milieu' 1940–1944*, p. 142.
5 Ernst Jünger, *A German Officer in Occupied Paris: The War Journals, 1941–1945* (New York: Columbia University Press, 2019).
6 Philippe Aziz, *Tu Trahiras sans Vergogne*, p. 173.
7 Eric Guillon, *Abel Danos, Le Mammouth*, p. 318.
8 Ibid., p. 129.
9 Philippe Aziz, *Tu Trahiras sans Vergogne*, p. 176.

10: *TOUT VA TRÈS BIEN, MADAME LA MARQUISE*

1 Mary Spelling McAuliffe, *When Paris Sizzled: The 1920s Paris of Hemingway, Chanel, Cocteau, Cole Porter, Josephine Baker, and their Friends* (Lanham: Rowman & Littlefield, 2016).
2 Allan Mitchell, *Nazi Paris: The History of an Occupation, 1940–1944*.

3 Cyril Elder, *Les Comtesses de la Gestapo* (Paris: Grasset, 2006), p. 32.
4 Rowland W. Black, *Histoire et Crimes de la Gestapo Parisienne*, p. 83.
5 Ibid., p. 72.
6 Ibid., p. 74.
7 Nicholas Shakespeare, *Priscilla: The Hidden Life of an Englishwoman in Wartime France*.
8 Serge Jacquemard, *La Bande Bonny-Lafont*.
9 Ibid.
10 Philippe Aziz, *Tu Trahiras sans Vergogne*, p. 147.
11 Ibid., p. 148.

11: THOSE DAMNED AND FALLEN

1 Jacques Bielinky, *Journal, 1940–1942: Un Journaliste Juif à Paris Sous L'Occupation* (Paris: Cerf, 1992), p. 269.
2 Alice Yaeger Kaplan, *The Collaborator: The Trial and Execution of Robert Brasillach* (Chicago: University of Chicago Press, 2000), p. 29.
3 Allan Mitchell, *Nazi Paris: The History of an Occupation, 1940–1944*.
4 Serge Jacquemard, *La Bande Bonny-Lafont*.
5 Philippe Aziz, *Tu Trahiras sans Vergogne*, p. 201.
6 Kenneth Mouré, 'Black Market Fictions: Au Bon Beurre, La Traversée de Paris, and the Black Market in France', *French Politics, Culture and Society* (Spring 2014), vol. 32, no. 1, pp. 47–67.
7 Serge Jacquemard, *La Bande Bonny-Lafont*.
8 Jacques Bonny, *Mon Père L'Inspecteur Bonny*.
9 Philippe Aziz, *Tu Trahiras sans Vergogne*, p. 168.
10 Ibid., p. 180.
11 Ibid., p. 183.
12 Ibid., p. 184.
13 Ibid., p. 185.
14 Eric Guillon, *Abel Danos, Le Mammouth*, p. 161.

12: HALF A FLAMING SUN

1 Nicole Attia, *Jo Attia: Mon Père* (Paris: Éditions Gallimard, 1976), p. 70.
2 Thomas Maeder, *The Unspeakable Crimes of Dr. Petiot*.
3 David King, *Death in the City of Light*.
4 Philippe Aziz, *Tu Trahiras sans Vergogne*, p. 262.
5 Rowland W. Black, *Histoire et Crimes de la Gestapo Parisienne*, p. 158.

13: IN THE CELLARS OF RUE LAURISTON

1 Serge Jacquemard, *La Bande Bonny-Lafont*.
2 Jacques Bonny, *Mon Père L'Inspecteur Bonny*.
3 Ibid.
4 Ibid.
5 Philippe Aziz, *Tu Trahiras sans Vergogne*, p. 168.
6 Ernst Jünger, *A German Officer in Occupied Paris: The War Journals, 1941–1945*.
7 Philippe Aziz, *Tu Trahiras sans Vergogne*, p. 247.
8 Ibid., p. 160.
9 Bertram M. Gordon, 'Review of *La France du Marché Noir (1940–1949)* by Fabrice Grenard'.
10 Robert Paxton, *Vichy France: Old Guard and new Order 1940–1944*, p. 671.
11 Jacques Bonny, *Mon Père L'Inspecteur Bonny*.
12 Eric Guillon, *Abel Danos, Le Mammouth*, p. 175.

14: A NORTH AFRICAN CONNECTION

1 Rowland W. Black, *Histoire et Crimes de la Gestapo Parisienne*, p. 175.
2 Philippe Aziz, *Tu Trahiras sans Vergogne*, p. 253.

3 Kenneth Mouré, 'The Faux Policier in Occupied Paris', p. 108.
4 Rowland W. Black, *Histoire et Crimes de la Gestapo Parisienne*, p. 176.
5 Peter Kemp, *The Thorns of Memory: Memoir* (London: Sinclair-Stevenson, 1990), p. 157.
6 Philippe Aziz, *Tu Trahiras sans Vergogne*, p. 308.
7 Allan Mitchell, *Nazi Paris: The History of an Occupation, 1940–1944*.
8 Ibid., p. 317.
9 Jacques Bonny, *Mon Père L'Inspecteur Bonny*.
10 Philippe Aziz, *Tu Trahiras sans Vergogne*, p. 323.
11 'Procès Bonny-Lafont' (1944), Transcripts 3, p. 102.
12 Ibid., p. 103.
13 Serge Jacquemard, *La Bande Bonny-Lafont*.
14 Jacques Bonny, *Mon Père L'Inspecteur Bonny*.

15: SS MOHAMMED

1 Jacques Bonny, *Mon Père L'Inspecteur Bonny*.
2 Philippe Aziz, *Tu Trahiras sans Vergogne*, p. 255.
3 J. Mehlman, 'The Joinovici Affair: The Stavisky of the Fourth Republic', *French Politics, Culture & Society* (Spring 2014), vol. 32, no. 1, pp. 101–10.
4 Jacques Bonny, *Mon Père L'Inspecteur Bonny*.
5 Lucien Rebatet, *Les Mémoires d'un Fasciste, Vol. 2: 1941–1947* (Paris: Pauvert, 1976).
6 Grégory Auda, *Les Belles Années du 'Milieu' 1940–1944*, p. 174.
7 Philippe Aziz, *Tu Trahiras sans Vergogne*, p. 257.
8 Jacques Bonny, *Mon Père L'Inspecteur Bonny*.
9 Pierre Nord, *My Comrades-in-Arms are Dead: Vol. 2*, translation of *Mes Camarades Sont Morts: Tome 2* (US Army Special Warfare School Fort Bragg, North Carolina, 1963, CIA-RDP85-00671R000200180001-2), p. 81.

16: THE COMEDY IS OVER

1 Cyril Elder, *Les Comtesses de la Gestapo*, p. 90.
2 Jean-Marc Belierre, *Police des Temps Noirs: France, 1939–1945* (Paris: Perrin, 2018).
3 Serge Jacquemard, *La Bande Bonny-Lafont*.
4 'Procès Auxiliaires Français de la Gestapo' (1947), Transcripts II, p. 7.
5 'Procès Bonny-Lafont' (1944), Transcripts 3, p. 141.
6 'Procès Bonny-Lafont' (1944), Transcripts 7, p. 53.
7 Rowland W. Black, *Histoire et Crimes de la Gestapo Parisienne*, p. 183.
8 Jean Monange, 'Un du 93 rue Lauriston', 1 April 2005, https://www.histoire-genealogie.com/Un-du-93-rue-Lauriston?lang=fr (accessed April 2020).
9 Patrice Rolli, *La Phalange Nord-Africaine en Dordogne: Histoire d'une Alliance Entre la Pègre et la Gestapo (15 Mars–19 Août 1944)*, (Éditions L'Histoire en Partage, 2013), p. 64.
10 Jean Monange, 'Un du 93 rue Lauriston'.
11 Philippe Aziz, *Tu Trahiras sans Vergogne*, p. 360.
12 Ibid., p. 361.

17: *LA TOUR DE BABEL*

1 Kay Chadwick (ed.), *Philippe Henriot: The Last Act of Vichy, Radio Broadcasts January–June 1944* (Liverpool: University of Liverpool Press, 2011), p. 7.
2 Ernst Jünger, *A German Officer in Occupied Paris: The War Journals, 1941–1945*.
3 Bruce Chatwin, 'An Aesthete at War'.
4 Agnès Catherine Poirier, *Left Bank: Art, Passion and the Rebirth of Paris 1940–1950* (London: Bloomsbury, 2018).
5 Philippe Aziz, *Tu Trahiras sans Vergogne*, p. 92.
6 J. Willging, '"True down to the Last Detail": Narrative and Memory in Marguerite Duras's "Monsieur X"', *Twentieth Century Literature* (Autumn 2000), vol. 46, part 4, pp. 369–86.

7 Philippe Aziz, *Tu Trahiras sans Vergogne*, p. 365.
8 Ibid., p. 367.
9 Serge Jacquemard, *La Bande Bonny-Lafont*.
10 Raymond Arnette, *De la Gestapo à L'OAS: L'Itinéraire Atypique d'un Homme de Dieu* (Paris: Filipacchi, 1996), p. 111.
11 Patrice Rolli, *La Phalange Nord-Africaine en Dordogne: Histoire d'une Alliance Entre la Pègre et la Gestapo (15 Mars–19 Août 1944)*, p. 65.
12 Alan Riding, *And the Show Went On*.
13 Francis P. Sempa, 'Review of The Liberation of Paris: How Eisenhower, de Gaulle, and von Choltitz Saved the City of Light', *New York Journal of Books*, https://www.nyjournalofbooks.com/book-review/liberation-paris (accessed April 2020).

18: *DAS SCHLOSS*

1 Louis-Ferdinand Céline, *L'Ecole des Cadavers* (Paris: Éditions Denoël, 1938), p. 219.
2 Allan Mitchell, *The Devil's Captain: Ernst Jünger in Nazi Paris, 1941–1944* (Oxford: Berghahn Books, 2011), p. 76.
3 Richard Griffiths, A Certain Idea of France: Ernst Jünger's Paris Diaries 1941–44, *Journal of European Studies* (March 1993), vol. 23, pp. 101–20.
4 Pierre-André Taguieff et Annick Duraffour, 'Céline Contre les Juifs ou L'École de la Haine', *Études du CRIF* (13 March 2018), no. 48.
5 Heinrich Frey, 'Louis Malle and the 1950s: Ambiguities, Friendships and Legacies', *South Central Review* (Summer 2006), vol. 23, no. 2, pp. 22–35.

19: PICKING MUSHROOMS

1 'La Brigade du Crime', *Ce Soir*, 5 September 1944.
2 Jacques Bonny, *Mon Père L'Inspecteur Bonny*.
3 Ibid.
4 Ibid.
5 Ibid.
6 Eric Guillon, *Abel Danos, Le Mammouth*, p. 136.
7 Anthony Beevor and Artemis Cooper, *Paris: After the Liberation, 1944–1949* (London: Penguin, 2007).
8 Rowland W. Black, *Histoire et Crimes de la Gestapo Parisienne*, p. 204.
9 Cyril Elder, *Les Comtesses de la Gestapo*, p. 63.
10 Laure Adler, *Marguerite Duras* (Paris: Gallimard, 1998), p. 202.
11 *Ce Soir*, 10 September 1944.
12 Cyril Elder, *Les Comtesses de la Gestapo*, p. 103.
13 Ibid., p. 99.
14 Eric Guillon, *Abel Danos, Le Mammouth*, p. 205.
15 Malcolm Muggeridge, *Chronicles of Wasted Time, Vol. 2: The Infernal Grove* ([S.I.]: Collins, 1973), p. 243.

20: THE TRIAL

1 Jacques Bonny, *Mon Père L'Inspecteur Bonny*.
2 Rowland W. Black, *Histoire et Crimes de la Gestapo Parisienne*, p. 221.
3 Alice Yaeger Kaplan, *The Collaborator: The Trial and Execution of Robert Brasillach*, p. 107.
4 Rowland W. Black, *Histoire et Crimes de la Gestapo Parisienne*, p. 224.
5 Ibid., p. 227.
6 Cyril Elder, *Les Comtesses de la Gestapo*, p. 29.
7 Rowland W. Black, *Histoire et Crimes de la Gestapo Parisienne*, p. 133.
8 'Procès Bonny-Lafont' (1944), Transcripts 6, p. 2.
9 Rowland W. Black, *Histoire et Crimes de la Gestapo Parisienne*, p. 234.
10 Jacques Bonny, *Mon Père L'Inspecteur Bonny*.

11 Ibid.
12 Ibid.
13 Rowland W. Black, *Histoire et Crimes de la Gestapo Parisienne*, p. 216.
14 Philippe Aziz, *Tu Trahiras sans Vergogne*, p. 377.

21: LONG LIVE FRANCE, ANYWAY

1 Alphonse Boudard, *L'Étrange Monsieur Joseph*, p. 152.
2 Serge Jacquemard, *La Bande Bonny-Lafont*.
3 'French Gestapo Men', *Western Mail*, 28 December 1944.
4 '"Gestapo Gang" Shot in France', *Daily Telegraph – Sydney*, 29 December 1944.
5 Henri Rousso, *Pétain et la Fin de la Collaboration: Sigmaringen 1944–1945* (Paris: Éditions Complexe, 1984), p. 422.
6 *Le Figaro*, 31 October 1946.
7 Philippe Aziz, *Tu Trahiras sans Vergogne*, p. 232.
8 André Goldschmidt, *L'Affaire Joinovici: Collaborateur, Résistant et Bouc Émissaire* (Paris: Privat, 2002), p. 12.
9 Robert Paxton, *Vichy France: Old Guard and new Order 1940–1944*.
10 J. Mehlman, 'The Joinovici Affair: The Stavisky of the Fourth Republic', p. 106.
11 Alice Yaeger Kaplan, *The Collaborator: The Trial and Execution of Robert Brasillach*, p. 79.

22: AN OLD PHOTOGRAPH OF OUR YOUTH

1 'Accused Drug King Waits in Latin Jail', *Miami Herald*, 29 June 1972.
2 'Intelligence Memorandum: International Narcotics, Series no. 3: Paraguay, Heroin Crossroads of South America' (CIA-RDP85T00875R001700020019-8 Ricord).
3 Bettina Stangneth, *Eichmann Before Jerusalem: The Unexamined Life of a Mass Murderer* (New York: Knopf, 2014).
4 Eric Guillon, *Abel Danos, Le Mammouth*, p. 234.
5 Ibid.
6 Ibid., p. 412.
7 Ibid., p. 414.
8 Patrick Modiano, *Pedigree: A Memoir* (New Haven: Yale University Press, 2015).

23: GHOSTS OF PARIS

1 Agnès Catherine Poirier, *Left Bank: Art, Passion and the Rebirth of Paris 1940–1950*.
2 Jean Genet, *The Thief's Journal* (London: Grove Press, 1964), p. 149.
3 'The Selected Correspondence of Louis-Ferdinand Céline', trans. by Mitch Abidor, *The Brooklyn Rail*, October 2014, https://brooklynrail.org/2014/10/fiction/celine-september (accessed April 2020).
4 Marc Dambre, Hugo Frey and Louis Malle, 'Ascenseur Pour L'Échafaud (Elevator to the Gallows, 1957): An Exclusive Interview with Louis Malle', *South Central Review* (Summer 2006), vol. 23, no. 2, pp. 12–21.
5 The film's protagonist is fictional but there was a real Louis Lacombe, a *Milice* man who was sentenced to forced labour for life after the war; there are also similarities with the teenage Aimé Ariès from Cazaril-Tambourès, who was turned down by a resistance group because of his age and became involved in collaboration.
6 Paul Jankowski, 'In Defense of Fiction: Resistance, Collaboration, and Lacombe, Lucien', *Journal of Modern History* (September 1991), vol. 63, no. 3, pp. 457–82.
7 Alexandra Schwartz, 'Patrick Modiano's Postwar World', *New Yorker*, 9 October 2014, https://www.newyorker.com/books/page-turner/patrick-modianos-postwar (accessed April 2020).
8 Serge Jacquemard, *La Bande Bonny-Lafont*.

ABOUT THE AUTHOR

Author photo © Anna Wiśniewska

CHRISTOPHER OTHEN IS AN English writer currently based in Eastern Europe. His day jobs have included journalist, legal representative for asylum seekers and English language teacher. In off-the-clock adventures he has interviewed retired mercenaries about war crimes, discussed lost causes with political extremists and got drunk with an ex-mujahid who knew Osama bin Laden.

He is the author of four other books, including *Franco's International Brigades: Adventurers, Fascists, and Christian Crusaders in the Spanish Civil War* and *Katanga 1960–63: Mercenaries, Spies and the African Nation that Waged War on the World.*

BIBLIOGRAPHY

Adler, Laure, *Marguerite Duras* (Paris: Gallimard, 1998).

Arnette, Raymond, *De la Gestapo à L'OAS: L'Itinéraire Atypique d'un Homme de Dieu* (Paris: Filipacchi, 1996).

Attia, Nicole, *Jo Attia: Mon Père* (Paris: Éditions Gallimard, 1976).

Auda, Grégory, *Les Belles Années du 'Milieu' 1940–1944: Le Grand Banditisme dans la Machine Répressive Allemande en France* (Paris: Michalon, 2002).

Aziz, Philippe, *Tu Trahiras sans Vergogne: Histoire de Deux 'Collabos', Bonny et Lafont*. (Paris: Fayard, 1970)

Beevor, Anthony, and Artemis Cooper, *Paris: After the Liberation, 1944–1949* (London: Penguin, 2007).

Berlière, Jean-Marc, *Police des Temps Noirs* (Paris: Perrin, 2018).

Black, Rowland W., *Histoire et Crimes de la Gestapo Parisienne* (Brussels: Exclusivités de Vente ASA, 1945).

Bonny, Jacques, *Mon Père L'Inspecteur Bonny* (Paris: Éditions Robert Laffont, 1975).

Boudard, Alphonse, *L'Étrange Monsieur Joseph* (Paris: Pocket, 1998).

Bouysse, Grégory, *Légion des Volontaires Français, Bezen Perrot & Brigade Nord-Africaine* (Paris: Lulu, 2012).

Delarue, Jacques, *Trafics et Crimes sous L'Occupation* (Paris: Fayard, 1968).

Eder, Cyril, *Les Comtesses de la Gestapo* (Paris: Grasset, 2006).

Guillon, Éric, *Abel Danos, Le Mammouth: Entre Résistance et Gestapo* (Paris: Fayard, 2006).

Hellman, John, *The Knight-Monks of Vichy France* (Quebec: McGill-Queen's University Press, 1993).

Jacquemard, Serge, *La Bande Bonny-Lafont* (Paris: French Pulp, 2016).

Jünger, Ernst, *A German Officer in Occupied Paris: The War Journals, 1941–1945* (New York: Columbia University Press, 2019).

Kaplan, Alice Yaeger, *The Collaborator: The Trial and Execution of Robert Brasillach* (Chicago: University of Chicago Press, 2000).

King, David, *Death in the City of Light: The Serial Killer of Nazi-Occupied Paris* (Crown, 2011).

Lambert, Pierre Philippe, and Le Marec, Gérard, *Partis et Mouvements de la Collaboration: Paris 1940–1944* (Paris: Jacques Grancher, 1993).

Maeder, Thomas, *The Unspeakable Crimes of Dr. Petiot* (New York: Open Road Media, 2016).

Mauthner, Martin, *Otto Abetz and his Paris Acolytes: French Writers who Flirted with Fascism, 1930–1945* (Brighton: Sussex Academic Press, 2017).

Meletta, Cédric, *Jean Luchaire: L'Enfant Perdu des Années Sombre* (Paris: Perrin, 2013).

Miller, Michael B., *Shanghai on the Métro: Spies, Intrigue, and the French between the Wars* (Berkeley: University of California Press, 1994).

Mitchell, Allan, *The Devil's Captain: Ernst Jünger in Nazi Paris, 1941–1944* (Oxford: Berghahn Books, 2011).

Mitchell, Allan, *Nazi Paris: The History of an Occupation, 1940–1944* (New York: Berghahn Books, 2008).

Modiano, Patrick, *Pedigree: A Memoir* (New Haven: Yale University Press, 2015).

Muggeridge Malcolm, *Chronicles of Wasted Time, Vol. 2: The Infernal Grove* ([S.I.]: Collins, 1973).

Paxton, Robert O., *Vichy France: Old Guard and New Order, 1940–1944* (New York: Knopf, 2015).

Riding, Alan, *And the Show Went On: Cultural Life in Nazi-Occupied Paris* (New York: Knopf, 2010).

Robb, Graham, *Parisians: An Adventure History of Paris* (London: Picador, 2010).

Rolli, Patrice, *La Phalange Nord-Africaine en Dordogne: Histoire d'une Alliance Entre la Pègre et la Gestapo (15 Mars–19 Août 1944)*, (Éditions L'Histoire en Partage, 2013).

Rousso, Henry, *Pétain et la Fin de la Collaboration: Sigmaringen 1944–1945* (Paris: Éditions Complexe, 1984).

Rousso, Henry, *The Vichy Syndrome: History and Memory in France Since 1944* (London: Harvard University Press, 1944).

Sapin, Louis, and Galante, Pierre, *La Grande Filière: Croissance, Déferlement et Débâcle de la 'French Connection'* (Paris: Éditions Robert Laffont, 1979).

Sebba, Anne, *Les Parisiennes: How the Women of Paris Lived, Loved and Died in the 1940s* (London: Weidenfeld & Nicolson, 2016).

Sergg, Henry, *Joinovici: L'Empire Souterrain d'un Chiffonnier Milliardaire* (Paris: Le Carousel-FN, 1986).

Shakespeare, Nicholas, *Priscilla: The Hidden Life of an Englishwoman in Wartime France* (New York: Harper, 2014).

Soucy, Robert, *French Fascism: The Second Wave, 1933–39* (New Haven: Yale University Press, 1995).

INDEX